Learn, Teach...
Succeed...

With **REA's TExES™ Pedagogy and Professional Responsibilities EC–12 (160)** test prep, you'll be in a class all your own.

We'd like to hear from you!
Visit **www.rea.com** to send us your comments

TExES™

TEXAS EXAMINATIONS OF EDUCATOR STANDARDS™

PEDAGOGY AND PROFESSIONAL RESPONSIBILITIES EC-12 (160)

Beatrice Mendez Newman, Ph.D.
The University of Texas-Pan American

Research & Education Association

Research & Education Association
61 Ethel Road West
Piscataway, New Jersey 08854
E-mail: info@rea.com

TExES™ Pedagogy and Professional Responsibilities EC–12 (160) With Online Practice Tests

Published 2015

Printed in the United States of America

Library of Congress Control Number 2013954897

ISBN-13: 978-0-7386-1142-6
ISBN-10: 0-7386-1142-5

The competencies presented in this book were created and implemented by the Texas Education Agency and Educational Testing Service (ETS®). Texas Examinations of Educator Standards and TExES are trademarks of the Texas Education Agency. All other trademarks cited in this publication are the property of their respective owners.

Cover image: Jamie Grill/Getty Images

Developed and produced by Focus Strategic Communications, Inc.

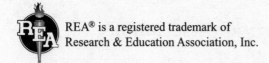

Contents

CONTENTS

About the Author

Dr. Beatrice Mendez Newman is a professor in the English Department at The University of Texas-Pan American where she regularly teaches first-year writing courses and writing methods classes. Her PhD is from Texas A&M University where she specialized in rhetoric and composition and linguistics. She has a lifetime Texas teaching certificate in secondary English and Journalism with ESL certification and works extensively with local teachers in creating student-centered, engaging writing units.

Dr. Newman's book, *English Teacher Certification Exams in Texas,* published by Allyn and Bacon in 2005, is a study guide for the TExES ELAR exams. Dr. Newman's research has been published in collections on teaching writing at Hispanic serving institutions and writing center pedagogy; her recent articles have appeared in *Voices from the Middle, HETS Online Journal,* and the *English Journal.*

Dr. Newman is very active in the National Council of Teachers of English, serving as an NCATE reviewer, as a reader for NCTE journal manuscripts, and as a national judge for the NCTE Achievement Awards in Writing.

About Research & Education Association

Founded in 1959, Research & Education Association (REA) is dedicated to publishing the finest and most effective educational materials—including study guides and test preps—for students in middle school, high school, college, graduate school, and beyond.

Today, REA's wide-ranging catalog is a leading resource for teachers, students, and professionals. Visit *www.rea.com* to see a complete listing of all our titles.

Acknowledgments

We would like to thank the people at Focus Strategic Communications, Inc., for their work on this test prep. We extend special gratitude to Focus's principals, Adrianna Edwards and Ron Edwards, for developing and producing the entire manual as well as putting together, overseeing, and supervising the writing, editorial, and production teams. We thank First Image for meticulously and patiently laying out and formatting the pages.

We would also like to thank Pam Weston, Publisher, for setting the quality standards for production integrity and managing the publication to completion; John Paul Cording, Vice President, Technology, for coordinating the design and development of the REA Study Center; Larry B. Kling, Vice President, Editorial, for his overall direction; Michael Reynolds, Managing Editor, for coordinating development of this edition; and Christine Saul, Senior Graphic Designer, for designing our cover.

INTRODUCTION

Passing the TExES Pedagogy and Professional Responsibilities EC–12 (160) Test

Passing the TExES Pedagogy and Professional Responsibilities EC–12 (160) Test

Congratulations! By taking the TExES Pedagogy and Professional Responsibilities (PPR) EC–12 (160) test, you are on your way to a rewarding teaching career. Our book and the online tools that come with it give you everything you need to succeed on this important exam, bringing you one step closer to being certified to teach in Texas.

Our *TExES PPR* Book + Online Prep package includes:

- Complete overview of the TExES Pedagogy and Professional Responsibilities EC–12 (160) test

- Comprehensive review of all four domains and 13 competencies

- Online diagnostic test to pinpoint your strengths and weaknesses and focus your study

- Two full-length practice tests, both in the book and online, with powerful diagnostic tools to help you personalize your prep

- Detailed answer explanations that not only identify correct answers, but also explain why the other answer choices are incorrect

There are many different ways to prepare for the TExES Pedagogy and Professional Responsibilities EC–12 exam. What's best for you depends on how much time you have to study and how comfortable you are with the subject matter. Our book and online tests give you the tools you need to customize your prep so you can make the most of your study time.

■ How to Use This Book + Online Prep

About Our Review

The review chapters in this book are designed to help you sharpen your command of pedagogical skills so you can pass the TExES PPR. Whether you're a recent graduate of a traditional teacher education program or you've gone the alternate route, our review will reinforce what you've learned and show you how to relate the information you have acquired to the specific competencies on the exam.

Our targeted review chapters are grouped by domain, and cover what you need to know to succeed on the exam. Each chapter outlines a specific competency and includes must-know terminology, practical classroom examples, and end-of-chapter review questions modeled after actual PPR exams. After studying our review, you will have an excellent grasp of the subject matter and a solid foundation for passing the exam.

About the REA Study Center

We know your time is valuable and you want an efficient study experience. At the online REA Study Center (*www.rea.com/studycenter*), you will get feedback right from the start on what you know and what you don't know to help make the most of your study time.

Here is what you will find at the REA Study Center:

■ **Diagnostic Test**—Before you review with the book, take our online diagnostic test. Your score report will pinpoint topics where you need the most review, to help you focus your study.

■ **2 Full-Length Practice Tests**—These practice tests give you the most complete picture of your strengths and weaknesses. After you've studied with the book, test what you've learned by taking the first of two online practice exams. Review your score report, then go back and study any topics you missed. Take the second practice test to ensure you've mastered the material and are ready for test day.

Each online test comes with:

■ **Automatic Scoring**—Find out how you did on your test, instantly.

■ **Diagnostic Score Reports**—Get a specific score on each competency, so you can focus on the areas that challenge you the most.

■ **Detailed Answer Explanations**—See why the correct answer is right, and why the other answer choices are incorrect.

■ **Timed Testing**—Learn to manage your time as you practice, so you'll feel confident on test day.

All TExES tests, with the exception of Braille (183), are given only as **computer-administered tests (CATs),** so we recommend you take the online versions of our practice tests to simulate test-day conditions.

Getting Started

Before you work through this book, we strongly recommend that you download a copy of the *Preparation Manual 160 Pedagogy and Professional Responsibilities EC–12* from the official Texas Education Agency (TEA) website: *http://texes.ets.org*. Our review is presented in accordance with this guide and, for best results, we advise using the two guides in conjunction with each other.

At the TEA website you'll also find the most current information on the exams, including registration information, testing sites, testing format, test-day advice, registration cost, and TEA-developed test preparation materials.

An Overview of the Test

What is Tested on the TExES PPR EC–12 Test?

The TExES PPR EC–12 (160) test ensures that you have the essential knowledge and skills to teach the state-required curriculum, known as Texas Essential Knowledge and Skills, or TEKS.

Whether you are a student, a graduate from a Texas state-approved teacher preparation program, or an educator who has received certification in another state, you should consult the requirements for pedagogy and professional responsibilities provided at the official TEA website.

The TExES PPR is a required component of full certification in teacher preparation programs in Texas. The PPR focuses on knowledge and skills relevant to teaching, classroom practices, student characteristics, and professional responsibilities that an entry-level educator should have. The exam consists of 100 multiple-choice questions (90 of which are scored) based on the four domains and 13 competencies as outlined in the *TExES Preparation Manual* (available for download at *www. texes.ets.org*).

The competencies represent the knowledge that teams of teachers, administrators, subject-area specialists, and others have determined to be important for beginning teachers who work in the state's public schools. Each competency is further divided into descriptive statements, which articulate the specific ways in which the competency is manifested in teaching situations. These descriptive statements offer the best indication of the type of items that will be on the test because each test item is a direct measurement of a specific descriptor in a specific competency.

In addition, the descriptive statements include very specific terms that help define the parameters of each competency. Frequently, the specific terms appear as parenthetical lists that illustrate the concept presented in that particular descriptive statement—and which may be reflected in a test-item stem.

Here is the approximate percentage of the total exam devoted to each domain, as outlined by the TEA:

Domains: Approximate Percentage of Exam		
Domain I	Designing Instruction and Assessment to Promote Student Learning	34%
Domain II	Creating a Positive, Productive Classroom Environment	13%
Domain III	Implementing Effective, Responsive Instruction and Assessment	33%
Domain IV	Fulfilling Professional Roles and Responsibilities	20%

What Is the Format of the TExES PPR EC–12 Test?

The multiple-choice questions on the TExES PPR are designed to assess your knowledge of the competencies and the related skills required to become a teacher in Texas.

In general, the multiple-choice questions require critical thinking—mirroring the classroom imperative to promote exactly this among your future students. You are expected to demonstrate more than an ability to recall factual information; you may be asked to evaluate the information, comparing it with knowledge you have, or you may be asked to evaluate information in a scenario or to make a judgment about a teaching situation.

Each question has four choices, labeled A, B, C, and D. The items, or questions, are of two general types: single items (which you can think of as "stand-alone" items, meaning that no other items are connected to them) and grouped items. In grouped items, a scenario, teaching situation, or stimulus (a student-produced artifact or an illustration) connects several items. Note that ETS refers to grouped items as Questions with Stimulus Material, Clustered Questions, or Decision Sets. We'll help you attack them all.

The *TExES Preparation Manual 160 Pedagogy and Professional Responsibilities EC-12* includes a detailed description with examples and explanations of the various types of items included on the exam. You should study those pages carefully. Additionally, you should acquaint yourself with the number of items you can expect on the test, the minimum passing score, and score reporting details.

The TExES PPR is scored based on the number of questions you answer correctly, and no points are deducted for wrong answers. Therefore, do not leave any item unanswered, since you will not be penalized for guessing, and you have at least a one in four chance of getting it right.

You are given five hours to complete the test—which may seem like a lot—but be aware of the amount of time you are spending on each question so you allow yourself time to complete the whole test. Five hours is 300 minutes, which averages out to just three minutes per question, so pace yourself. You may be able to read and answer some questions quickly, perhaps in a matter of seconds. Other questions will require slow, careful consideration of the scenario because you will be asked to make decisions about the teaching situation presented in the items.

Taking our online practice tests with timed testing conditions at the REA Study Center will help you use your time efficiently. However, if you choose to take the printed versions of the tests in the book, be sure to time yourself.

According to the Texas Education Agency, all TExES exams are developed following a specific, systematic approach:

1. Review of relevant portions of the Texas Essential Knowledge and Skills— TEKS—the state-mandated curriculum for each grade level in each content area.

2. Creation of *educator standards* based on TEKS that reflect knowledge and skills a beginning educator should have in order to promote students' achievement of expectations delineated in TEKS.

3. Identification of broad *domains* and *competencies* that reflect educator standards. TExES test items are designed to measure performance in these competencies.

It might help to visualize these test components as a continuum:

TEKS → Educator Standards → Test Domains and Competencies → Test Items

Thorough preparation for the PPR test must include all of these elements. A bit of advice: do not dismiss any of these components in your preparation. Collectively, they offer a comprehensive view of the depth and breadth of PPR content. Later in this introduction, you'll read a section explaining how you can relate these components to develop your test-readiness.

How to Read PPR Exam Items

A major part of succeeding on the PPR exam (or any TExES exam) is figuring out how to decode the items as efficiently as possible. Regardless of the type of question (stand-alone or grouped), each individual item reflects a specific competency and descriptive statement. This is why it is so important to learn the PPR competencies.

Each sample test item included in the *TEA Preparation Manual* is labeled according to the relevant competency; on the actual test, you will not know what competency pertains to each item. However, there will be clues and limiters in the item stem to help you figure out the domain and competency addressed by the item. Picking the correct response item depends on your ability to identify the competency implied in the item stem and select the response that matches the parameters established in the stem.

What makes TExES exams challenging is that in many cases, all of the responses seem to be viable choices for dealing with the situation presented in the stem. As you consider the four options, you might think, "There's nothing wrong with any of these responses," and you would be right because each option could describe an objectively good teaching practice.

Therefore, picking the correct response does not mean that the other responses represent abjectly poor teaching actions or obviously wrong response choices. Instead, you need to consider which response *best* fits the parameters of the stem. In other words, the correct response is subjective because it applies specifically to the situation presented in the stem.

But there are several other strategies you need to use in responding effectively to PPR items:

1. Read the item stem slowly and carefully. You will be looking at a computer screen, but you will be given scratch paper on which you can make relevant notes to help you work through the items.

2. Pay attention to any limiters included in the stem, such as *initial, best, most, first.* In items that include these terms, the limiters will enable you to eliminate response options that might work in the scenario but might not fit the limitation established by the stem.

3. On the basis of the previous two strategies, identify the PPR competency that seems to be addressed by the stem. Inferring the targeted competency will enable you to eliminate response options that do not apply to that competency. Identifying the competency represented by the item stem is the most crucial step in ensuring that you respond correctly to the item.

4. Read each response option carefully. This is not a time for skimming. You should circle and underline any terms that seem particularly important in the responses. Do not expect obvious wrong answers or "trick" responses. TExES exam items are constructed to activate higher-order thinking skills that reflect the certification candidate's breadth of knowledge in the test domains.

5. Do not pick your response too quickly. As you go about eliminating three of the four response options, make sure you can articulate why the response is wrong—why does it not fit the parameters established by the stem?

6. When you make your response choice, double-check yourself by asking how the response fits the limitations established by the stem. It might help if you think of the stem as a puzzle piece with an indentation that can be filled perfectly by only one of the response options.

Let's analyze a sample item to see how these strategies can help you respond effectively to a representative PPR item:

Sample PPR Item	Analysis Using Response Strategies
Students in a grade 6 social studies class are having trouble remembering the location of major bodies of water (rivers, lakes, and oceans) in the countries of the world. Which of the following instructional strategies would most effectively engage learners in meeting the teacher's objective?	Circle grade 6—this will help you make some inferences about the students' developmental level. Circle "remembering"—this suggests that students are having trouble connecting the location to the geographic feature (the bodies of water). Finally, notice the limiters in the question: "most effectively" and "engage learners." From your Competency chart and notecards, you should connect this item stem to Competency 008, which focuses on engaging learners in the learning process, specifically Descriptive Statements 008B and 008C. Look at those right now to verify the connections. Although, on the surface, these responses all describe good instructional activities, three do not form a smooth match with the stem.
(A) The teacher has students work collaboratively to label bodies of water on maps of countries of the world. The teacher encourages students to color and decorate the maps creatively and post them on the class Social Studies board.	(A) is incorrect because it does not include a means to help the students remember. This response might seem correct because the collaborative work is likely to engage learners in the immediate activity; however, the collaboration is irrelevant to the problem identified in the stem.
(B) The teacher gives each group a list of bodies of water and has students work collaboratively at computer stations to find where they are located.	(B) is incorrect because no mechanism for remembering is included in the Internet-based activity. This response might seem right, however, because of the integration of technology to help learners complete a classroom task.

(continued)

Sample PPR Item	Analysis Using Response Strategies
(C) The teacher administers a series of quizzes that ask students to match bodies of water to the countries in which they are located. Each subsequent quiz covers only the items that all or almost all the students got wrong.	(C) is incorrect because quizzing is not considered an optimum means of engaging learners. However, this response might seem correct because of the retesting to give learners a chance to succeed. This response also fails to address the remembering problem identified in the stem.
(D) Working in groups, students create a song that imitates the lyrics and music of a favorite song but that focuses on connecting major bodies of water to their global locations.	(D) is the correct response because it perfectly fits the parameters of the item stem. There is quite a bit of research demonstrating that students remember things when they are set to music. Additionally, the teacher is integrating students' prior knowledge of popular music and creating an opportunity for them to meaningfully complete an instructional task.

When you start working through the online practice tests, and later when you take the actual PPR exam, make sure you use the process illustrated in this sample item analysis to respond correctly to the items. It really works!

Each of the chapters that follow will show you how to identify the core concepts that distinguish each competency so that you will be adept at connecting test items to the relevant competency and thereby be able to select the correct response option confidently.

■ TExES PPR Study Strategies

To prepare effectively for the PPR exam, you need a well-conceived study plan that enables you to proceed logically and purposefully toward the exam date—and toward success on the exam. The following basic study strategies should be part of your plan.

Study Strategy 1

1. Assemble some study "tools." Get a spiral notebook or a ring binder for your notes, and use it to take notes as you study from this test prep and your other PPR materials (including your textbook, class notes, and so on). Alternatively, you may prefer to take notes electronically, but whatever method you use, be sure to organize your notes according to the PPR competencies. You might consider creating a folder for each competency.

2. Make flashcards to help you learn the PPR competencies and core concepts in the descriptive statements. The review chapters include a list of core concepts for each competency compiled by analyzing the descriptive statements. To learn the competencies, you need to know what core concepts define each competency.

Study Strategy 2

Download all the TEA and ETS documents relevant to the PPR test from the official website. You should have the following documents at hand (preferably in print form so you can annotate them as you work through this book):

1. *Preparation Manual 160 Pedagogy and Professional Responsibilities EC–12* (available at *http://texes.ets.org*). This manual is the official TEA preparation booklet. Although it includes basic information on test format and a short sample test, it does not include discussion or definition of concepts or terms in the competencies. That's why you need a resource like this test prep.

2. The TExES Pedagogy and Professional Responsibilities (PPR) EC–12 (160) Test at a Glance (available at *http://texes.ets.org*). This document presents a thumbnail view of the test (including the time limit for the exam, the number of items, the competencies measured on the test, and the percentages allotted to each competency on the test).

3. The PPR Educator Standards EC–12 (accessible on the TEA webpage titled Approved Educator Standards—*www.tea.state.tx.us*). Educator standards are presented in two columns: one column lists knowledge statements (k) and the other lists corresponding skills statements (s) that collectively present what beginning teachers should know and be able to do. You will find these helpful in interpreting the PPR competencies and descriptive statements.

4. The Technology Applications Standards for All Teachers, which are integrated into the PPR exam (accessible on the TEA webpage titled "Approved Educator Standards"—*www.tea.state.tx.us*). The *PPR Preparation Manual* explains where these technology application standards are integrated into the test framework.

Study Strategy 3

Review your content-area TEKS. If you have taken your content-area exam, you are familiar with the TEKS relevant to your subject. The PPR exam will not include content-specific items; however, your content-area TEKS stipulate knowledge and skills that students are expected to have at the end of each grade. Thus, by reviewing TEKS, you can infer the types of knowledge that teachers should have in order to help students meet those expectations. For example, notice how this excerpt from grade 7 TEKS for Mathematics implies certain types of teacher knowledge and skills:

1. Mathematical process standards. The student uses mathematical processes to acquire and demonstrate mathematical understanding. The student is expected to:

   (C) select tools, including real objects, manipulatives, paper and pencil, and technology as appropriate, and techniques, including mental math, estimation, and number sense as appropriate, to solve problems;

   (D) communicate mathematical ideas, reasoning, and their implications using multiple representations, including symbols, diagrams, graphs, and language as appropriate.

Embedded in this excerpt are the following PPR-relevant strategies: (1) hands-on activities promote learning; (2) communicating a content-area concept demonstrates understanding. While in this specific excerpt these strategies are contextualized in mathematics TEKS, hands-on learning and encouraging students to articulate content-area ideas are recognized as good teaching practices in all disciplines. This is the type of content addressed on the PPR exam. Thus, your PPR preparation should include a brief review of your content-area TEKS. If you do not already have a copy of TEKS for your subject and grade level, download it from the TEA website on the page titled "Texas Essential Knowledge and Skills"—*www.tea.state.tx.us*.

Study Strategy 4

Read the PPR competencies and educator standards carefully. To perform well on the exam, you need to understand the rationale behind the test items. Knowing the competencies and the educator standards will give you a context for every item. Furthermore, if you juxtapose the PPR competencies and the PPR educator standards, you will notice quite a bit of redundancy. So, the TEA documents related to the PPR exam do not represent distinct sets of material you need to learn. Instead, TEKS, PPR educator standards and PPR competencies are interrelated and complementary.

An important early step in your test preparation is to learn the PPR competencies so that you can recognize the terms and concepts associated with each competency when you are looking at the exam items on the practice tests and the actual test. The chart on the next page offers a summarized version of the PPR domains and competencies to facilitate your ability to remember each competency. As you look through the chart, you should refer to your PPR domains and competencies printout, circling and underlining terms reflected in the chart.

DOMAIN I	Instruction, Assessment, and Student Learning
Competency Number and General Topic	**Core Ideas from Descriptive Statements**
001 Learner Characteristics	• Developmental characteristics • Stages of cognitive, social, physical, and emotional development • Cognitive development at different ages • Developmental characteristics at early elementary, elementary, middle-school, and high-school ages • Behaviors, challenges, and risk taking manifested at different ages • Adolescents and peer pressure
002 Student Diversity	• Knowledge of diversity (ethnicity, gender, language background, and exceptionality) • Understanding of how diversity can enrich teaching and learning • Knowledge of English language learner needs • Familiarity with English Language Proficiency Standards (ELPS)
003 Designing Effective Instruction	• Knowledge of TEKS and state assessment systems • Effective planning • Instruction that reflects students' developmental levels and learning readiness • Familiarity with teacher actions that promote learning
004 Teacher Actions that Promote Learning	• Knowledge of learning theory • Understanding of cognitive differences at different age levels to create developmentally appropriate instruction • Developmentally appropriate learning activities that promote higher-order thinking skills • Integration of time management and study skills • Awareness of how teacher behaviors impact student learning • Integration of ELPS • Understanding of impact of home and community factors on students' classroom experiences

(continued)

DOMAIN II	Creating a Positive Learning Environment
Competency Number and General Topic	**Core Ideas from Descriptive Statements**
005 **Creation of a Positive Classroom Environment**	• Classroom environment reflecting learners' developmental stage • Classroom environment values diversity, promoting respect, encouraging collaboration, nurturing students, and conveying high expectations • Classroom configuration promoting learning
006 **Classroom Management**	• Knowledge and application of classroom management theories and practices • Creation of age-appropriate classroom routines and schedules that support learning • Effective implementation of developmentally appropriate cooperative and collaborative strategies • Promotion of age-appropriate interpersonal skills for effective classroom interactions
DOMAIN III	**Effective and Responsive Instruction and Assessment**
Competency Number and General Topic	**Core Ideas Summarized from Descriptive Statements**
007 **Effective Communication**	• Communication skills targeted at students' developmental levels • Effective integration of communication skills (oral language) to promote student learning
008 **Engaging Instruction**	• Application of strategies designed to engage learners • Ongoing assessment of effectiveness of teacher actions • Targeted instruction for ELL students
009 **Integration of Technology**	• Familiarity with technology and opportunities for classroom applications • Integration of technology to promote student learning
010 **Feedback and Assessment**	• Effective use of various assessment methods • Use of feedback to promote student learning

(continued)

DOMAIN IV	Teacher's Professional Roles and Responsibilities
Competency Number and General Topic	Core Ideas Summarized from Descriptive Statements
011 **Family** **Involvement**	• Effective communication with families • Awareness of diverse family backgrounds • Efforts to engage families in students' educational experiences
012 **Professional** **Development**	• Collaboration with local colleagues to promote student learning • Effective use of district resources to promote student achievement • Effective use of professional development resources for individual professional growth
013 **State** **Educational** **Structure** **and Legal** **Requirements**	• Knowledge of state educational structures as presented in state documents • Knowledge of legal requirements and teacher responsibilities in education issues • Understanding of how state assessments fit into the state educational framework

Study Strategy 5

Assemble your textbooks, supplementary materials (such as handouts from your professor, online posts, and so on), notes, and other class materials (tests, reviews, research papers you wrote, PowerPoint lessons, class forums, etc.). Have these at hand as you study. When you start learning the competencies and the descriptive statements, you will very likely need to refer to these materials for definitions and explanations of core concepts.

Study Strategy 6

Get serious about studying. Once you decide when you are going to take the exam, you need to establish a dedicated time each day for studying. It is never too early to start studying for the TExES PPR exam. The earlier you begin, the more time you will have to sharpen your skills and focus your efforts. Do not procrastinate. Cramming is not an effective way to study, since it does not allow you enough time to learn the test material. Work out a study routine and stick to it. Reviewing your class notes and textbooks along with our book will provide you with an even better foundation for passing this exam.

Study Schedule

Although our study plan is designed to be used in the six weeks before your exam, if necessary, it can be condensed to three weeks by combining each two-week period into one. Be sure to set aside enough time—at least two hours each day—to study. The more time you spend studying, the more prepared and relaxed you will feel on the day of the exam.

When you take the online practice tests at the REA Study Center, simulate the conditions of the test as closely as possible. Turn your television and radio off, and sit down at a quiet table free from distraction.

As you complete each test, review your score reports, study the diagnostic feedback, and review the explanations to the questions you answered incorrectly. Concentrate on one problem area at a time by reading the question and explanation, and by studying our review until you are confident that you have mastered the material. Give extra attention to the review chapters that cover your areas of difficulty, as this will build your skills in those areas.

Week	Activity
1	Take the online Diagnostic Test at the REA Study Center. Your detailed score report will identify the topics where you need the most review.
2-4	Study the review chapters. Use your score report from the Diagnostic Test to focus your study. Useful study techniques include highlighting key terms and information and taking notes as you read the review. Learn all the domains and competencies by making flashcards and targeting questions you missed on the diagnostic test.
3	Take Practice Test 1 online. Review your score report and identify topics where you need more review.
4	Reread all your notes, refresh your understanding of the exam's competencies and skills, review your textbooks and class notes you've taken. This is also the time to consider other supplemental materials, (such as official test bulletins) your advisor or the TEA suggests.
5	Take Practice Test 2 online. Review your score report and restudy any topics you missed.
6	Review your score reports from the Diagnostic Test and both Practice Tests, read the detailed answer explanations for the questions you got wrong, and study those competencies. If you have extra time, take Practice Test 1 again and see how much your score has improved.
Note: If you are studying and do not have Internet access, you can take the printed versions of the tests in the book. These are the same practice tests offered online, but without the added benefits of timed testing conditions, automatic scoring, and diagnostic score reports.	

Official TExES PPR Practice Test

If you want even more practice before exam day, take the free full-length interactive PPR practice test available on the TEA/ETS website.

As you take the TEA/ETS PPR practice test, jot down terms you do not know, and make sure you look them up prior to taking the actual exam.

Test-Day Preparation

Make sure you follow all instructions provided by ETS regarding your exam day, time, and all other test-day requirements (see *registration bulletin*). The instructions include information about what you are required to bring (types of ID), what materials are restricted in the test area, and what time you are expected to arrive.

If you are not familiar with the test center, you should take a practice drive to the site to ensure you know where it is, to anticipate potential traffic problems, and to estimate the time it takes to get there. The rules for administering the exam are non-negotiable; if you arrive late, you will not be allowed to take the exam. You must also have your exam admission ticket, which you can print from the official website. The website also provides details about your score access and availability.

During the test, procedures will be followed to maintain test security. Once you enter the test center, follow all of the rules and instructions given by the test supervisor. If you do not, you risk being dismissed from the test and having your scores canceled. Make sure you ask about breaks during the test so that you do not violate testing procedures.

When you finish your test, hand in your materials and you will be dismissed. Then, go home and relax—you deserve it!

Good luck on the TExES PPR!

TExES PEDAGOGY AND PROFESSIONAL RESPONSIBILITIES EC-12 (160)

Domain Reviews

PART I: DOMAIN I

Designing Instruction and Assessment to Promote Student Learning

Designing Instruction and Assessment to Promote Student Learning

Domain I addresses Competencies 001, 002, 003, and 004, focusing on the responsibility of the teacher to reach a diverse student body by using well-considered, effective pedagogical methods and teaching strategies that take learners' developmental features into account.

Before continuing through this chapter, carefully read and annotate the four competencies and descriptive statements in Domain I from the *Preparation Manual 160 Pedagogy and Professional Responsibilities EC–12.* Underline key terms, mark terms you do not know, and pay special attention to the terms in parenthesis because those provide very specific indicators of the parameters of the competency. Here are the four competencies in Domain I, as outlined in the TEA PPR *Preparation Manual*:

Competency 001: The teacher understands human development processes and applies this knowledge to plan instruction and ongoing assessment that motivate students and are responsive to their developmental characteristics and needs.

Competency 002: The teacher understands student diversity and knows how to plan learning experiences and design assessments that are responsive to differences among students and that promote all students' learning.

Competency 003: The teacher understands procedures for designing effective and coherent instruction and assessment based on appropriate learning goals and objectives.

Competency 004: The teacher understands learning processes and factors that impact student learning and demonstrates this knowledge by planning effective, engaging instruction and appropriate assessments.

You should also carefully read the Pedagogy and Professional Responsibilities Educator Standards (the introduction explains how to access this document and why it's relevant to your PPR prep). Remember that standards include specific information about what beginning teachers should know and should be able to do; the knowledge statements (k) and the skills statements (s) from the standards will offer insights into the meaning of the descriptors for each competency. According to the official TEA PPR *Preparation Manual*, Domain I addresses PPR Educator Standard 1: The teacher designs instruction appropriate for all students that reflects an understanding of relevant content and is based on continuous and appropriate assessment.

Take a few minutes to study the content of PPR Standard I, paying particular attention to the way the knowledge (k) and skills (s) statements illuminate the descriptive statements for the Domain I competencies. As you read this chapter, you should have both the PPR competency pages and the PPR standards at your study area so that you can connect the information presented here to the TEA materials.

Competency 001

Competency 001

The teacher understands human development processes and applies this knowledge to plan instruction and ongoing assessment that motivate students and are responsive to their developmental characteristics and needs.

Competency 001 addresses **learner characteristics** and is explained through 16 descriptive statements, which cover the following general areas:

- Developmental factors that apply to all ages (cognitive, social, physical, and emotional)

- Developmental characteristics that apply to early childhood through students in grade 12

- Creating a positive learning environment

- Knowing how to address the needs of students at different age levels

- Risky behaviors that students may engage in

Competency 001 Key Terms

The following key terms are integral to fully understanding the scope of Competency 001. You should consider creating flashcards to remind you of what they mean so that you can recognize the direct or implied references to these terms in the test items.

Competency 001 Key Terms		
adolescence	developmental processes and instructional decisions	organizational skills
cognitive development	emotional development	peer pressure
decision making	equity	physical development
developmental characteristics: adolescence and early adulthood	goal setting	positive learning environment
developmental characteristics: EC through grade 4	health and school performance	risky behaviors
developmental characteristics: middle school	high expectations	skills
developmental differences	importance of play	social development
developmental processes	learning community	workplace skills

Developmental Processes

Teaching effectively requires extensive knowledge of the learners in our classrooms. Having a breadth of knowledge of the content area is only part of what is needed to be an effective teacher. To promote student learning, a teacher must also understand where the learners are developmentally, what strategies get their attention, what personal events and changes are impacting them, and even what forces are causing problems for them. To plan and deliver effective lessons, a teacher must take all of these factors into account. Developmental differences manifested at different age levels are generally categorized as cognitive, affective, social, and physical changes.

Piaget's Stages of Cognitive Development

Jean Piaget is a predominant figure in the field of cognitive psychology. His theory of cognitive development is based on the notion that cognitive abilities (one's ability to think) are developed as individuals mature physiologically and they have opportunities to interact with their environment. On the basis of years of observation and notes on children, including his own daughters and son, Piaget asserted that behaviors and ways of thinking occur in stages that last multiple years as the individual progresses to higher levels of cognition. According to Piaget, there are four stages of cognitive development, beginning with the sensorimotor stage (birth through age two) and culminating in the formal operational stage (early adolescence to young adulthood). The chart below summarizes Piaget's stages.

Piaget's Stages of Cognitive Development

Stage	Age Range	Cognitive Characteristics	Brief Explanation
Sensorimotor	Birth to two	• Reality-based schemes • Centrism • Object permanence	• Experience processed by reaching, grasping, and moving about • Experience centered on the child's own body • The child gradually learning that objects exist even if out of sight
Preoperational	Preschool years	• Language development • Symbolic functions • Symbolic play • Egocentrism	• Intentional use of language; acquisition of language structures • Representational thought: child can represent objects and events removed in time and space • Play demonstrates increasing imaginative capacity • Inability to understand another's perspective
Concrete operational	Elementary grade years	• Conservation • Class inclusion • Seriation • Decentering	• Understanding that format or shape do not affect mass • Recognizing of subset relationships • Ordering ability • Integration of self into physical and social environment
Formal operational	Early adolescence forward	• Abstract thinking • Logic • Thinking in hypotheses	• Ability to think in and of possibilities • Ability to think deductively • Ability to plan

Chart adapted from Pressley and McCormick

Piaget used the term "operation" to mean the ability to conceptualize something that previously the child could do only physically. The stages delineate the child's cognitive development starting with the sensorimotor stage, a reality-based world in which the infant positions himself or herself at the center of the world and learns by processing the impact of his or her actions on the environment. Significant cognitive accomplishments in this first state include the creation of sensorimotor schemes, such as moving from sucking as a reflex to sucking as a means of learning about new objects. The development of object permanence is considered a major accomplishment of this period: the realization that when objects are not visible they have not disappeared altogether.

The **preoperational stage** covers the preschool years when children begin to use language deliberately in contrast to the "babble" and experimental articulations of babyhood. A major accomplishment in this stage is the acquisition of language that proceeds from random, imitative babbling through rudimentary syntax to language that enables children to be understood by people beyond their family circle. Because of the development of language, the child at this stage can represent events and objects in a variety of symbolic ways: words, images, gestures, and recall. Play is a critical developmental component in this stage as children demonstrate the ability to play symbolically—pretending that ordinary objects represent other things or acting out scenarios in which they themselves represent other individuals or creatures.

In the **concrete operational stage**, thinking becomes more sophisticated but is still largely based on concrete objects and immediate situations. However, important cognitive skills that develop at this stage include the ability to subdivide objects into subsets referred to as class inclusion or just classification. One-dimensional seriation—the ability to arrange or order objects on the basis of a single characteristic—is a cognitive ability that develops at this stage. Understanding of conservation is another significant development; children in the concrete operational stage gradually understand that objects conserve their mass or volume when they are transferred to or transformed into different shapes. Children at this age begin to decenter which Piaget describes as transitioning from the earlier state in which the baby centers all experience on his or her own body to a "decentered" state in which children begin to see themselves objectively positioned among other people and within an environment (Piaget, 1969, p. 94).

The **formal operational stage** begins in later childhood (about age 11) and extends through adulthood. Learners at this stage of cognitive development can engage in logical, abstract, and hypothetical thought; they can use the scientific method, meaning they can formulate hypotheses, isolate influences, and identify cause-and-effect relationships. They can engage in both deductive and inductive reasoning, and they can operate on verbal statements exclusive of concrete experiences or examples. These cognitive abilities characterize the highest levels of thought, which continue to develop throughout adulthood, although many child development experts believe that some individuals never make it completely through the formal operational stage (Piaget, 1969; Santrock, 2009, pp. 182–199; Presley & McCormick, 2007, pp. 61–65).

Despite the overwhelming influence of Piaget on education, it is important to remember that his cognitive stages are not absolute, which means that teachers must look not simply at students' ages, but at their behaviors and abilities. Piaget himself pointed out that the stages are incremental, gradually moving the child toward integration of cognitive, social, affective, and moral accomplishments into a unified whole (Piaget, 1969, p. 128). Piaget's stages should not be used to categorize but to understand why children do certain things at certain ages and to plan instruction that addresses their current intellectual abilities and moves them toward higher levels. Competency 004 addresses how teachers can use knowledge of these developmental stages to plan effective, engaging instruction and assessment.

Erikson's Theory of Psychosocial Development

Another influential theoretical approach to understanding human development is offered by Erik Erikson, who concentrated on how human development reflects the individual's social affiliations. For each of eight stages, Erikson hypothesized a "crisis" from which the individual "re-emerges with an increased sense of inner unity, with an increase of good judgment, and an increase in the capacity 'to do well' according to his own standards and to the standards of those who are significant to him" (Erikson, 1968, p. 92). According to Erikson, negotiating each crisis effectively is essential in constructing and maintaining identity. The crisis at each stage is not a "catastrophe" but an opportunity to grow and to thrive. The stages span from birth through death (Erikson, 1968, p. 96). The chart on the next page outlines Erikson's stages of development.

Erikson's Stages of Development

Stage	Age	Crisis	Brief Description
1	Birth through first year	Trust versus mistrust	Although apparently helpless, infants learn to "get" what they need from their caregivers, and the quality of that giving shapes the individual's negotiation of the trust versus mistrust crisis.
2	Toddler	Autonomy versus shame, doubt	In asserting his or her free will, the child begins to recognize boundaries that must be observed in order maintain cooperation with others. This creates an on-going tension between the individual's propensity for self-insistence (autonomy) and the need to exercise self-control (shame and doubt).
3	Third year	Initiative versus guilt	Recognizing what he or she is now able to do creates in the individual a sense of guilt brought on by developing conscience when he or she considers the possibilities and consequences of acting on new potential.
4	Early school years	Industry versus inferiority	The desire to produce, to make things, to imitate adult productivity is a major part of entering the school environment; however, inferiority may be caused by the child's lack of readiness for the tasks attempted or for "replacing" the family/home environment with the social setting of the school.
5	Adolescence	Identity versus identity confusion	The individual recognizes the pending need to assume an adult role but feels confusion and resistance over possibly having to settle on a role that may not reflect his or her will.
6	Late adolescence through young adulthood	Intimacy versus isolation	Intimacy is a manifestation of "true" identity as the individual shares his or her identity with others; isolation results when interpersonal relationships do not adequately address the individual's need for intimacy.
7	Adulthood through early senior years	Generativity versus stagnation	Generativity means concern for making meaningful contributions to guide the next generation; failing to achieve that sense of contribution and personal enrichment results in stagnation.
8	Old age	Integrity versus despair	A sense of integration is caused by satisfaction over the individual's sense of comradeship with people who lived before and will come after; despair comes from dissatisfaction over the life lived and the inability at this late stage to start over and make alternate choices.

Chart based on Erik Erikson's *Identity: Youth and Crisis*

Three of Erikson's stages are salient to the EC–12 teacher. Stage 4, industry versus inferiority, marks the child's entry into the school environment where the child has to negotiate a new social setting involving teachers instead of parents and a lot more children. Industry, according to Erikson, is the natural drive at this stage as the child attempts to imitate adult competencies and to produce things that may win him or her recognition. A sense of inferiority may result if the child's ability has not yet reached his or her desire to produce; the potential to produce may not be realized until a later stage (Erikson, 1968, pp. 122–128).

Around the time students enter junior high, they begin the developmental task of achieving identity—Erikson's Stage 5, identity versus identity confusion. According to Erikson, the struggle to achieve identity is one of the most important developmental tasks and one that creates serious psychosocial problems for adolescents. For example, even the individual who has successfully achieved all the important developmental milestones from the previous stages (such as initiative and industry) now finds himself or herself in a state of flux: everything (body, feelings, thoughts) is changing. The adolescent starts to ask, "Who am I? Who can I trust? What will I do when I grow up?" Individuals at this stage seek answers to big questions but may resist and question what authoritative grownups tell them, the resistance caused by the realization that accepting adult beliefs and expectations interferes with individual free will. Erikson believed that if adolescents find out what they believe in, what their goals, ideas, and values are, then they attain identity achievement; failure to discover these things leads to identity confusion and impacts later stages (Erikson, 1968, pp. 128–135).

In high school, students are entering the stage of young adulthood—for Erikson, a psychosocial stage characterized by the polarities of intimacy and isolation. Individuals at this stage of development begin to think about forming lasting friendships, even marital unions. Erikson would argue that many psychosocial problems experienced by young adults have their origin in the individual's failure to achieve identity during the preceding stage; the young person who does not know who he or she really is cannot achieve true intimacy, and the result is isolation brought on by the unwillingness to risk true intimacy because of the potential impact on identity (Erikson, 1968, pp. 135–138).

Piaget's and Erikson's frameworks generalize about expected behaviors, attitudes, and capabilities young people demonstrate at the developmental stages these two theorists define. In reality, teachers deal with students who do not fit perfectly into Piagetian and Eriksonian molds. Moreover, both Piaget and Erikson explained that stages are not absolutely linear: vestiges of behaviors, attitudes, and cognitive abilities from previous stages persist in later stages. However, understanding these developmental theories does offer insights into the cognitive, social, physical, and emotional states of children, and these understandings should inform the instructional decisions teachers make.

Other Developmental Characteristics

It would seem that the developmental characteristics that teachers should be concerned about are strictly cognitive, but other learner characteristics impact student readiness and ability to participate in classroom activities. The cognitive and psychosocial stages attributed to Piaget and Erikson have affective manifestations as well. For example, according to Erikson's theory, if the crisis presented at each stage is not effectively negotiated by the individual, the result is "maladjustment" (Erikson, 1968, p. 96). Integrating Erikson's theory into the classroom environment suggests an expected "norm" for children and young people at the various Eriksonian stages. Thus, a child who seems timid, nonparticipatory, academically and socially lethargic is the opposite of what Erikson describes as the behavior outcomes of a child who has successfully negotiated the initiative versus guilt stage (Erikson, 1968, p. 114).

Similarly, a child who seems to lag behind in Piaget's cognitive stages may exhibit frustration, anger, and low self-esteem because apparently "developmentally appropriate" tasks are beyond his or her ability. Competency 001 focuses on the teacher's ability to recognize developmental characteristics; later competencies cover specific teacher actions that demonstrate responsive instruction that appropriately addresses students' needs.

Play Development and Classroom Expectations

Play is an important part of childhood and should thus be an integral part of classroom experiences. Play is what occupies most of a child's day up until he or she enters school; so children start school with a great deal of experience in using play to learn. Play can be symbolic, constructive, solitary, social, indirect, intellectual, or physical (Santrock, 2009, pp. 460–463). Many of the skills necessary for academic success are acquired through the self-initiated play that children engage in during the preoperational stage: problem solving, persistence, creativity, organization, cooperation. Consequently, teachers can use play as a teaching strategy in presenting new concepts. In early elementary grades, children equate school day events with play, reporting play as a key activity in their accounts of school day routines (Fein & Wiltz, 1998).

When teachers integrate play into academic activities, they provide opportunities for learners to develop oral language skills, observation skills, critical thinking skills, social skills, and motor skills. Indeed, play can be integrated into any academic subject (Brewer, 2007).

Classroom play is important even for older students. In self-initiated play situations, older children learn cooperation, reciprocity, courtesy, verbal and nonverbal communication, and aggressive and nonaggressive behaviors. As they move into the concrete operational and formal operational stages, children's play—self-initiated and classroom structured—integrates gender roles, confidence based on physical ability, cooperation, rule-setting, literacy development, and technology-related cognitive skills. When older students describe a class as being "fun," they frequently are referring to such things as learning new content through games, integrating kinesthetic activities into the class routine, and using role playing to demonstrate new knowledge. In general, children and young people consider play voluntary, pleasurable, and meaningful; thus, educators see benefits in integrating play activities and behaviors into class activities. In fact, play seems to contribute to learning and academic achievement (Manning, 1998, p. 155–159).

Beyond Content: Real-World Issues in the Classroom

The theories of development summarized above reinforce the reality that the classroom is not just a place where students learn academic subject matter. The school space functions as a site where young people interact meaningfully in situations that mimic the "real world." Students spend about eight hours each day in school (more if they are involved in extracurricular activities). Thus, the school space necessarily contributes to skills necessary for success in venues outside school.

Community and Acceptance

Seeing the classroom as a *learning community* is a common approach to integrating life skills into the school space. From the learning community perspective, learners operate as participating members of a group. Such membership requires mutual respect, the ability to negotiate with other members of the community, recognition of diverse qualities that members bring to the community, and a general expectation that the individuals will thrive.

Clearly, the teacher facilitates the creation of community in the classroom through specific attitudes and actions that begin the moment the students enter class on the first day. Harvey Daniels talks about familiarity as the core of community formation: if students do not know each other, they will not be able to form a community. Thus, he recommends a highly effective first-day strategy—meet five people in five minutes—in which students mingle with each other, ask each other get-to-know-you questions, and learn each other's names (Daniels, 2012). If this activity is repeated a few times in the opening days of a semester, students will be well on their way to learning who their classmates are, and this is a core component of the community setting.

One of the "problems" evident in the reactions of young children and adolescents to stressful situations is their easy reliance on insult. A teacher can avert (or reduce) such occurrences by creating a culture of respect and success in the classroom by modeling desirable behaviors. For example, student work can be showcased equitably so that not just the high achievers' work is displayed. Students can be given opportunities to work together to help underachieving classmates earn higher scores. Grades should not be presented as a competition where only a few students can attain top scores. The classroom should be a space that inspires assurance of success for everyone, not a place that symbolizes failure. A scene from the film *Dangerous Minds* (Simpson, 1995) illustrates how cinematic teacher LouAnne Johnson cultivates a culture of success and community in her class of underachieving students. On the second day of class, she tells her students that they all have an A and all they have to do is keep it. Although the students are initially incredulous, they eventually rely on this promised A as they move through the challenging assignments she gives them. Through this relatively simple gesture, the teacher has created a culture of success, high expectations, and community in the class.

Teachers can create assignments that allow students to integrate their real worlds into class activities. When teachers value and integrate the knowledge and experience that students bring from their home lives and real-world experiences, they are implementing a "funds of knowledge" approach (Moll, Amanti, Neff, & Gonzalez, 1992). Here's an example. Teacher Mindy Barry Hanson (2003) writes about Dusty, a 19-year-old senior who had to write a traditional literary research paper as a graduation requirement, but he felt he couldn't do it. In talking with Dusty, the teacher learned that he knew quite a bit about racing cars; they negotiated and he wrote a research paper on the history of the Daytona 500. The teacher's comment about Dusty's experience offers an excellent explanation of the results of how the funds of knowledge approach fosters high expectations: "Dusty himself taught me that if I hope for the best in a student, I may just get it. Also, I realized that getting students involved in their learning is half the battle. Once the desire is there, students are often surprisingly willing to try" (Hanson, 2003, p. 34).

Complications from the Real World

Bringing the real world into the classroom, however, also means acknowledging the problems that students bring into the classroom: drug use, disruptive home lives, and risky behaviors.

Teachers must be aware of the multiplicity of issues affecting physical growth and maturation and which directly impact students' classroom behavior, academic performance, and social interaction. For example, teachers must take into account the role of proper nutrition, adequate rest and physical activity. For this reason, school breakfast and lunch programs provide free meals to students with limited financial resources. For some students, these free meals may be their only source of nutrition.

Children need enough sleep to be able to stay awake and participate in their classes. A recent study of young people's sleep patterns suggests that 10-year-old children need about 10 hours of sleep, and younger ones need more. Older children need less sleep except when they are going through puberty, when they need about 10 hours. This study also reports that 85 percent of adolescents are "mildly" sleep deprived and 10 to 40 percent are significantly sleep deprived. In the classroom, sleep deprivation results in lower grades, decreased motivation, and problems in concentration, attention, and coherent reasoning. Furthermore, insufficient sleep reduces memory, self control, and speed of thinking and increases errors (Bergin & Bergin, 2009/2010). While teachers can do little to improve students' sleeping habits, they can recognize how this problem impacts students' cognitive, social, physical, and emotional development.

Children whose parents are using illegal drugs or who use illegal drugs themselves will also often present troubling behaviors that disrupt classrooms and the learning of others, not to mention the negative effects on their own academic progress. Drug use impairs judgment, reaction time, and reduces inhibitions.

Because peer pressure mounts during the preteen and teenage years, it is important that teachers deal with the topic and provide students with tools to combat negative peer pressure. Peer pressure may drive students to engage in dangerous behavior: drug use, violence, and gang affiliations. Being able to discuss ideas and feelings without fear of ridicule or criticism is important, as are opportunities to examine life values and goals.

The impact of external factors is frequently manifested through poor school achievement, poor school attendance, numerous school suspensions, difficulty with social skills, poor peer relations, and difficulty controlling impulses and emotions, all of which directly impact the student's class participation and achievement.

Students' involvement in risky behavior could disrupt normal educational routines. Competency 013 in Domain IV addresses teachers' responsibilities in handling such problems. Competency 001, however, simply acknowledges the potential impact on the affected student's development and learning. In other words, knowing the manifestations of risky behavior will keep teachers from labeling a student lazy or unmotivated; instead, the teacher will know that the student's classroom performance is being impacted by real-world problems that need to be addressed as explained in Competency 013.

Review Questions

1. A grade 5 teacher wants to teach his class about the classification system in the animal kingdom. He introduces the unit with this activity: He brings to class a cardboard box filled with 30 household items, displays the contents on a table, and asks the students, in groups of three or four, to put like items into piles and to explain why they placed certain items into a particular pile. Which of the following rationales best explains the developmental appropriateness of this instructional activity?

   (A) The assignment moves students into higher-order thinking skills

   (B) The assignment allows students to make home-school connections

   (C) The assignment focuses on categorizing, a skill that calls for explaining inter-relationships

   (D) The assignment will enable students to practice socialization skills

   The correct response is **(C)**. According to Piaget's theory of cognitive development, students at this age are at the stage of *concrete operational* thought. Grouping based on similarities and differences is a cognitive accomplishment characteristic of this stage. Response (A) is incorrect because the students are probably about 10 years old and still firmly in concrete operational thinking rather than the higher order thinking that characterizes Piaget's fourth stage. (B) overlooks the academic reasoning behind the activity: the teacher wants students to practice classifying, not to make home-school connection. (D) is a side effect of the activity but not the primary pedagogical intention behind the sorting activity.

2. As part of a high school's career day, a high-school teacher invites several professionals from the community to talk to students about their responsibilities and how they contribute to the community. This activity is developmentally appropriate for this age level because the students are in which of the following stages of Erikson's psychosocial development?

    (A) Industry versus inferiority

    (B) Identity versus identity confusion

    (C) Intimacy versus isolation

    (D) Integrity versus despair

The correct response is **(B)**. Interest in career is a hallmark of Erikson's identity versus identity confusion stage which corresponds to adolescence. Responses (A), (C), and (D) are incorrect because these stages do not correspond to the age level and class activity specified in the stem.

3. A middle-school teacher constructs a unit on peer pressure. Which of the following initial unit activities would most effectively demonstrate awareness of students' current developmental levels?

    (A) The teacher has students write a short essay on their experiences with peer pressure and read their essays orally. After the readings, the teacher directs a class discussion about the problems caused by peer pressure.

    (B) The teacher has students interview each other to ask questions about experiences with peer pressure.

    (C) The teacher shows students several news clips of young people injuring themselves through actions attributed to peer pressure.

    (D) The teacher creates open-ended scenarios in which characters face peer pressure. Each group is assigned a scenario, which they dramatize to the class; the groups explain the rationale for how they resolve the peer pressure situation.

The correct response is **(D)**. This response is the most likely in this scenario to create a comfortable class setting for investigating the importance of peer pressure, peer acceptance, and conformity to group norms. The open-ended dramatization allows students a great deal of autonomy in speculating about peer pressure without admitting to individual problems related to peer pressure. (A) and (B) show a lack sensitivity to students' individual stories about peer pressure; requiring students to share their stories is likely to create discomfort in all the students. (C) suggests that peer pressure leads to danger; this response does not allow for consideration of the positive aspects of peer pressure or for discussion of the significance of peer-related issues in adolescents' experiences.

CHAPTER

Competency 002

2

Competency 002

The teacher understands student diversity and knows how to plan learning experiences and design assessments that are responsive to differences among students and that promote all students' learning.

Competency 002 addresses the broad topic of **student diversity** and is explained through nine descriptive statements, which cover the following general areas:

- Understanding, acceptance, and increasing awareness of student diversity

- Knowledge of how to use diversity to enrich students' learning experiences by planning instruction that is responsive to differences

- Knowledge of English Language Proficiency Standards (ELPS) in TEKS

Competency 002 Key Terms

The following key terms are integral to fully understanding the scope of Competency 002. You should consider creating flashcards to remind you of what they mean so that you can recognize the direct or implied references to these terms in the test items.

Competency 002 Key Terms		
cultural diversity	ELPS	IDEA
culturally relevant pedagogy	English language learners	learning styles
differentiated instruction	ethnicity	linguistic differences
disabilities	exceptionality	social characteristics
diversity	gender	socioeconomic differences

Recognizing Diversity

PPR Competency 002 addresses the various ways in which teachers can recognize diversity, celebrating difference as a means of enriching students' classroom and holistic educational experiences. Homogeneity does not exist in our classrooms; instead, diversity has increasingly become the most salient characteristic of our classrooms. Recognizing the diversity that students bring to the classroom is an important part of knowing our students.

Federal and state statistics reveal the growing diversity of our student populations. In educational contexts, diversity encompasses a broad range of differences: cultural, socioeconomic, ethnic, linguistic, academic proficiency, developmental, special needs. Nationally, 52.4 percent of students enrolled in public elementary and secondary schools are classified as white, and 47.5 percent are from other races and ethnic groups (U.S. Department of Education, NCES, 2013, Digest of Education Statistics, Table 45). Nationally, English language learners make up 9.8 percent of the total U.S. student population, 48.1 percent qualify for free or reduced lunch programs, and 13 percent are designated as disabled by the *Individuals with Disabilities Education* (IDEA) *Act* (U.S. Department of Education, NCES, 2013, Digest of Education Statistics Table 47, Table 46, Table 51).

Beyond legally defined types of diversity is the diversity that comes from being a distinct individual. In the classroom, celebration of diversity means that the teacher values each learner and fosters a culture of inclusivity in the classroom. The following seven principles illustrate how a teacher can use instructional activities to help learners value each others' differences.

1. Establishing and maintaining a classroom community is central to celebrating diversity. The teacher should use icebreaker activities at the beginning of the school year to ensure that students know each other and know *about* each other. Throughout the year, the teacher should integrate community-building activities to maintain cohesiveness among learners.

2. Whenever class misunderstandings can be traced to diversity issues, the teacher should take the opportunity to explore the root of the conflict. For example, racist remarks, gender-related insults, jibes about disabilities, etc. need to be addressed directly. The teacher should do everything possible to show students that difference means distinctiveness not deficit.

3. Major assignments should include options that enable individual learners to showcase their strongest abilities.

4. Displays of classwork should include all learners' products, not just the work of the class "stars."

5. Students should be taught how to work with each other in collaborative settings to avoid exclusivity and to recognize individual contributions by every group member. Students need guidance for working effectively in groups. For example, the teacher could use a fishbowl demonstration to explain how to integrate every group members' contribution, how to deal with group conflict, and how to motivate a nonproductive group member.

6. Lessons should include meaningful integration of characters, situations, and events reflecting cultural, gender, ability, and socioeconomic differences in authentic rather than stereotypical situations.

7. If necessary, instruction should be differentiated to take into account individual learner's needs while still addressing curricular goals.

Multiculturalism

When we consider that almost half of learners in American classrooms are classified as members of distinct racial or ethnic groups, the exigency of integrating diversity into classroom routines and instruction is evident. Multiculturalism should embrace the accomplishments of all cultural and ethnic groups, thereby strengthening our classroom communities (Competency 001) instead of fragmenting them into small sets of insular, exclusive groups.

An example from the film *Freedom Writers* (DeVito, Shamberg, & Sher, Producers, 2006) illustrates how a teacher strives to create community and inclusiveness out of fragmentation. Based on real-life teacher Erin Gruwell, the film focuses on how initially fragmented groups eventually grow to embrace their commonalities. In a pivotal scene, cinematic teacher Erin Gruwell stands outside watching students isolate themselves into groups on the school grounds. The next day, she has the students in her class play "the line game." She lays a strip of masking tape on the classroom floor, has students stand at the line, asks them a series of questions about their backgrounds, and has them step away from the line whenever they can answer positively to the question. The questions start out with popular rap music and films but gradually move to the details that inform the students' real lives: how many have been in a detention facility, how many have lost friends or loved ones to street violence. At the end of the scene, no one is standing at the line. This scene operationalizes the descriptive statements in Competency 002: diversity and difference should be celebrated as a crucial component of community in the classroom.

Special Needs Students

Exceptionality is the pedagogical term frequently used to describe special needs students whose needs are addressed by the *Individuals with Disabilities Education Act* (IDEA) (U.S. Department of Education, 2013). IDEA provides explicit federal guidelines for identifying students with Specific Learning Disabilities (SLD). While the teacher can be involved in the formal evaluation of the student, the teacher's most important responsibility comes in adapting and modifying classroom procedures and content to ensure that SLD students are able to progress effectively toward expected educational goals. IDEA is linked to the *No Child Left Behind Act* in the overarching goal to ensure educational equity for all students in America. The components of IDEA stipulate that children identified as SLD are educated with nondisabled students in "the least restrictive environment" (National Dissemination Center for Children with Disabilities, 2012).

However, teachers need to recognize that accommodations for special needs students should include efforts to integrate students with disabilities into the classroom community without eliciting a deficit response among class members. Accommodations typically include adjustments that make learning accessible to the learner without diffusing or reducing the content. Logical adjustments include such things as allowing the learner additional time to complete assignments, providing additional one-on-one time with the teacher, delivering instruction in methods that best meet the learner's needs, and collaborating with special education specialists to stay on the learner's Individualized Education Plan (Burden & Byrd, 2013, pp. 37–38). In terms of Competency 002, the teacher should make sure that SLD students are an integral part of the class community and that their exceptionality is valued as part of the classroom diversity. Students tend to be eager to help a disabled classmate participate in class activities: they are solicitous, kind, helpful, and generally inclusive. But teachers do need to be aware that occasionally, students may deliberately or inadvertently make insensitive comments or display unkind or even cruel behavior. This is why celebrating diversity must be a key component of a teacher's efforts to plan learning experiences responsive to all students' needs.

It is important to realize that special education requires specialized preparation and designated credentials. Competency 002 integrates exceptionality as a reality of our diverse classrooms, but it does not address the special preparation and legal guidelines relevant to students with disabilities. The discussion of Competency 013 addresses some of those federal regulations.

A quick PPR preparation strategy for familiarizing yourself with special education expectations in Texas is to review the competencies for the TExES examinations on special education which you can access from the Texas Education Agency webpage on the Texas Examination of Educator Standards (*http://cms.texes-ets.org* and search for "preparation materials").

Socioeconomic Differences

Socioeconomic differences may not be as obvious as differences in ethnicity, gender, linguistic background, or exceptionality. Socioeconomic categories reflect income, occupation, and education (Burden & Byrd, 2013, pp. 38–39). A low socioeconomic status generally suggests inequities in access to resources and opportunities, which substantively impact students' educational experiences (Kauchak & Eggen, 2012, p. 57). For example, students whose parents have little or no formal education usually cannot depend on parents to help them with homework, and many times, teachers, especially at lower grades, expect that parents will be able to help children do challenging homework. Students whose families have low incomes may not be able to purchase supplementary class materials. They may have limited or no access to technologies that may be required for class projects. Parents may have jobs that prevent them from taking children to school-related activities. Families may not have discretionary funds for students to participate in extracurricular activities. Low socioeconomic status may even impact students' basic nutritional and health needs.

Teachers need to address such differences sensitively without making the learners feel deficient or inferior or without calling undue attention to their socioeconomic status.

Regardless of students' financial resources, teachers can support equity in the classroom by modeling goal-setting, celebrating the distinct backgrounds and skills that each learner brings to the classroom, setting high expectations for all learners, and creating opportunities for all learners to experience success.

English Language Learners

According to the Texas Education Agency, 17 percent of the total number of students in state public schools are classified as English language learners (TEA, 2013, Limited English Proficiency Initiatives). English language learners are students who are in the process of acquiring English, who have a language other than English as their home language, and who have difficulty completing class work in English (Texas Constitution and Statutes, 2013). Teachers who teach in sections of the state with a very high Hispanic population (such as border areas and some major metropolitan areas) can expect a much higher percentage of ELLs in their classrooms. In Texas, the diversity borne out of the large ELL population of students contributes significantly to diversity in our classrooms. As with other types of diversity addressed by Competency 002, language diversity should be celebrated, respected, and embraced in all classroom situations.

An ever-increasing set of federal and state guidelines regulating the education of ELLs reflects the broad goal to provide educational equity for all students. In Texas, a variety of bilingual and ESL programs are implemented to meet the needs of ELLs as they progress toward L2 acquisition. While some of these programs segregate ELL students in order to provide L1 support as students acquire basic and academic fluency in L2, the goal for all programs is to eventually have students exit ESL programs and move into mainstream classrooms. Within the classroom, in day-to-day teaching, ELL students who are in transitional stages of their ESL program must be integrated equitably into the classroom community. Their developing language abilities should be considered a distinction rather than a deficit.

The classroom diversity created by ELL students offers opportunities for prolific teaching, student-centered instruction, and inclusive pedagogy. Many research and practice-based studies offer abundant strategies for accommodating ELL students without singling them out as deficient (Freeman & Freeman, 1998; Peregoy & Boyle, 2008). Additionally, the Texas Essential Knowledge and Skills includes English Language Proficiency Standards (ELPS) as part of state-mandated curriculum requirements (TEA,

2013, Texas Essential Knowledge and Skills). ELPS are appended to TEKS to guide all teachers, not just language arts teachers, in helping students meet curricular expectations for English proficiency in listening, speaking, reading, and writing. Additionally, ELPS include criteria for recognizing students' proficiency levels as beginning, intermediate, advanced, or advanced high, distinctions that are salient in making instructional adaptations to meet ELL students' educational needs.

Understanding the personal, social, cultural, and academic diversity of ELL students means making necessary pedagogical accommodations that celebrate the students' diversity rather than create a deficit view of the difference they bring to classroom. In classes with large numbers of ELL students, teachers are encouraged to integrate culturally relevant pedagogy that showcases the cultures represented in the classroom. Best teaching practices, however, are the same for all students; accommodations necessary for ELL students in mainstream classes could include integrating visual materials, pairing students so that native speakers help ELL students in collaborative work, hands-on instructions, vocabulary-development strategies, and attention to metacognitive strategies for acquiring L2.

A quick PPR preparation strategy for familiarizing yourself with ELL expectations in Texas is to review the competencies for the TExES ESL Supplementary Exam, which you can access from the Texas Education Agency webpage for the Texas Examinations of Educator Standards (*cms.texes-ets.org* and search for "preparation materials"). Additionally, REA's *TExES Special Education EC-12 (161)* is an excellent resource for familiarizing yourself with this important area of general pedagogical responsibilities.

Review Questions

1.   A grade 11 teacher assigns an Internet research project: working in groups, students identify a college or university to research. Students will prepare a PowerPoint presentation on their findings. The teacher allows one class period for students to organize the project and assign group tasks and gives the students a weekend to complete the assignment out of class. Several students approach the teacher after class to explain that they do not own computers and thus have no access to the Internet at home. Which of the following adjustments should the teacher make to ensure equitable treatment of all the students?

(A) The teacher should create a different assignment for the students who do not have Internet access

(B) The teacher should revise the assignment timeline to include several class sessions at the school's computer lab

(C) The teacher should pull out students with no home Internet access and have them work at the computer lab during class

(D) The teacher should excuse the students with no Internet access from this assignment and offer a makeup assignment later in the semester

The correct response is **(B)**. This response takes into account differential access to technology without singling out the students who have no home access to technology. It presents an equitable pedagogical adjustment to accommodate all learners' circumstances. (A) and (C) are incorrect because they call undue attention to the students with no Internet access, creating a deficit and exclusionary response to the learners' needs. (D) is incorrect because this option excludes the students with no internet access at home from participating meaningfully in this assignment.

2. A middle-school teacher starts the school year by having students create a Profile Wall. The teacher allows students to pick sheets of construction paper and then tells them to create a Profile Page that includes information such as their favorite movies and games, where they were born, something they want to accomplish in life, things they are good at, and so on. They are also supposed to include a snapshot or illustration that shows them doing something they enjoy doing. When all the profiles are complete, each learner will briefly present his or her Profile Page to the class and then post it on the wall. The Profile Wall will primarily address which of the following instructional goals?

(A) Integration of a variety of skills to allow students to be creative

(B) Connection between the classroom and the real world

(C) Recognition of diversity among learners in the class

(D) Beginning a new school year with a project that engages students in a fun activity

The correct response is **(C)**. Having students create individual profiles and present them to the class appropriates a strategy from social networking in a class activity designed to create a class community. (A) and (D) are incorrect because the details of the activity show that it is far more than a venue for creative expression or fun. (B) is incorrect because, while the activity is modeled on social networking profiles, the details of the activity do not focus on real-world-classroom connections.

3. A grade-3 teacher is scheduling a parents' morning to showcase science projects students have completed. She has students write invitations to deliver to their parents. Julia, an ELL student, writes the following note.

> To pleze come for the science day. Is because to celebrate. We make the project on school.

Julia's note suggests she is at which of the following ELPS writing proficiency levels?

(A) Beginning

(B) Intermediate

(C) Advanced

(D) Advanced High

The correct response is **(B)**. The writing demonstrates the student's ability to address grade-appropriate writing tasks in a limited way—the prime descriptor for intermediate ELPS level. (A) is incorrect because the student's writing demonstration exceeds the ELPS descriptors for beginning-level writing. (C) and (D) are incorrect because the student's writing sample does not yet meet advanced or advanced high ELPS descriptors.

CHAPTER

Competency 003

3

Competency 003

The teacher understands procedures for designing effective and coherent instruction and assessment based on appropriate learning goals and objectives.

Designing effective instruction is the broad area addressed by Competency 003. Eight descriptive statements in this competency cover the following general topics:

- Understanding of TEKS and connections to instructional goals

- Developing and implementing learning goals

- Formative assessment based on class performance and state assessment data

- Integrating resources to enhance student learning

- Devising varied learning activities

Competency 003 Key Terms

The following key terms are integral to fully understanding the scope of Competency 003. You should consider creating flashcards to remind you of what they mean so that you can recognize the direct or implied references to these terms in the test items.

Competency 003 Key Terms		
age-appropriateness	developing instructional goals	relevance
alignment	formal assessment data	resources
appropriateness of learning goals	formative assessment	significance
clarity	logically sequenced units	sufficient time
connections to real world	multicultural experiences	TEKS and instructional goals
cooperative learning	multiple perspectives	thematic units
cross-disciplinary content		

Designing Instruction

PPR Competency 003 covers pragmatic aspects of teaching: design instruction including setting instructional goals that reflect the teacher's content knowledge, support curricular expectations, reflect students' learning readiness, guide students toward higher levels of achievement, demonstrate the teacher's breadth of knowledge of effective pedagogy, and coordinate with state instructional expectations. Competency 003, in a nutshell, addresses skills needed to transform content-area knowledge into coherent instruction. Competency 003 reminds us that effective teaching revolves around two questions: what will you teach (content), and why will you teach it (goals)?

In Texas, the Texas Essential Knowledge and Skills (TEKS) present the state's curriculum standards in English language arts and reading, mathematics, social studies, and science. However, TEKS only identify the topics that need to be addressed at each grade level with minimal reference to strategies and approaches. Let us look at an excerpt from the grade 6 Social Studies TEKS (TEA, 2011):

- Citizenship. The student understands that the nature of citizenship varies among societies. The student is expected to:
  (A) describe roles and responsibilities of citizens in various contemporary societies, including the United States;

To teach this curricular component, teachers need to know *how* to teach it to students. Knowing how involves contextualizing this specific TEKS excerpt in the bigger social studies picture, figuring out how to make this specific TEKS component accessible, meaningful, and interesting to students, and devising appropriate assessment strategies. These concerns are addressed by Competency 003 and its descriptive statements.

Instructional design begins with planning. Ideally, every lesson has a place in an instructional hierarchy that starts with daily lessons, moves through units, grading periods, semesters, and the academic year. At the top of the instructional design hierarchy are the state-wide curricular standards established by TEKS. Teachers, however, need to factor in district-developed curriculum, best-teaching practices for the content area, student needs, the teacher's own dispositions, and a variety of other components.

Effective planning shows purpose and design. While it is possible to teach chapters out of a book, the kind of instructional design described in Competency 003 moves far beyond simply following a textbook presentation of a topic or whole subject.

Effective teachers know how to plan so that their curriculum guides, lesson plans, actual lessons, and tests and assessments are correlated. They plan in advance, explain the unit's goals and objectives to the students, and devise activities that will help the class reach the desired outcomes.

Why are you teaching this? What do students need to know? How will students show or demonstrate that they do know? These are important considerations that allow teachers to set appropriate learning goals and objectives. Frequently, educators use the terms goals, objectives, standards, and outcomes interchangeably to describe what students are supposed to know and be able to do. Effective instructional design should reflect a coherent approach to what students should be able to do as a result of a specific lesson, unit, or semester-long course of study. For decades, teachers have looked to Bloom's Taxonomy of Educational Objectives for guidance in designing instruction.

Bloom's Taxonomy

Bloom's Taxonomy of Educational Objectives dates back to 1956 when Benjamin Bloom and his colleagues classified instructional objectives using six categories of cognitive activities. Since then, this taxonomy has been revised several times by other researchers, but the basic tenets persist (Burden & Byrd, 2013, pp. 99–102). In the context of planning instruction, the taxonomy offers a robust check on the way lessons reflect well-considered objectives, age-appropriate activities, and assessment possibilities. In short, Bloom's Taxonomy affords teachers a system for designing effective, coherent instruction.

Briefly stated, Bloom's Taxonomy of Educational Objectives poses six hierarchical categories of intellectual activities to describe specific instructional expectations.

Bloom's Taxonomy Categories

Bloom's Taxonomy Category	Category Label	Definition	Example from a High-School English Class
1	Remembering	Retrieve objective knowledge	List the English verb forms
2	Understanding	Demonstrate comprehension	Identify the verbs in a short newspaper article
3	Applying	Use knowledge to carry out a learning task	Write an original sentence that includes two different verb forms
4	Analyzing	Examine something to determine how component parts work together	Determine how verb choices contribute to a specific writer's style
5	Evaluating	Offer judgment based on sound knowledge	Consider whether you are using verb forms effectively in a rough draft
6	Creating	Generate a product that integrates knowledge	Revise your rough draft to include a wide variety of verb forms that effectively convey your meaning

Chart adapted from Anderson and Krathwohl, 2001

In Bloom's categorization, the categories move from least to most intellectually challenging. Category 1 (Remembering) is considered a "low-level" cognitive skill, while Category 6 (Creating) is considered the highest, most cognitively challenging. The categories do not apply to levels of difficulty; instead, within a particular grade level, the representative activities reflect the learners' developmental level at that grade. For example, a second-grade student might find it intellectually challenging to construct an illustrated story booklet about a time when he or she learned an important lesson (which would qualify as a Category 6 activity), but without substantive adjustment, such an activity would be too simplistic for a tenth-grade learner. For a tenth-grade learner, a similar Category 6 activity would be to create a story modeled after John Updike's "A&P."

In the context of designing instruction, Bloom's categories help teachers identify instructional results, outcomes, and potential changes in learners (Anderson & Krauthwohl, 2001, p. 17). The value of using Bloom's Taxonomy is that teachers can target instruction to move students to higher levels of accomplishments; however, understanding the levels can also prevent teachers from frustrating learners by creating lessons that are beyond students' zone of proximal development or that are so nonchallenging that learners are bored.

Additionally, a teacher can determine whether teaching activities are disproportionately targeting a limited number of Bloom's Taxonomy categories. For example, are most teaching activities clustered in the Remembering and Understanding categories? Is an activity in the Creating category being assigned without sufficient preparation? Bloom's Taxonomy presents a robust system that enables teachers to look critically at assignments from the perspectives of learner readiness, developmental appropriateness, and enhanced student learning.

Turning Content-Area Knowledge Into Lessons

At the core of Competency 003 is the reminder that teaching means far more than standing in front of a classroom talking about a subject. Competency 003 addresses key skills that teachers need in order to make content-area knowledge accessible to learners.

In Texas, TEKS identifies essential topics for core academic areas, but individual teachers still have considerable leeway in how content-area material is presented and assessed in the classroom. You should notice that TEKS statements start with active verbs that reflect Bloom's Taxonomy: *identify, describe, observe, predict, differentiate, recognize, explore, classify*, etc. TEKS, however, does not include specific classroom means for achieving those objectives. In outcomes-oriented learning, teachers define specific outcomes, or what they want students to know and be able to do when they complete a required course of study. Establishing goals and outcomes allows teachers to create coherent instruction, which means that the teacher can articulate the expected outcomes and knows how to convey those expectations to students. Integral to effective outcome-oriented planning is the teacher's understanding of his or her students' learning readiness and predictions about students ability to move toward higher levels of achievement. The key to effective outcome-oriented planning is to consider what outcomes must be achieved and then determine which teacher behaviors and which student behaviors will improve the probability that students will achieve the outcomes.

Behavioral Outcomes

Outcome-based planning starts with the end product—what must be learned or accomplished in a particular course or grade level or a particular semester. For example, an algebra teacher may decide that the final outcome of his or her algebra course would be that students transfer real-world thinking skills in solving algebraic problems. He or she then works "backward" to determine prerequisite knowledge and skills students need to have in order to accomplish this outcome. By continuing to ask these questions about each set of prerequisites, the teacher finds a starting point for the subject or course, develops goals and objectives, constructs units, and eventually creates daily lessons.

Behavioral outcomes specifically state what student actions are expected at the end of a lesson or lesson cycle (Burden & Byrd, 2013, pp. 95–99). A behavioral objective may simply describe the expected student action or may include conditions and criteria for the expected action. Here are some examples of behavioral objectives on a history lesson covering the *Stamp Act*:

- **Descriptive:** Students will know the connections between the *Stamp Act* and the beginning of the American Revolution.

- **Behavioral:** Working in groups, students will create a chart showing the colonists' reaction to specific events related to the *Stamp Act*.

- **Behavioral:** Students will score 85 percent or higher on a 25-item multiple-choice exam that covers the two lessons on the *Stamp Act*.

You will notice that the second and third examples establish conditions and name specific learning products. Creating behavioral objectives allows teachers to integrate instructional design components such as learner readiness, developmental appropriateness, cooperative and independent work, and assessment.

Lessons

Generally, a daily lesson does not stand on its own; it could be a component of a unit in which multiple objectives and a wide variety of instructional activities address the unit goals, or it could be an integral part of series of lessons targeting a specific goal. On a day-to-day basis, lessons are structured around objectives that can be met in a classroom period.

Lessons, first of all, must fit in the designated time period, whether the daily period is 50 or 90 minutes. That "fit" needs to reflect learner readiness, special needs, previous learning, and adequate time for the teacher to present necessary new material and for learners to complete appropriate learning tasks. Lessons should never be rushed to reflect necessary "coverage" of material; instead, the teacher's systematic, deliberate planning should reflect attention to the learners' needs. In fact, the term "learner-driven instruction" refers to lessons that reflect students' response to new material. In contrast, curriculum-driven lessons mean that a teacher moves through a lesson primarily to "cover" material mandated by state, district, or campus curriculum without regard to student comprehension.

Typically, a lesson should start with a short, introductory activity that engages the learners in the new material. It could be an activity to stimulate learners' prior knowledge about the topic of the new lesson. It could be as simple as a question that invites learners to speculate about the new topic or a quick activity targeted at getting students to discover how they can relate to the new lesson. For a lesson that is part of a longer unit, the introductory activity might simply be a concise summary of what has been covered thus far in the unit. The point is that the introductory activity should be used to help learners position themselves in the new lesson.

The presentation of new knowledge is the core of the lesson. The presentation can be via lecture, demonstration, video, mini-lessons, short collaborative activities, teacher-guided activities, whole-class questioning, or a variety of other strategies. Critical to the presentation is the teacher's informal assessment of the learners' understanding of the new knowledge. This is where Bloom's Taxonomy figures in. The teacher needs to decide what level of learner understanding is appropriate for the learners and for the new learning task. To maintain learner engagement, the teacher should devise activities that are interesting, relevant, developmentally appropriate, and targeted on the new knowledge.

Time allocation is an essential component of effective instructional design. Time on task and academic learning time refer to how much time learners spend directly on an instructional activity. Academic learning time—how much time learners need to master new knowledge successfully—depends on the learners' familiarity with the content, on learner readiness, on developmental appropriateness, and on the clarity of the teacher's presentation (Burden & Byrd, 2013, pp. 88, 206). A well-crafted lesson does not run all the way up to the end of the class, with students rushing out as the bell rings. Instead, a lesson should allow the teacher time to bring the lesson to a meaningful closure, perhaps by summarizing key points, by having a question-and-answer session, by briefly mentioning the next lesson, or by having students jot down their "take-aways" from the lesson.

Units

Units bring together a series of connected, coherent lessons covering larger segments of content structured around a broad goal(s). Units can cover a relatively long instructional period—for example, an entire grading period (six weeks, nine weeks, or whatever grading period is used in the district). Or, a unit can be as short as a week. What distinguishes a unit from other types of lessons is the coherence provided by the overall goal(s) for the unit and the deliberate coordination of all lessons to reflect the unit goal (Kauchak & Eggen, 2012, pp. 130–136). Typically, in English classes, novels are presented in units rather than as individual lessons. In social studies classes, historical periods are covered in units.

Units can be structured around a curricular requirement, or they may be thematic, which is why most textbooks are organized by units. Units enable teachers to devise a wider variety of learning activities, to make cross-disciplinary connections, to integrate technology, to introduce multiple viewpoints on the topic, and to incorporate multicultural perspectives. Units, especially multiweek units, allow teachers to incorporate a wide variety of data sources such as library visits, online research, community connections, family involvement, oral presentations, multimedia products, guest speakers, and many other creative applications of content-area material. Units typically end with a culminating activity that allows learners to create a product, individually or collaboratively, that showcases their understanding of the unit material. Quite often, teachers accommodate learner needs by giving students options on the culminating activity.

Units can be structured around curriculum, as these examples demonstrate:

- **English:** a unit on *To Kill a Mockingbird*
- **Social Studies:** a unit on the American Revolution
- **Math:** a unit on basic fractions
- **Science:** a unit on the structure of a cell
- **Art:** a unit on Impressionism

Many educators believe that thematic units significantly enhance student learning. Thematic units are generally structured around topics that the teacher believes are relevant to students and are thus likely to result in greater student engagement. Thematic units are also advocated as means of increasing comprehensible input for ESL students because of the redundancy provided by having multiple sources of data to draw on; the integration of listening, speaking, reading, and writing skills; the possibilities for interdisciplinary connections; and the extended time devoted to a specific topic (Peregoy & Boyle, 2008, pp. 93–98). For example, a thematic unit on decision making could include a short story, a real-world scenario that integrates mathematics, a visit to a virtual shopping center, a scene from a historical event, a clip from films in which characters are shown making important decisions, and personal narratives drawn from students' own experiences.

Assessment

Classroom-based assessment takes two broad forms: summative and formative. Summative assessment is final; it comes at the end of a learning period perhaps as a formal test, a writing project, or a major project. Once students complete and submit the assessment instrument, there is no opportunity for improvement of the score on that particular assignment. Summative assessment may seem draconian, but if you consider that other types of assessment can prepare students for the finality of summative assessment, then it seems less academically drastic.

In formative assessment, teachers identify students' strengths and weaknesses in order to guide them toward greater understanding of the topic under study. In comparison to summative assessment, formative assessment permits opportunities for continual improvement—up until the project is submitted for summative assessment. For example, in writing assignments, the drafting-conferencing-revising cycle is considered formative assessment. In math classes, teachers can review students' work on problems and show them how to apply operations correctly in new problems. Formative assessment allows students to work continually at demonstrating that they understand new material and to resubmit materials for scoring that reflects improvement. However, formative assessment also includes the teacher's analysis of learner needs and exploration of why learners might not be proceeding smoothly through a particular lesson(s). Formative assessment calls for adjustment of learning goals and class activities to address students' strengths and weaknesses.

Authentic assessment is a type of informal assessment conducted on a daily basis. Authentic assessment brings together the topics covered in Competency 001 (teacher's understanding of learner characteristics) and Competency 002 (student diversity). In many cases, simply observing students' response to a lesson allows a teacher to authentically assess the learners' understanding. A teacher can be attuned to the learners' demeanor and gestures and immediately respond. For example, a teacher might say something like, "I see some of you are frowning a little. Maybe I should explain the definition once again." Or a teacher could have students pair up and do a quick summary of a minilesson. A status-of-the-class session, where each learner is given the opportunity to talk about his or her current progress on an assignment, is another example of authentic assessment. Questions raised during a formal lesson or whole-class discussion also permit a teacher to conduct authentic assessment.

The overarching purpose of all types of assessment is to move learners toward higher levels of achievement. However, assessment also allows teachers to adjust objectives, to change learning approaches, to integrate different types of activities, and to self-evaluate the effectiveness of teaching activities. Assessment fundamentally involves constant measurement (informal or formal) to determine whether learning objectives are being met. Ultimately, the goal of assessment is to help all learners meet learning objectives.

Results of mandated exams should be integrated meaningfully into overall assessment. On the one hand, the results of mandated tests are summative because scores are used to evaluate formally learners' achievement on state-mandated objectives, such as the TEKS readiness standards on the State of Texas Assessments of Academic Readiness (STAAR) or the English proficiency ratings from the Texas English Language Proficiency Assessment System (TELPAS). However, teachers can use such scores to modify class instruction so that all learners are guided toward higher levels of achievement on state-mandated objectives.

Review Questions

1. Mrs. Rodriguez, a tenth-grade English teacher, is planning a unit on *Julius Caesar*. Acknowledging that students may have difficulty relating to the events and circumstances of the play, she wants to devise teaching activities that engage students meaningfully and that help students relate to the play. Which of the following introductory activities for this unit would most effectively activate students' prior knowledge about the political events in the play?

(A)   Writing a study guide that summarizes each act of the play and giving students a pretest based on the guide

(B)   Listening to a reading of Mark Anthony's funeral oration and asking students to do an analysis of the rhetorical strategies used in the speech

(C)   Showing clips of films and documentaries on assassinations of modern political figures such as J.F. Kennedy, Martin Luther King, and Benazir Bhutto

(D)   Showing students a film version of the play and having them write a response paper about what they liked about the film

The correct response onse addresses the teacher's concern that udents may not find *Julius* evant. Connecting the Caesar's assassina-tion to modern political assassinations will activate students' prior knowledge and heighten their interest in this classic play. (A), (B), and (D) are incorrect because none of these responses addresses the teaching objective presented in the stem. These responses could all be beneficial activities in the unit, but they do not address the teaching objective to activate prior knowledge.

2.   Ms. Sanchez is a middle-school math teacher. She has reviewed her students' scores on the state-mandated exam. Which of the following instructional plans would best use the assessment results to improve student learning?

(A)   The teacher creates and administers a series of sample tests to give students practice on challenging components of the exam

(B)   The teacher matches her lesson plan objectives to the readiness standards for the state-mandated exam that will be administered in the current school year

(C)   The teacher identifies the learners' strengths and weaknesses and creates lessons that target common challenges in understanding math concepts

(D)   The teacher devotes 10 minutes of each day to reviewing a sample test item and making sure all students know how to select the correct response

The correct response is (C). This response takes into account how scores on state-mandated exams can be used in classroom applications to improve student learning. (A) is incorrect because administering more tests without first identifying students' strengths and weaknesses will not address the teacher's objective. (B) does not integrate data from mandated state exams to improve student learning. (D) is incorrect because knowing the correct answers to released test items does not identify learners' strengths and weaknesses and does not promote achievement.

3. A grade 3 teacher is currently covering the multiplication tables; the students have reached the 5s. To assess whether students have memorized the 5 x sequence, the teacher dedicates a morning to have students practice reciting the 5 x table and then quizzes them by having them write the 5 x table through 5 x 12. This learning activity reflects which of the following categories of Bloom's Taxonomy of Educational Objectives?

(A) Creating

(B) Remembering

(C) Collaborating

(D) Understanding

The correct response is (B). Learning the times tables and demonstrating mastery is a straightforward remembering class activity. The instructional activities presented in the stem are aimed at determining whether students have memorized the times table for 5s. (A) and (D) are Bloom's Taxonomy categories that do not fit the scenario presented in the stem. (C) is not a Bloom's Taxonomy category.

4. A middle-school teacher wants to integrate formative assessment into his science class. Which of the following activities would best support this teacher's instructional plan?

(A) The teacher assigns homework based on each day's lesson. The next day, students score each other's homework. Then, the teacher gives the class a few minutes to work individually to correct any items they got wrong.

(B) The teacher assigns homework based on the day's lesson. The next day, the students work in pairs to complete items that they were unable to do on their own.

(C) The teacher assigns an independent class activity based on the day's lesson. The teacher scores the assignment. The next day, the teacher works with students in small groups to explain strategies for understanding items that they missed.

(D) The teacher gives students time to review the previous day's lesson and then administers an objective quiz based on the lesson. Students who pass the quiz are assigned a new chapter, while the teacher reteaches the lesson to the students who failed the quiz.

The correct response is (C). This response presents the best example of formative assessment. by scoring the independent assignment, the teacher determines strengths and weaknesses in the students' understanding of the lesson. The follow-up involving explanations of concepts the students did not understand is a hallmark of formative assessment. (A) and (B) are incorrect because these options do not include teacher intervention in the form of identifying students' strengths and weaknesses. (D) is incorrect because this response does not show that the teacher is identifying students' strengths and weaknesses and is instead creating two groups of students on the basis of the overall score.

Competency 004

Competency 004

The teacher understands learning processes and factors that impact student learning and demonstrates this knowledge by planning effective, engaging instruction and appropriate assessments.

The broad area addressed by Competency 004 is **how students learn**. Sixteen descriptive statements in this competency cover the following general topics:

- Learning theory
- Learning strategies applied to different developmental levels
- Promoting higher-order thinking skills
- Classroom logistics and student learning
- Metacognition and learning
- Teacher behaviors and student learning
- Integration of home, family, culture, and community into classroom learning
- Learning styles
- Integrating learning theory applications to ELPS

Competency 004 Key Terms

The following key terms are integral to fully understanding the scope of Competency 004. You should consider creating flashcards to remind you of what they mean so that you can recognize the direct or implied references to these terms in the test items.

Test-taking tip: Pay close attention to specific terms embedded in the descriptive statements and especially those included in parenthesis. Connecting those specific terms to Competency 004 will provide necessary clues in responding correctly to test items that target this competency. Study strategy: Make note cards to help you associate these terms with Competency 004.

Competency 004 Key Terms		
abstract thinking	linguistic accommodation	research skills
appreciating diversity	middle-schoolers: transitional stage	respectful exchange of ideas
attention span	motivation	risk taking
career goals	need for physical activity	search for identity
cooperation	organizational skills	self-directed learning
ELPS and learning strategies	ownership of learning	student roles
higher-order thinking skills	play and learning	study skills
home and community	positive contributions	teacher behaviors
importance of peers	prior knowledge	teacher roles
inquiry	problem solving	time management
learning styles	questioning values	young children and concrete thinking
learning theory	relevance	

Learning Theory

Learning theory explores how students learn and offers suggestions about teacher actions that promote learning. In some ways, learning theory is an application of the "natural" learning that takes place starting at birth. Learning theory poses questions such as what do we know about how babies and very young children learn "naturally," and how can we apply those strategies in classroom environments? How can we help students look at academics with the same curiosity that they apply in real-world, self-motivated learning? What teacher actions can sustain core learning behaviors so as to promote higher cognitive abilities in learners?

Learning theory includes the following fundamental principles:

- Prior knowledge supports new learning.

- Relevance makes learning meaningful (connection to the real-world, authentic learning experiences).

- Learning is a social activity (includes responsibility for own learning)

- Learners construct their own understanding of new knowledge (students are not empty vessels waiting to be filled).

- Learners organize knowledge using scaffolds that connect existing knowledge to new knowledge.

- Teacher actions, behaviors, and attitudes can impact learning positively or negatively.

(Jacobson, Eggen, & Kauchak, 2006, pp. 6–12)

Learning involves change. Whether it is a toddler's recognition that the ball that rolled behind the couch did not permanently disappear or a kindergartener's realization that the symbols on the pages of a book can be decoded into meaningful words, new knowledge changes the learner. But, learning is rarely immediate or sudden; instead, it is a process. Furthermore, as one researcher puts it, learning is not something that is *done* to students but that students do on their own (Ambrose et al. 2006, p, 3). This change, these processes, and knowledge construction result from ongoing negotiations between teachers and learners.

Learning theory is crucial to effective teaching in several ways: (1) learning theory helps us identify the types of teacher actions, behaviors, attitudes, and understandings that promote learning; (2) learning theory helps us understand how learners learn; (3) learning theory can be operationalized as classroom interactions and activities that genuinely promote learning.

◼ Learner Characteristics and Learning

If you recall, Competency 001 included descriptive statements that address stages of cognitive, social, physical, and affective development. The developmental characteristics that learners exhibit at a particular age are important in understanding how they learn and in planning age-appropriate instruction and assessment.

Developmental Levels: Age-Appropriate Activities

Planning effective learning experiences for young children must take into account their need for motor and sensory input, their developmental tendency toward concrete thinking, and their relatively short attention span. Elementary classrooms are frequently set up with tables and chairs rather than desks to encourage social development; centers are set up to allow students to move about the room as they complete class activities; school supplies, such as scissors, paper, and books, reflect the students' current motor development; the room is decorated in bright colors; periods for working on content-area learning may be as short as 20 minutes; and manipulatives are available to help students make concrete connections to new knowledge. Young students tend to be egocentric, impulsive, and apparently unconcerned with consequences. For example, a first-grader might solve a disagreement over who sits in the blue chair by knocking his classmate to the floor. The teacher needs to recognize that this decision is not malicious but representative of the child's current developmental level.

Middle-school students are transitioning from childhood to adolescence and thus need educational experiences that straddle those two stages. Behaviorally, middle-schoolers may seem disinterested, unfocused, lively, generally immature, and unconcerned about consequences for ill-considered behavior. Developmentally, such behaviors manifest the transition from childhood to young adulthood.

To work successfully with middle-schoolers, teachers need to understand their behaviors and anticipate ways of helping them succeed in classroom tasks. While older elementary and middle-school-age students retain some egocentric behaviors from earlier developmental stages, they seek independence, pursue social affiliations, and explore their identity. Intellectually, they think more abstractly and logically (Santrock, 2009, p. 16, 23–24). However, middle-schoolers also enjoy doing class activities that allow the sort of freedom they enjoyed in elementary grades: creative projects, dramatizations, role playing, meaningful collaboration, and support from the instructor. But, because they are developmentally on the route toward young adulthood, adolescents also need to see tangible, authentic connections between educational experiences and the real world. In a sixth-grade class, a student might articulate confusion over a history lesson not by asking a question, but by saying, "This is so lame." From the developmental perspective, this student's metamessage is, "Show me why this should matter to me."

Older students (later middle-school and high-school age) are entering adulthood but are still transitioning from one developmental stage to another. Vestiges of childlike behavior may persist in the craving for attention and irrational behaviors that crop up in high-school classrooms, but students at this age are well on their way to adulthood. As such, they are starting to consider life choices, recognizing the positive and negative influence of peers, questioning values, and deliberately shaping themselves into distinct individuals through the choices they make (Santrock, 2009, p. 24). A high-school student placed in a group that includes none of her friends might resist participation by not responding to group members or by not doing any of her group tasks. Although the student may seem to be recalcitrant, developmentally, she could be "testing" a hypothesis—*even though the teacher puts us in groups, he won't do anything if we don't participate.* Understanding motivations for students' behavior in classroom situations can be enhanced through knowledge of behaviors, attitudes, and capabilities at different developmental levels.

Enhancing Student Learning

Teacher actions and behaviors impact student learning. Teacher actions influence the way students perceive new knowledge, the way students position themselves in classrooms, and the way classroom interactions impact students' social and personal development. The constructivist view of learning places a great deal of responsibility on the learner: learning happens when the learner assimilates new knowledge into existing organizational schemes. However, the teacher bears a great deal of responsibility as well because constructivism casts the teacher as a participant in facilitating acquisition of new knowledge. The teacher does not simply dispense information to a receptive learner who readily records the knowledge (Jacobsen, Eggen, Kauchak, 2006, p. 6). Instead, in the constructivist view, teachers draw on natural propensities that promote learning in the real world: curiosity, relevance, inquiry, problem solving, manipulation, social settings, and connection of new knowledge to prior knowledge.

The classroom, in some ways, is an artificial learning environment given the routine and regimentation, but effective teachers know that certain teacher behaviors promote learning. For example, teachers should encourage learners to try for higher levels of achievement. Teachers should be facilitators rather than directors. When students do not meet expectations, teachers should respond in ways that do not discourage learners but that instead inspire the learner to keep trying. A teacher's demeanor is crucial in creating and maintaining learner motivation.

Motivation is particularly important as teachers integrate higher-order thinking skills into lessons. Abstract thinking and reasoning should reflect the learners' developmental stage. As learners move into higher levels of cognitive abilities, tasks may become more challenging, and learners may feel discouraged by failure. Teacher responsibilities include showing learners that new, more challenging learning tasks reflect the real world and can meaningfully impact the learners' lives. Teacher responsibilities also include fostering feelings of accomplishment and satisfaction in learners (Jacobsen, Eggen, & Kauchak, 2006, pp 8–9). Ultimately, learners should develop a sense of ownership and responsibility for their learning, and to a great extent, such self-directed learning results when teachers consistently devise learning and assessment activities that reflect the fundamental principles of effective learning: prior knowledge, relevance, social context, and scaffolding.

Learning Styles

The realities of the classroom environment behoove teachers to be attuned to students' approaches to learning. Learners are heterogeneous: no two learners learn exactly the same way. If a teacher persists in maintaining the myth of learner homogeneity, even carefully crafted, content-sound lessons can fall apart. Teachers need to incorporate different learning styles into instructional practices. Learning styles—auditory, visual, tactile, kinesthetic, verbal—refer to learners' preferred ways of processing information Additionally, some research suggests that environmental factors—lighting, temperature, time of day, seating configuration, sound—impact how students learn (Jacobson, Eggen, & Kauchak, 2006, pp. 279–281).

Logistically, however, it would be impossible for any one teacher to adjust lessons to meet each individual student's apparent learning style. Instead, a more pragmatic approach is to take the variety of possible learning styles into account in instructional practices. For example, instead of always presenting material through lecture format, a teacher could include demonstrations, posters, videos, recordings, Internet information, whole- and small-group discussion. And, instead of always requiring paper-and-pencil products for informal and formal assessments, teachers could provide options including multimedia presentations, posters, skits, reader's theater, technology-based outputs, and other products that reflect students' learning preferences.

Understanding learning styles can keep teachers from misinterpreting student behavior. An apparent lack of understanding could be cleared up by approaching a lesson from a different angle. A student's apparent nonparticipation could be explained by the student's inability to complete a task in a traditional format. Behaviors that suggest a student is wasting time could be emblematic of a preference for a different way of processing new information.

Teachers should explore the impact of environmental preferences on student performance (such as integration of music, seating configurations, students' preferences for lighting, and best work times). Teachers should be aware that students work at different paces: some work like sprinters and are able to complete almost any task quickly; at the other extreme, some students appear to work slowly, almost as if they do not understand the material. Class work should make allowances for all learning paces without embarrassment or punishment for students who seem to need more time to complete assignments.

Logistics and Strategies for Enhancing Learning

Classroom organizational routines seem far removed from actual learning, but because the classroom is a prime learning site in our educational system, organizational structures and time-management skills are important components of students' learning experiences. Routines create expectations, regularity, and organization, all of which contribute to sustaining the class community. Additionally, participating in maintaining organizational structures promotes students' sense of involvement. Whether it is passing out workbooks or simply arriving on time, maintaining organizational routines is a vital component of delivering effective, engaging instruction.

Age-appropriate study skills are another fundamental component of educational success. Teachers should not assume that students already know how to use metacognitive strategies to promote learning or how to use classroom-specific skills like note taking, graphic organizers, and research processes to complete instructional activities. Teachers should model how such skills apply specifically to the content area and create instructional materials that encourage learners to use study skills productively to enhance their acquisition of content-area knowledge.

Effective instruction should also take into account the impact of family, home, and community influences in students' educational experiences. Teachers should partner with parents to convey clear expectations about student performance, explain to students how community resources can be accessed for learning applications, and make efforts to integrate social and cultural factors into instruction.

Accommodations for ELL Students—ELPS

If you have not already read and annotated the English Language Proficiency Standards (ELPS) (accessible via the Texas Essential Knowledge and Skills webpage on the TEA website—*http://ritter.tea.state.tx.us/rules/tac*), you should download them now. According to the Texas Education Code Chapter 74, school districts shall implement this section [ELPS] as an integral part of each subject in the required curriculum (TEA, 2007). This means that all content-area teachers are responsible for teaching language proficiency skills to ELL students.

ELPS includes specific descriptors that detail language-proficiency expectations in listening, speaking, reading, and writing. Additionally, ELPS includes criteria for categorizing students as beginning, intermediate, advanced, and advanced high ELL proficiency. To ensure that ELL students meet ELPS expectations and move toward higher levels of language proficiency, teachers are expected to make appropriate linguistic and content-area accommodations. Teachers should realize that "accommodation" does not mean oversimplifying content; accommodations should be based on knowledge of ELL students' needs and should reflect a teacher's ability to adjust instructional materials to make them accessible to second-language learners.

■ Review Questions

1. A third-grade teacher assigns 20 math problems each Thursday for students to complete independently during the usual math period. The teacher has been using this strategy for three weeks as a way of informally assessing students' ability to apply the lessons from the week. Students who complete all 20 items get a red star on their class-activities chart. On Friday, the teacher has students check each others' problems and work collaboratively to correct any problems they got wrong. Several

students have been unable to complete the 20 items. Which of the following strategies would most effectively promote motivation in the students who cannot complete the 20 problems?

(A)   The teacher encourages the students by explaining that they will get a silver star if they can complete more problems than they did the previous week

(B)   The teacher allows the students who cannot complete the assignment in class to finish it for homework

(C)   The teacher pairs the noncompleters with students who finish the assignment early and has the faster students show the other students how to work the problems

(D)   The teacher creates a shorter list of problems for the students who are having trouble completing the 20 items

The correct response is **(A)**. Repeated inability to complete a task is likely to reduce student motivation to keep trying; thus, by recognizing improvement, the teacher is attempting to encourage the students who are having difficulty completing the class activity. (B) does not address the students' inability to complete the 20 items in class; assigning the uncompleted problems for homework changes the assignment for these students. (C) assumes that the students have not been able to complete the 20 items because they do not know how to work the problems, but there is no evidence in the stem that this is the problem. (D) is incorrect because this option singles out the noncompleters by changing the learning task; additionally, if some students have fewer items to complete, an element of inequity is introduced into the assignment.

2.   A grade 5 science teacher has several beginning-level ELL students in her class. After each science lesson, which the teacher presents through demonstration, manipulatives, and group work, she has students write a three- to five-sentence science journal explaining what they learned from the lesson. Today's lesson was on absorption. The ELL students participated readily in the groups and asked questions during the demonstrations; however, they are having trouble writing their journals, so the teacher gives them the following format to follow and tells the ELL students they can complete the blanks with one or more words:

The lesson was about _____. The water made the dirt _____. A new science word I learned today is _____. The most interesting part of the lesson was _____. I think the water would not have poured through _____.

This accommodation addresses English Language Proficiency Standards for writing in which of the following ways?

(A)   The teacher is creating a simplified version of the assignment to provide comprehensible input for the ELL students

(B)   The teacher is providing linguistic scaffolding to facilitate the students' acquisition of content-area knowledge

(C)   The teacher is providing differentiated instruction to enable the ELL students to meet their learning goals

(D)   The teacher is changing the assignment to ensure that ELL students are not frustrated by their inability to complete the assignment

The correct response is **(B)**. The sentence stems offer scaffolding for the ELL students, enabling them to access content-area knowledge through an accommodation that corresponds to ELPS. (A) incorrectly identifies the scaffolding strategy as a simplification when, in fact, it is an accommodation. (C) is incorrect because it overstates the accommodation described in the stem; differentiated instruction would have changed the approach to perhaps an oral response or a visual representation. (D) is incorrect because the teacher has not changed the assignment for the ELL students; the scaffolding provided by the teacher preserves the original objective and the original assignment.

3.   Elva Rodriguez teaches fourth grade. She has structured her class so that students can spend 30 minutes daily after lunch in sustained silent reading (SSR) with books and reading materials of their own choosing. Which of the following adjustments to the SSR period most effectively recognizes varied student-learning approaches?

(A)   The teacher allows students to choose whether they will read at their desks or move to a reading area where they sit on floor cushions or recline on floor mats

(B)   The teacher makes sure that all students have selected appropriate reading materials

(C)   The teacher plays classical music on a tape player to enhance student learning

(D)   The teacher dims the lights in the classroom in order to increase students' reading comprehension

The correct response is **(A)**. This response takes into account differences in learning preferences among learners by giving them options as to how and where they will read. (B) deviates from the principles of SSR—in classic SSR situations, students read materials that they have self-selected. (C) and (D) show attention to the preferences of only some of the students.

4. A high-school history teacher assigns the U.S. Constitution for students to read for homework. The next day, he starts a discussion and quickly realizes only a handful of students did the assignment. When he asks the class why they did not do the assignment, the students explain that the reading was difficult and that they could not understand what it meant. Which of the following teacher actions would best model appropriate use of metacognitive strategies to approach a challenging reading task?

(A) The teacher does a think-aloud of the first few paragraphs, explaining the questions that come to mind as he reads and musing about meanings of phrases. He then has student volunteers do the same with a few more paragraphs.

(B) The teacher reads the entire U.S. Constitution orally to the students and asks them to interrupt the reading when they have questions.

(C) The teacher stops the lesson and has students spend the class period reading the U.S. Constitution silently.

(D) The teacher shows the students an Internet site that explains key points of the U.S. Constitution and offers historical background on its creation.

The correct response is **(A)**. The think-aloud strategy is considered a highly effective means of modeling how we process challenging reading and shape comprehension. (B), (C), and (D) do not address the comprehension problem identified by the students.

PART II: DOMAIN II

Creating a Positive, Productive Classroom Environment

Creating a Positive, Productive Classroom Environment

Domain II focuses on the how classroom space can be configured literally and operationally to promote learning. In talking about classroom space, we use terms such as classroom climate, classroom routines and schedules, managing student behavior, creating a nurturing environment, and arranging classroom furnishings. While classroom space refers to dimensionalities and furnishings in a literal sense, it also refers to the way the space is perceived by the learner as a place that invites and promotes growth. Domain II, then, addresses attitudinal, pedagogical, and logistical concerns that contribute to creation of a learner-centered classroom environment.

Before continuing through this chapter, carefully read and annotate the two competencies and descriptive statements in Domain II from the *Preparation Manual 160 Pedagogy and Professional Responsibilities EC–12*. Underline key terms, mark terms you do not know, and pay special attention to the terms in parenthesis because those provide very specific indicators of the parameters of the competency. Domain II covers these two competencies:

Competency 005: The teacher knows how to establish a classroom climate that fosters leaning equity and excellence and uses this knowledge to create a physical and emotional environment that is safe and productive.

Competency 006: The teacher understands strategies for creating an organized and productive learning environment and for managing student behavior.

Standard II of the Pedagogy and Professional Responsibilities Educator Standards applies to Domain II; you should look over those knowledge and skills statements to reinforce your understanding of the scope of Domain II.

Competency 005

5

Competency 005

The teacher knows how to establish a classroom climate that fosters learning equity and excellence and uses this knowledge to create a physical and emotional environment that is safe and productive.

Competency 005 addresses **classroom climate** and is explained through seven descriptive statements, which cover the following general areas:

• Creating a classroom community

• Fostering excellence

• Creating a safe, comfortable classroom environment

Classroom climate refers to the way classroom space fosters a positive learning environment. Classroom space is much more than the physical dimensions and configuration of the educational area; classroom space is symbolic and metaphorical as much as it is real. Competency 005 addresses actions and attitudes teachers can demonstrate that make students feel that the classroom space is a good place to be. Furthermore, creating a positive classroom climate cultivates expectations of excellence and promotes equity.

Competency 005 Key Terms

The following key terms are integral to fully understanding the scope of Competency 005. You should consider creating flashcards to remind you of what they mean so that you can recognize the direct or implied references to these terms in the test items.

Competency 005 Key Terms		
arranging physical space	high expectations	space and safety
collaboration	learning equity	student-student interactions
cooperation	respect for diversity	teacher enthusiasm
developmentally appropriate classroom environment	respect for student dignity	teacher-student interactions
excellence	space and emotional needs	

The Classroom Space: Creating Community

Classroom climate refers to the atmosphere and pervasive mood in which teacher and students interact. The classroom should feel welcoming, and it should be a space in which learners and the teacher are comfortable for the duration of the school day. As one researcher puts it, "When you walk into a classroom where students are actively engaged in learning and are cooperating with the teacher and others, you can almost feel the *good vibrations* [my emphasis] given off by the class" (Burden, 2006, p. 98).

Establishing a classroom community based on mutual respect, cooperation, and personal and shared responsibility is a good beginning point to creating a positive classroom climate. Creating a sense of community is a major teacher responsibility, and it starts even before the students enter the classroom. As explained below, getting the classroom ready for students is a first step in creating a positive, productive classroom environment.

Community is created attitudinally as well as operationally. For example, a teacher who stands at the door to greet students as they enter the class is conveying an attitude of receptiveness. Similarly, starting out the school year with activities designed to get learners to know each other is an important step in fostering mutual respect. Such activities should be designed to show learners connectivity through shared experiences while recognizing individuality and diversity. Community has to be based on a feeling of affective safety: learners must feel valued as members of the class community. When a teacher strives to get learners to respect each other and to celebrate difference, students will feel good about sharing ideas, speaking up in class, risking wrong responses, laughing, volunteering, and doing all the other things that sustain community.

Collaboration with peers is considered a major means of promoting community. But collaboration is not an intrinsic quality among young people. Recall the discussions in Domain I about the egocentrism that young people carry with them through adolescence. For very young children, collaboration might take the form of learning to share and taking turns. Teachers of young elementary-level children might promote collaboration by creating simple team projects in which each group member is assigned a specific responsibility or by limiting available resources so that children practice equitable access to, let us say, one pair of scissors or four crayons or one piece of construction paper or one storybook.

Older learners need direction in learning how to work effectively in groups. A lesson that most teachers learn early in their classroom experience is that you have to teach students how to work in groups. At one extreme is the highly orchestrated division of group labor advocated by individuals who research and write about group dynamics where group tasks include such responsibilities as recorder, researcher, time manager, presenter, etc. A more community-based approach might be a demonstration using a fishbowl setting where the teacher models desired collaborative actions by demonstrating with a few volunteers so that the whole class can observe and ask questions about productive group behaviors.

Working effectively in groups also requires knowing how to listen, debate, ask questions, consider alternate points of view, disagree politely, argue productively, and reach consensus. Such behaviors should be modeled using real classroom volunteers or perhaps watching film clips that illustrate desirable and undesirable group behaviors. Collaboration should be valued as means of promoting the discovery of new ideas, fostering connectivity that expands and completes individual thinking, and making creativity possible (Johnson, 2010, pp. 21–22).

Creating a collaborative learning environment does much to establish a level educational field for all learners. Competition certainly is an important part of an individual's growth, but it can also blur the value of individual worth and contribution. Learners need to feel equitable access to success in the classroom. While not every class activity should be conducted as a collaborative effort, overall, the classroom climate should make every learner feel proud of his or her accomplishments. For example, learning artifacts should be displayed equitably: instead of showcasing the "best" products, the teacher should create opportunities for sometimes displaying all contributions.

How the teacher responds to learners is another vital component of sustaining a positive, productive classroom environment. At the core, students should trust the teacher as someone who will respond positively to their questions, who will address their needs, and who generally helps them enjoy being in the classroom. Each learner should feel valued by the teacher. This puts a great deal of responsibility on the instructor for ensuring that individual learners *know* that community depends on each individual's contribution and mutual respect. Teachers should also be aware that learners may perceive slights where none was intended. Sarcasm, irony, and even humor may be misunderstood, so teacher-student communication must be direct, polite, and attentive to the individual learner's developmental level. Teachers need to strive to convey emotional objectivity to avoid overreaction to learner behaviors that might be considered inappropriate. However, learners appreciate empathy and understanding, even if they are in the wrong. Competency 006 more fully addresses strategies for managing student behavior. Competency 005, however, reminds us that even when student behavior is disruptive or inappropriate, the teacher's response should sustain a positive classroom climate.

The Classroom Space: Fostering Excellence

Learners love teachers who are dynamic, enthusiastic, and happy about being in the classroom. A teacher's enthusiasm for the subject and for learning in general spills over onto the learner. Enthusiasm for the subject is manifested by the teacher's real-world references to his or her own involvement with learning. For example, teachers can talk about books they are currently reading and bring copies of those books to class to help students connect the classroom to the real world. Through demeanor, tone of voice, and general manner, teachers should convey the attitude that every classroom activity is important. In other words, teachers should not make comments like, "I know you don't like to look words up, but..." Or, "You're all probably very tired of doing our benchmarks, but the school requires these scores, so let's just do it."

As the lead member of the classroom community, the teacher needs to remember that the rest of the community takes its cues from the teacher's attitude about being in the classroom. Teachers need to remember that smiles and physical vitality motivate learners. In a way, the teacher is a cheerleader rallying the students to be excited about learning.

Enthusiasm for learning is also demonstrated by the variety of methods used to present course content and to help students engage meaningfully in their own learning. (This aspect of the classroom environment will be covered fully in the section on Domain III.) Teachers need to remember that some delivery methods, such as lecturing or independent workbook drill and practice, do not engage students actively.

Enthusiasm for learning is also sustained when every learner feels that success is accessible. Teachers need to understand the learners' current developmental levels (see Domain I) to ensure that lessons, activities, and expectations promote success. For activities that need to be completed in class, teachers need to factor in students' varied work paces, acknowledging that some learners need far more time than others to complete the same assignment. Penalizing a student who works at a slower pace but clearly understands the material conveys a sense of inequity that could diminish the student's interest in learning.

The Physical Space: Nurture, Safety, and Learning

The configuration of furnishings and areas for movement is considered a vital aspect of the classroom environment. Each year, before the school year starts, teachers spend days "getting the room ready." In part, the teacher displays content-related visuals and artifacts around the room, creates attractive bulletin boards, and prepares spaces for displaying student works. Some teachers decorate the door, changing the decorations seasonally.

Quite a bit has been written about arrangement of desks so as to promote highest levels of learner engagement. The arrangement of desks is also considered to be a manifestation of the teacher's approach to authority relations in the classroom. For example, in a classroom with desks arranged in rows that face the front of the classroom where the teacher's desk and presentation spaces are located, authority is centralized in the teacher, and to get information (and knowledge), students must direct their gaze and attention toward that central authority figure. Theoretically, such an arrangement promotes a "banking" theory of education where the teacher, the possessor of knowledge, "bestows" that knowledge on students who are essentially empty vessels waiting to be filled by the bestower, and "communication" occurs monologically with the teacher at the front of the room controlling all aspects of the classroom discourse (Freire, 1970, p. 53; Gale, 1996, p. 11–12). Clearly, many teachers would agree that this is an extreme conceptualization of the classroom environment; however, these theoretical constructs of classroom authority are frequently used as the rationale for departing from the trappings of students-sitting-in-rows-with-the-teacher-in-the-big-desk-at-the-front configuration. Classroom configurations that preserve the one-way directionality of information from the teacher to the learner do not promote intellectual risk taking by the learner and do not create the good feelings that make learners feel emotionally safe. Consider, for example, the fact that in a rows arrangement, learners can see only the backs of the children in front of them and the only face-to-face connection is between the learner and the teacher at the front. If a classroom community is the desired goal, learners must be able to interact meaningfully with each other and with the teacher, and such connections are fostered through visual access to other learners in the classroom.

Although configuration of desks in rows that face the front of the room seems to be the traditional arrangement, many experts suggest clustering desks or tables together to create groups that allow for high levels of cooperative and collaborative inactions among learners. Teachers can arrange groupings in which four to six learners face each other. Other groupings include U-shaped arrangements or even circling desks around the perimeter of the room.

A major consideration in the dynamics of room arrangement is where the teacher's desk and presentation spaces will be. The teacher's "big desk" is considered a symbol of authority; spatially, the desk can create a psychological boundary between the students' space and the teacher's space. Pragmatically, the desk represents the teacher's center of operations, a vantage point from which to keep an eye on students. This is why some experts suggest putting the desk at the back of the room where the teacher can watch students. The vantage-point idea simultaneously suggests an expectation of trouble (which would be why the students need to be watched), but it also pragmatically addresses the need for the teacher to be receptive to learners' needs. If the teacher can see everyone in the classroom, the teacher is attuned to student actions that suggest needed attention or particularly effective interactions among learners.

Classroom space also includes arrangement of centers, storage areas, presentation platforms, and technological aids (such as computers). The classroom space should provide easy access to such areas so that those areas become attractive sites for extending learning. Centers, however, should also allow students to work comfortably either individually or collaboratively. Centers should not be crowded against each other in ways that create inference as learners try to concentrate. Furthermore, center sites should be conducive to extended learning experiences; students should *want* to go to the centers. For example, getting to the computer station should not involve having to squeeze through several groups of desks or having to move backpacks out of the way or having to clear off stacks of workbooks. For the six or eight hours that students inhabit the classroom site, that space should be considered an environment that in every way promotes positive, productive feelings about learning.

Finally, room arrangements must be physically safe, allowing for easy access and egress in emergency situations and ensuring that children can move about freely without physical obstacles that compromise personal safety.

Review Questions

1. A middle-school history teacher wants to arrange student desks in a configuration that optimally promotes collaboration, positive interaction, and communication. Which of the following classroom-organizing strategies most effectively facilitates the teacher's goals?

    (A) The teacher arranges the desks into traditional rows, with the teacher's desk at the front, to reinforce students' expectations for authority and delivery of information

    (B) The teacher asks for student input in arranging classroom furniture in ways that reflect student preferences for class configuration

    (C) The teacher creates a U-shaped classroom by arranging the desks around the perimeter of the room, leaving a wide open space at the center for lesson delivery

    (D) The teacher clusters the desks into group configurations that allow students to talk with each other while still having a clear view of all presentational areas

    The correct response is (D). Theories of cooperative learning suggest grouping configurations that allow face-to-face interactions among students. This response also takes into account the need for students to be able to see teacher presentations. (A)

is incorrect because room arrangement should not emphasize power relationships but should instead create optimum opportunities for learning. (B) seems to offer a democratic, student-centered way to address classroom configuration; however, the teacher should be responsible for arranging the room in a way that maximizes student learning. (C) is incorrect because a U-shaped arrangement in a typical classroom creates a lot of space between learners at opposite ends of the U and leaves the middle of the class open. Additionally, U-shaped arrangements can obstruct students' ability to move freely to other learning areas in the room or to exit the room.

2. It is the third day in a row that Steffy, a fourth-grade student, has failed to bring her completed homework to class. The teacher wants to encourage Steffy to start doing her homework. Which of the following teacher reactions would be most likely to support a positive teacher-student interaction regarding the incomplete homework?

    (A) The teacher laughs, and says, "Third day in a row. That's okay. I'm sure you'll have tomorrow's homework ready."

    (B) During independent work time, the teacher steps outside with Steffy to talk about why she is not doing her homework. The teacher suggests that Steffy give up recess for one day if she needs extra help in understanding the homework assignments.

    (C) In order to sustain an equitable classroom environment, the teacher asks for volunteers to help Steffy complete her homework during independent work time.

    (D) To ensure that Steffy gets back on track and starts doing her homework, the teacher sends a note home requesting that her parents sign Steffy's homework when she completes it.

The correct response is **(B)**. Not completing homework for three days in a row probably points to a problem, so the teacher needs to try to figure out what might be going on. *Suggesting* that the child use recess to ask for extra help gives the learner an opportunity to assume responsibility; additionally, the teacher is demonstrating concern that might encourage the student to get back on track. In responses (A) and (C), the teacher makes no effort to understand the cause of the problem or to encourage the student to correct the behavior. (D) is incorrect because the teacher still does not know why the student is not completing her homework; asking parents to sign the homework seems punitive rather than encouraging.

3. A high-school history teacher is lecturing on the role of John Brown's raid in the events leading up to the Civil War. The lights are off, and he is projecting images from period newspapers as well as illustrations from well-known historical accounts of the raid. Several of the students have fallen asleep. Which of the following strategies

would most effectively address the disruption while showing students the teacher's enthusiasm for the lesson?

(A)   Not wanting to embarrass the sleeping students, the teacher turns on the lights and continues the lecture and slide show.

(B)   The teacher turns on the lights and says, "John Brown's raid is a pivotal moment in the events that brought our country to civil war. Let's take a moment to individually jot down three reasons why this event is so important."

(C)   The teacher turns on the lights and calls on several of the sleeping students to come up to the board. He says, "It is difficult to remember all the reasons that this event is so important in U.S. history. These volunteers and I are going to draw a timeline that you need to copy into your spiral."

(D)   The teacher turns on the lights, asks students to clear a space in the center of the room, leads the class in writing a timeline of the event on the board, and calls on several students to act out the key events.

The correct response is **(D)**. This response is the most likely in this scenario to show the teacher's enthusiasm for the subject. Dealing with sleeping students could trigger an emotional response from the teacher and could completely derail the lesson, but staying focused on the learning activity and switching from the dark classroom and passive lecture format should revitalize the learners and allow the teacher to stay upbeat about the lesson. (A) only superficially addresses the problem by altering the environment in a minor way. (B) inserts a punitive factor into the lesson; instead of showing the teacher's enthusiasm for the subject, jotting down reasons for the importance of the event has a quiz-aura about it, which seems triggered by the teacher's reaction to the sleeping students. (C) shows levity in dealing with the situation, but the teacher risks exposing the students to embarrassment in front of the whole class and derailing the lesson.

Competency 006

6

Competency 006

The teacher understands strategies for creating an organized and productive learning environment and for managing student behavior.

The broad area addressed by Competency 006 is **classroom organization**. Ten descriptive statements in this competency cover the following general topics:

- Classroom routines and procedures

- Managing student behavior

Organizational strategies for the way the classroom time is managed and the way learners interact can have a significant impact on student learning and achievement. Competency 006 addresses the realities of managing a classful of young people for a whole day or for designated periods while maintaining a classroom environment that optimally promotes learning.

Competency 006 Key Terms

The following key terms are integral to fully understanding the scope of Competency 006. You should consider creating flashcards to remind you of what they mean so that you can recognize the direct or implied references to these terms in the test items.

Test-taking tip: Pay close attention to specific terms embedded in the descriptive statements and especially those included in parenthesis. Connecting those specific terms to Competency 006 will provide necessary clues in responding correctly to test items that target this competency. Study strategy: Make note cards to help you associate these terms with Competency 006.

Competency 006 Key Terms		
age-appropriate routines	organizing groups	restful activities
classroom routines	pacing lessons	rules
conduct standards	paraprofessionals	student behavior
dealing with misbehavior	play and learning	time management
movement activities	procedures	types of activities
noninstructional duties	promoting ethical behavior	volunteers

Classroom Routines and Scheduling

If you consider the stretch of time that constitutes a full day in a self-contained classroom, the need for carefully structured routines and pragmatic scheduling is obvious. The way instruction is delivered by the teacher and received by the student depends in large part on the way the classroom day or class period is configured.

In order to get to the instructional parts of the day, teachers of younger students who are in self-contained classrooms need to factor in management of all sorts of scheduling necessities—such as the students' arrival to class; dealing with attendance, lunch counts, absences; accommodating announcements from the main office; bathroom breaks and so on. Very young students whose concept of time is still developing need to understand how the day will be chunked into activities and lessons. Consequently, teachers of elementary-level children frequently use visual timelines and timers to help children understand how the day is divided into segments. Teachers of young children also frequently have a group activity at the start of the school day to help students transition into the class environment; it could be a group story time with learners clustered comfortably on the floor mats, or a similar collective activity that pulls everyone into the school day. Beginning-of-the-day routines must also include time for students to put away backpacks, stow away outer garments, and collect necessary materials for the school day (such as spirals, workbooks, pencils, crayons, etc.).

Clearly, in a self-contained environment, the teacher needs to schedule appropriate time segments for all subjects, but other time-related events need to be scheduled as well. Transitioning from one subject to another needs to be managed efficiently, not abruptly. Other transitions such as recess, lunch, and music, or other subjects handled out of the main classroom setting, need to be managed efficiently.

Classroom routines are important in creating an organized learning environment, and typical routines should be managed through procedural guidelines. For example, something as simple as sharpening pencils can be highly distracting if students are getting up throughout lessons or seat work. But a designated time for sharpening pencils alleviates the disruption. Alternatively, the teacher could have a container of sharpened pencils available whenever someone needs a new pencil. Procedures for entering and exiting the classroom not only maintain students' individual safety but also ensure that order in the learning environment is valued. Frequently, teachers appoint class helpers for routines such as handing out workbooks and worksheets to keep the entire class from milling about.

Effective time management contributes to a productive classroom environment. In self-contained classrooms, each content segment needs to be configured as a learning segment with a clear beginning, instructional activities, and a cohesive closing. Learners need to feel that there is a logical routine in the lesson segment. And teachers need to be highly aware of how students' developmental levels impact attention spans. A lesson that goes on too long creates potential chaos as students fidget or engage in disruptive behavior. When the teacher needs to address those interruptions, the quality of instructional time is compromised.

With older students who move from one content class to another throughout the day, lessons needs to be paced appropriately to include a relevant attention-getting opening to pull learners into the lesson, meaningful instructional activities that integrate several opportunities for learners to demonstrate understanding, and a closing segment that simultaneously provides closure for the lesson and prepares learners to transition into the next class.

Whatever their students' age level, teachers need to remember that students in a classroom must be treated as an audience. Teachers need to be realistic about the toll that being in classes from about 8 a.m. until 3 p.m. takes on learners. It is unrealistic to expect students to be as alert and receptive at the end of the day as they are earlier—which does not mean that teachers should consider the last classes of the day a waste of time. What this means is that teachers need to be dynamic instructors, use a variety of learner-centered delivery methods, and move lessons along at a good pace to keep learners actively engaged. Whole-class discussions should ensure that everyone in the class can participate. For example, prior to a whole-class discussion, students could do a short individual prep activity involving key questions, using manipulatives, or listing bullet points relevant to what the teacher just covered in the lesson. It is very easy for students to become non-participatory in a whole-discussion, especially if a few students can always be counted on to respond. Our discussion of Competency 005 is relevant here: if the teacher has created a class community that values connectivity, collaboration, and contribution, whole-class discussions can be more of a "grand conversation" than a dialogue between the teacher and a few students.

With very young students, teachers need to balance periods of activity, engaged participation, and restful time. For example, a science lesson on butterflies could include a relatively restful reading of a story or short chapter and move to a kinesthetic activity that might include making butterfly wings out of craft paper and demonstrating butterfly movements. Reading classes can integrate Readers' Theater, which allows students to act out in a creative way their version of the stories they have read.

Teachers of young children also need to integrate play into learning activities. Until they start school, play is the primary means of learning for children (we covered this in the discussion of Domain I). Integrating play into learning activities involves bringing role playing, pretense, and symbolic constructions of reality into the classroom setting in situations that allow children to engage in solitary as well as cooperative play. Theorists and researchers agree that play develops sensorimotor, social, and cognitive skills, so it should be an integral part of the classroom environment (Santrock, 2009, pp. 460–463). Additionally, many academic concepts can be taught through professionally produced or teacher-developed games.

Even older students need variety in the types of activities included in a lesson. Play at the level suitable for young learners would clearly be inappropriate for middle-school and high-school students, but learners at that age profit greatly from integrating playlike situations into lessons. Computer simulations, role playing, and outdoor settings for class lessons are considered age-appropriate ways of integrating play into learning for older students (Manning, 1998, pp. 157–160).

Teachers need to make sure that lesson after lesson does not put learners in a sedentary attitude. Instead, teachers need to work at managing classroom time to allow for meaningful integration of a variety of learning venues that integrate individual and social activities in a variety of learning tasks that promote creativity, understanding, analysis, and personal growth with understanding of academic content.

Group activities are considered a prime method of promoting social skills and individual responsibility through cooperative learning. However, group activities must be planned and managed carefully so as to promote the highest levels of learning among all students. Students do not automatically know how to work productively in groups, so teachers need to be proactive in explaining and demonstrating how cooperative tasks can be managed so that everyone assumes responsibility, practices collaborative skills, and makes genuine contributions to the collective task. Even if a group activity seems relatively unimportant within the broader scope of a lesson, teachers need to model what effective group work looks like. Fishbowl approaches are good ways to show students how group activities can work. For more formal group projects, teachers should provide extensive instructions on how to sequence the steps of the project, how to ensure everyone participates equitably, how to avoid nonparticipation, and how to genuinely cooperate. Teachers should also be realistic about the amount of out-of-school time that students can devote to group projects. Many students have at-home responsibilities after school, so group projects that require substantive out-of-school project time would create an inequitable learning requirement for such students. Teachers should schedule group projects to allow as much in-class work time as possible.

The teacher's classroom time with students can be significantly impacted through assistance provided by paraprofessionals and volunteers. In a major group project, for example, a paraprofessional can be a major help in keeping students on-task and in providing feedback and guidance as students work through the task. In regular classroom interactions, volunteers and paraprofessionals can facilitate students' work on individual activities, essentially multiplying the time available for individual teacher-student interactions. However, volunteers and paraprofessionals need to be trained and monitored to ensure that teaching goals are met and that learner-centered, appropriate approaches are used in interactions with students.

Finally, noninstructional duties can take up valuable instructional time. Teachers need to figure out how to manage such duties efficiently. Responsibilities such as reporting attendance or collecting permission forms can be completed while students are doing independent work. Handing out scored papers and passing out class materials should be managed in ways that optimize learning time. Scored papers, for example, can be returned while students are doing independent work. Class materials can be efficiently distributed by designated class helpers. Routine class work such as worksheets or minor homework assignments can be managed through in and out boxes to which students have access at the beginning of the class period.

Well-conceived routines are more than just a way to manage classroom time. Routines create a sense of normalcy in the classroom community; normalcy allows students to expect certain things to happen in a certain order, which creates a sense of comfort and safety in learners. Routine does not mean rigid regimentation; however, routine provides scaffolding for implementing effective, responsive instruction, which we will cover in our discussion of Domain III.

Managing Student Behavior

In order to create and sustain a positive, productive learning environment, teachers must develop and enforce rules for procedures and conduct. Procedural rules pertain to the routines described in the section above—entering and exiting the room, putting materials away at designated times, sharpening pencils, distributing materials, and other similar routines. Conduct rules are intended to set standards for desirable behaviors that positively impact the class community.

Ron Clark, a real-world teacher whose story was made into a TV movie, *The Ron Clark Story* (McNeil et al., 2006), is famous for his book *The Essential 55: An Award-Winning Educator's Rules for Discovering the Successful Student in Every Child* (2004). The title encapsulates the best reason for having rules: to support student learning by promoting behaviors that create a productive learning environment. In Clark's rule collection, rules for social etiquette, classroom procedures, and conduct standards are merged because, as he points out, his lessons "are about how we live, interact with others, and appreciate life" (Clark, 2003), but the fact that this is a best-selling book indicates how important rules are in sustaining a class community. Clark's Rule 1 is: "When responding to any adult, you must answer by saying 'Yes ma'am' or 'No sir.' Just nodding your head or saying any other form of yes or no is not acceptable." This extends far beyond the realm of classroom environment. However, Rule 4, "During discussions, respect other students' comments, opinions, and ideas" (Clark, 2004, p. 9) is directly in concord with Competency 006.

Classroom rules are intended let students know up front what behavioral standards are expected in the class community. Rules are intended as ways of establishing positive behaviors that contribute to maintaining order in the classroom. In contrast to procedural rules, conduct rules should articulate behaviors that teachers want to see in the classroom.

Depending on the model of discipline adapted by the teacher, rules establish different levels of control, ranging from low to high. A low level of control places a great deal of responsibility on the students for maintaining order in the classroom, and the teacher operates on the assumption that students value each other and are able to respond positively (and logically) to ensure that everyone's needs are met. Medium control generally involves collaboration between students and the teacher in establishing rules that protect individual needs while safeguarding the needs of the whole group. High-control approaches put the teacher in charge of controlling student behavior (Burden, 2006, pp. 17–36).

Regardless of the level of control represented by classrooms, there must be a plan for dealing with misbehavior. Teachers are supposed to establish consequences for violations of rules and to enforce rules consistently and fairly.

Reinforcement approaches are advocated as means of ensuring that students follow basic rules intended to preserve a positive classroom climate. Reinforcers reward positive behavior under the expectation that rewards will shape behavior to the desired standard. Reinforcers in class situations are relatively symbolic. The stars system, for example, works only if learners value the recognition signified by different colors of stars: if a gold star represents best behavior and a blue star the lowest level of compliance, the system works because the class community as a whole values gold-star behavior. Reinforcers can take many forms, including privileges such as being chosen teacher's helper, getting to be first in line for lunch or recess exit, or earning free time for self-selected reading. As the class community becomes more cohesive, the class can work as a whole toward a big reward, such as a movie and pizza day or a field trip; this type of reinforcer is sometimes used to encourage students to work diligently toward academic achievements such as meeting satisfactory standards on mandated exams.

Because rules will be broken, teachers need to respond appropriately to violations of class-conduct standards. Teachers need to remember that making students feel positive about the classroom environment is a vital part of promoting student learning, so when punishment is meted out for violations, the teacher needs to focus on maintaining the individual student's personal dignity while preserving the community cohesiveness that is supposed to be protected by rules.

Back to Clark's 55 rules—that is far too many rules! Experts agree that class-conduct rules should be limited in number (perhaps as few as five) and should be stated positively. For example, instead of a rule that states "No talking without raising your hand," the rule could be positively presented as "Remember to take turns when you want to talk in class."

Rules also need to reflect the students' developmental levels. Very young children, for example, need more guidelines as they learn general classroom codes of conduct that older students would be expected to know simply on the basis of their years of classroom experience. And older students who manifest the behaviors associated with Erikson's Stage 5 (refer to our Domain I discussion in Chapter 1) may need a greater variety of negative and positive reinforcers to encourage them to respect classroom rules.

Rules are an important component of establishing a positive, productive classroom climate. While rules may seem restrictive or perhaps even arbitrary, ultimately, rules contribute meaningfully to helping students function as vital members of the class community. Rules encourage ethical behavior such as academic integrity, mutual respect, negotiation skills, and general good-citizenship behaviors that will help students participate more productively in settings beyond the classroom.

Review Questions

1. At the beginning of the school year, a grade 3 teacher assigns students a number corresponding to the alphabetical order of the class roster. Each time students submit assignments, they write their number at the top of the page next to their usual heading and circle it. A designated classroom helper organizes the submissions in numerical

order, and the teacher quickly notes which numbers are missing. Which of the following rationales best explains this classroom management strategy?

(A)   The teacher knows that some student may not yet have mastered alphabetizing, and she wants student helpers to feel comfortable in organizing the submissions

(B)   The teacher is efficiently managing noninstructional classroom duties

(C)   The teacher creates an atmosphere of fairness because papers are scored anonymously by numbers rather than by names

(D)   The teacher wants students to understand the importance of following procedures for correctly identifying their class submissions

The correct response is **(B)**. Assigning numbers to students according to alphabetic rosters enables the teacher to organize submissions quickly and, in this case, to rely on a classroom helper to arrange papers. Additionally, even in a large class, the teacher can quickly take note of missing papers and take whatever action is part of the classroom routine for nonsubmissions. (A) is incorrect because this classroom-management technique is not related to students' abilities to alphabetize. (C) is incorrect because student names are still on the papers. (D) is incorrect because the scenario does not extend to consequences for failing to put the assigned number on classroom submissions.

2.   A middle-school science teacher wants her paraprofessional to help students work through a lesson involving learning the plant parts and their functions. Which of the following strategies would most effectively involve the paraprofessional in enhancing instruction for this lesson?

(A)   The teacher puts a copy of the lesson plan in the paraprofessional's folder.

(B)   The teacher asks the paraprofessional to do some supplementary reading on the lesson.

(C)   The teacher asks the paraprofessional to stay late on the day before the lesson. The teacher demonstrates what students will be expected to do on the day of the lesson.

(D)   On the day of the lesson, the teacher and the paraprofessional model the steps of the lesson.

The correct response is **(C)**. This option most effectively prepares the paraprofessional to participate meaningfully in promoting student learning. By offering some hands-on training for the paraprofessional, the teacher is equipping this assistant to work more effectively with students on the day of the lesson. (A) and (B) are passive attempts to involve the paraprofessional in instructional activities. (D) is incorrect because this option does not take into account the need to prepare the paraprofessional ahead of time.

3. A middle-school teacher wants to manage and monitor student behavior effectively while students work independently. Which of the following class-management decisions would most effectively help students understand connections between appropriate behavior and a productive learning environment?

(A) The teacher takes advantage of independent work sessions to catch up on required administrative work but encourages students to come to the front desk when they have questions.

(B) To create a sense of community among students, the teacher appoints class monitors to help keep classmates on task and to report any problems.

(C) The teacher walks around as students do seat work and other independent projects. She stops to encourage students who seem to slacking off and praises those who are working diligently.

(D) To give students an opportunity to develop independent working skills, the teacher sits at the desk at the front of the room so that all students are in his or her field of vision; whenever a student goes off task, the teacher says, "Mr. ___ (or Miss___), I'm watching."

The correct response is (**C**). Walking around the classroom as students work independently reinforces rules and procedures that should be in place for independent work, and it shows students that the teacher is readily available to help them with their work. (A) is probably a highly realistic choice given the amount of paperwork teachers have to do; however, it is not a classroom-management decision that creates a productive learning environment because students may feel reluctant to interrupt the teacher with questions. (B) puts some students in the uncomfortable position of policing their classmates, a relationship that hinders rather than promotes community among learners. (D) distances the teacher from the students and casts the teacher in the role of disciplinarian rather than facilitator.

PART III: DOMAIN III

Implementing Effective, Responsive Instruction and Assessment

PART III: DOMAIN III

Implementing Effective, Responsive Instruction and Assessment

Domain III addresses one of the most enjoyable and creative aspects of teaching: creating activities that enable learners to achieve instructional goals and objectives. Broadly, Competencies 007, 008, 009, and 010 connect effective delivery methods (how you teach) to understandings about how students learn. Whereas Domain I and II establish parameters for devising logical, coherent lessons that reflect well-crafted goals and objectives within a positive classroom climate, Domain III moves toward how those objectives are operationalized through specific, varied instructional activities.

Before continuing through this chapter, carefully read and annotate the four competencies and descriptive statements in Domain III from the *Preparation Manual 160 Pedagogy and Professional Responsibilities EC–12*. Underline key terms, mark terms you do not know, and pay special attention to the terms in parenthesis because those provide very specific indicators of the parameters of the competency. Domain III covers these four competencies:

Competency 007: The teacher understands and applies principles and strategies for communicating effectively in varied teaching and learning contexts.

Competency 008: The teacher provides appropriate instruction that actively engages students in the learning process.

Competency 009: The teacher incorporates the effective use of technology to plan, organize, deliver, and evaluate instruction for all students.

Competency 010: The teacher monitors student performance and achievement; provides students with timely, high-quality feedback; and responds flexibly to promote learning for all students.

Standard III of the Pedagogy and Professional Responsibilities Educator Standards applies to Domain III; you should look over those knowledge and skills statements to reinforce your understanding of the scope of Domain III, particularly to notice the reiteration of concepts and terms relevant to Domain III.

CHAPTER

7

Competency 007

Competency 007

The teacher understands and applies principles and strategies for communicating effectively in varied teaching and learning concepts.

Competency 007 addresses **communicative effectiveness** and is explained through four descriptive statements, which cover the following general areas:

- Effective communication skills
- Communication skills and student learning

As presented in Competency 007, a teacher's communicative effectiveness incorporates clear communication in general classroom transactions as well as communication techniques for promoting student learning. Competency 007 explores the way "teacher talk" can be a consciously constructed, carefully modulated means of promoting student achievement. Communicative effectiveness incorporates a teacher's awareness of how listening and speaking competencies can be used artfully to engage students meaningfully in lessons and in day-to-day classroom discourse.

Competency 007 Key Terms

The following key terms are integral to fully understanding the scope of Competency 007. You should consider creating flashcards to remind you of what they mean so that you can recognize the direct or implied references to these terms in the test items. Also make sure to review the Communication section of Standard III of the Pedagogy and Professional Responsibilities Educator Standards.

Competency 007 Key Terms		
accuracy	conveying directions	listening and speaking skills
age-appropriate language	discussion techniques	promoting learning through effective communication
clarity	interpersonal communication skills	questioning skills

Communication Skills

New teachers are usually chagrined to discover how easy it is for students to misunderstand communication that the teacher assumed was perfectly clear. Do you remember the teacher from the Charlie Brown cartoons? The teacher whom we never saw but whose disembodied, distorted voice we heard? That is an extreme of fiction, of course, but there is a bit of underlying reality here: in the context of the many, many different activities and stimuli that students face from day to day in a classroom, it is easy to tune out the teacher. But, the teacher is the main agent for delivering instruction and conducting the other business of the classroom (which we covered in Domain II). Thus, the effectiveness of teacher communication is directly linked to the creation of a productive learning environment.

In many ways, the teacher's communication skills are connected to the classroom climate, which we discussed in Domain II. Everything from the first impression that the teacher makes as students enter the room for the first time to the way the teacher explains concepts is connected to the teacher's communication skills. Communication involves conscious awareness of an audience, and in the classroom, that audience is the students. This is why clarity and accuracy are beginning points in establishing effective classroom communication. Teachers need to remember that students sometimes listen to teacher talk selectively, retaining only fragments of what the teacher is saying. Clarity is achieved by providing information directly, by repeating vital information, by breaking chunks of information into manageable listening segments, and by inviting questions for further clarity. Clarity also means anticipating potential areas of misunderstanding.

Teachers should think of every class as a "performance," utilizing the strategies that speakers use in effectively reaching an audience. To begin with, teaching is a speechlike event. The teacher (speaker) needs to be precise, coherent, and highly audience-aware. Precision means using age-appropriate terms and being exact. Coherent means constructing classroom communication as orderly, easy-to-follow discourse. Being audience-aware means remembering that students, like any other audience members, can lose interest, drift off, or simply stop listening.

Regardless of the formality of the communicative event (giving simple instructions or conducting a pivotal lesson), teachers can use communicative techniques to keep the students focused. For example, props (sometimes called "realia") can be used to help students clearly and accurately visualize whatever is being discussed. Using visuals to call attention to particularly important parts of teacher speech is a good idea. Even something as simple as giving students instructions on how to format an upcoming assignment can be facilitated by showing a sample on the document camera or by doing a mock-up on the board. Moving into the learners' space by leaving the presentation area at the front of the room is another effective strategy for keeping students' focused. Modulating the speed of delivery also keeps learners focused; if the teacher is talking so fast that learners are unable to retain any information or if the teacher's delivery is lugubrious, targeted outcomes are not likely to be achieved. Teachers can also keep students focused by calling on them during delivery of instructions or during a lesson (we will cover this more fully in the section on questioning later in this chapter). Effective speakers also use transitions to alert the audience of what is coming. Teachers can use transitions to help learners connect previous information to new information. For example, even in giving instructions, a science teacher could say, "When we completed Experiment 1, we were practicing basic lab procedures. Now, in Experiment 2, we're going to start exploring how botanists make connections among similar plants." As they move through classroom discourse, teachers can emphasize particularly important information in many ways. Stopping and saying, "These next three points are so important that we're going to take time to write them on the board as bullet points." Emphasis can also occur as worked-in silence to let students process the information that was just presented. Finally, teachers need to remember that being an enthusiastic, dynamic speaker goes a long way toward keeping students focused and alert.

In short, a teacher's communicative skills are a vital part of creating and sustaining the positive class climate described in Domain II. The teacher's interpersonal skills give students important clues and cues about how they themselves should participate in the class community. To reinforce the positive class climate, a teacher should smile, laugh, modulate his or her delivery pace, speak loudly enough to be heard clearly, and use body language to reinforce information. Interpersonal communication in the classroom extends also to dealing with rules infractions (which we discussed in Domain II). Effective communication in such circumstances enables the teacher to address the infraction without conveying anger.

Increasingly, electronic communication is becoming an important part of the classroom community. In districts equipped for high levels of computer access, email, blogs, discussion boards, and even social media can be used effectively to conduct class business and to extend the learning space into cyberspace. However, teachers should spend time teaching students conventions of electronic communication to ensure that all communicative and learning goals are met in these nonconventional venues.

Effective Communication and Learning

Scenario 1: Imagine a classroom in which the teacher shuffles in every day, does not greet the class, does not make eye contact with anyone, stands behind the podium, and reads in a monotone from a set of notes. Students are not asked questions. The instructor continues until the bell rings, and the students close their notebooks and exit the room.

Scenario 2: The school movie, *Teachers* (Russo, 1984) includes a famous and quite funny scene in which a teacher has trained his students so effectively to walk in, pick up worksheets, turn in worksheets, pick up more worksheets, and then exit that he literally does not have to communicate with the students. In fact, thinking he is sitting at his desk reading a newspaper, several classes walk in and out of the classroom for their designated periods before anyone realizes that the teacher has been dead for most of the day.

These two scenarios illustrate the type of teacher who does not use communication techniques to promote student learning. Effective, responsive instruction depends on actually *seeing* the learners in the classroom and being attuned to what they need, how they are understanding (or not understanding) a lesson, and on keeping them engaged. Every lesson is an opportunity for the teacher to use communication skills to move learners toward higher levels of achievement.

Two fundamental delivery methods—questioning and discussion—represent ways that communication skills are operationalized in helping students learn.

Questioning Strategies

A good place to start a discussion on questioning techniques is our discussion of Bloom's Taxonomy of Educational Objectives in Domain I. Questions fundamentally provide a quick, easy, versatile means of assessing students' understanding. Applying Bloom's Taxonomy to questioning establishes that questions can range from the lower-level skills (memorization) to higher-order skills (analysis). When a teacher integrates questions into a lecture, the dynamics of the presentation change: the teacher changes the directionality of the lesson from teacher to student delivery of information to interactive discourse in which learners are communicating with the teacher and with each other.

New teachers frequently write out key questions (which is a good strategy given that the teaching presentation might lag in places if the teacher cannot think of appropriate questions). However, good communication skills should be reflected in the teacher's ability to shape questions in response to students' comments or nonverbal cues as they listen to a lesson.

When teachers ask questions, they are using authentic assessment to determine the students' level of understanding. For example, in a science lesson in which the teacher has just explained the parts of a plant, a lower-level question to focus students' attention on this basic information might be, "Justin, can you repeat the parts of the plant before we move on to explore each part more fully?" If the student cannot answer this low-level question, the teacher has other options such as calling on a different student or repeating the information.

When students initiate questions, they are demonstrating active engagement with the lesson. As an effective communicator, the teacher should encourage students to ask questions, making sure students realize that if one student has a question about something in the lesson, it is likely that others do as well. If the teacher has created a comfortable, learner-centered class environment, students are likely to feel that their questions are welcomed. When a student asks a question, a teacher can also take the opportunity to invite the rest of the class to respond, which furthers the assessment-value of questioning.

As questions move into the upper levels of Bloom's Taxonomy, students need to be given ample time to process the question and construct a response. This is known as "wait time." Unfortunately, teachers sometimes feel fidgety about silence in the classroom, so they do not give students enough time to shape a response, or they call on students who may not be ready to respond. Wait time means that the teacher recognizes that students need more than a few seconds to construct a response that calls for synthesis, analysis, or evaluation. Additionally, English language learners also need more wait time to develop their responses.

Another concern in good questioning strategies is equity in calling on students. In every class, there are some students who quickly respond to almost any question the teacher asks. To create an equitable distribution of responders, teachers need to develop strategies for encouraging broader participation in respondents such as actually calling on students rather than waiting for someone to respond. While the teacher risks calling on students who may not know the answer, this strategy might also develop individual responsibility in the class as a whole if students do not grow complacent about having the more assertive students always respond.

Teachers should also be ready with prompting or follow-up questions when students are called on and do not know the answer. Above all, questioning should be an opportunity for students to feel that they are valuable members of the class community and that question-and-answer sessions provide an opportunity for the whole class to profit from construction of new knowledge. Teachers should realize that for many students, answering a question is a major risk either because they feel insecure in their understanding of the content or because they are uncomfortable about speaking up in class. Teachers should never respond sarcastically or insensitively to students who respond incorrectly.

In many cases, an incorrect response indicates the teacher's failure to present material clearly. Sometimes, a teacher can adjust the lesson on the spot through astute restructuring, by providing examples, or by more fully explaining complex concepts.

Class Discussions

Conducting whole-class discussion requires orchestration of the rhythms and synchronicity of the class community. If the teacher has effectively implemented the strategies described in Domain II for creating a positive class climate, that is a good foundation for effective class discussion. Class discussions are sometimes referred to as "grand conversations" because the assumption is that everyone in the class community is interested in participating in talking meaningfully about the subject at hand. For class discussions to work, the teacher has to have conducted a lesson that engaged the learners and that created a desire to pursue the topic through further conversation. Whole-class discussions give students an opportunity to demonstrate such skills as negotiation, debate, questioning, listening, acknowledgement, and disagreement.

Communication skills are demonstrated by the teacher in day-to-day basic transactions and in lesson presentation. The give-and-take of discussion and questioning offers teachers genuine insight into how learners are processing new knowledge. Eggen and Kauchak (2012) offer a succinct, powerful assessment of effective communication in the classroom: "Seeing the pleasure on students' faces when they are able to put their understanding into their own words is one of the greatest rewards in teaching" (p. 74).

Review Questions

1. A middle-school history teacher has just finished a lecture on the Bill of Rights. He asks, "Does anyone have any questions?" No one responds. Which of the following strategies would best implement effective communication strategies to promote student learning in this context?

    (A) The teacher calls on several students to explain which part of the Bill of Rights they consider most important

    (B) The teacher asks several open-ended questions designed to help students consider the basic content of the Bill of Rights

    (C) The teacher has students reread the chapter on the Bill of Rights

    (D) The teacher administers a quiz asking students to list the topic of each amendment in the Bill of Rights

    The correct response is **(B)**. When the students do not initiate questions, the teacher engages students in discussion by asking questions that promote their higher-level thinking about the topic. (A) is incorrect because calling on students after no one asked questions seems punitive; the students in this scenario seem to need encouragement to engage in meaningful consideration of the topic. (C) and (D) are incorrect because reading or taking a quiz does not address the instructional goal specified in the scenario—promoting student learning through effective communication.

2. A high-school English teacher is preparing a class discussion on the story students read for homework. Which of the following questioning strategies should the teacher use to promote effective class discussion?

    (A) The teacher prepares all the questions she wants students to discuss, writes them on the board, and asks the class which questions they would like answered.

    (B) The teacher hands out index cards and has each student to write down one question he or she wants answered. The teacher collects the cards and answers each question.

    (C) The teacher starts the discussion with several pivotal questions and then constructs new questions based on the students' comments during discussion.

    (D) The teacher prepares a question for each group. Working collaboratively, the students prepare their response and present it to the class.

    The correct response is **(C)**. This answer shows the teacher launching the discussion with questions to get the discussion going. Continuing the discussion with questions based on the students' comments shows the teacher's *automaticity* in questioning (the ability to devise questions on the spot in response to ongoing discussion). (A) is incorrect because it does not offer an optimum strategy for engaging students in exploring the content and ideas of the story. (B) is a teacher-centered activity; although the students created the questions, by answering the questions, the teacher is preempting students' engagement in meaningful, thoughtful discussion of the story. (D) does not allow for effective whole-class discussion. The group activity would be better *after* a preliminary discussion that raises key questions that need further exploration.

3. A grade 2 teacher is guiding students in writing a short narrative based on a time they learned an important lesson on the playground. Which of the following strategies would best communicate an explanation of how to construct a narrative?

    (A) The teacher reads aloud a children's book and then works with students to construct a storyboard that shows the basic narrative elements in the story

    (B) The teacher tells her own story about the time she finally was able to go across the monkey bars when she was five

    (C) The teacher puts students in a circle and has each student tell what he or she is going to write about

    (D) The teacher distributes a storybook to students in groups and has each group prepare a Reader's Theater presentation of their story

The correct response is **(A)**. (A) offers students a clear example of what a narrative is. Through the interactive construction of a storyboard, the teacher is clearly communicating procedures in the context of an example. (B) and (C) are good strategies for triggering students' own story ideas, but they do not communicate an explanation of how to construct a narrative. (D) does not address the instructional goal in the scenario. Students are likely to intuit the narrative elements by doing this activity, but second-graders would need explicit instruction and direction, such as is provided by option (A).

Competency 008

8

Competency 008

The teacher provides appropriate instruction that actively engages students in the learning process.

The broad area addressed by Competency 008 is **engaging instruction**. Ten descriptive statements in this competency cover the following general topics:

- Strategies that engage students in learning

- Motivation

- Evaluating instructional effectiveness

- Targeted instruction for English language learners

Competency 008 is built on the premise that the teacher is responsible for actively engaging learners. Learners have huge capacities to grow personally, socially, and cognitively in our classes, but they are not necessarily *inherently* interested in the subject matter. That reality of teaching is what is at the root of the need to devise lessons that engage learners, promote higher levels of understanding, and result in meaningful achievement.

Competency 008 Key Terms

The following key terms are integral to fully understanding the scope of Competency 008. You should consider creating flashcards to remind you of what they mean so that you can recognize the direct or implied references to these terms in the test items.

Test-taking tip: Pay close attention to specific terms embedded in the descriptive statements and especially those included in parenthesis. Connecting those specific terms to Competency 008 will provide necessary clues in responding correctly to test items that target this competency. Study strategy: Make note cards to help you associate these terms with Competency 008. Reinforcement: Look through the knowledge and skills in the "Engaging Students in Learning Section" of Standard III of the Pedagogy and Professional Responsibilities Educator Standards. Notice the terms and concepts that reiterate the material in Competency 008.

Competency 008 Key Terms		
discussion	instructional effectiveness	prior knowledge
ELPS	instructional techniques	problem solving
ELPS: listening and speaking expectations	intellectual involvement	relevance
ELPS: reading and writing expectations	lesson pace	student needs
flexible grouping	motivation	targeted ELL instruction
inquiry		

Instructional Strategies that Promote Engagement

Given that they come into our classrooms day after day, students may seem to be a captive audience, but we should remember that they are members of a class community whose intellectual growth is interwoven with social and personal growth. Thus, instructional approaches should focus on helping learners grow affectively, socially, and cognitively.

Remembering Bloom's Taxonomy is a good starting point. The discussion of Domain I briefly addressed the need to match instructional objectives to appropriate levels of Bloom's Taxonomy. Instructional approaches that concentrate on higher levels, such as evaluation, analysis, synthesis, and creating, are likely to be more challenging for learners, and instruction that challenges should be more interesting than instruction that calls for memorization, rote learning, or drills. For example, a third-grade science teacher could give students a drawing of the basic parts of a plant and ask students to color and label the parts; this would be an activity at the basic knowledge, comprehension, and application level. A more challenging approach would be to have students collect samples from their yards or school grounds so they can differentiate the basic plant parts in a variety of plant samples.

Class discussions, which we addressed in Competency 007, should be used to move more learners toward higher levels of understanding. Teachers should move beyond questions that call for "yes" or "no" responses or that call for basic information. Shaping discussion around "how" and "why" questions leads students to think critically about the topic. Back to the grade 3 plant example: class discussion could focus on explaining how each part contributes to the integrity of the plant's structure instead of simply identifying the parts. In a class of older students in a social studies class, students could be assigned a group project in which each group devises a "perfect" society, drawing on course content to explain how the various parts of the society work together and presenting arguments that support the group's conception of a perfect society.

Students should be constantly encouraged to engage in inquiry activities that help them delve deeply into topics ranging from ordinary to exceptional. Inquiry puts students simultaneously in the roles of critic and advocate. Questioning how and why something is the way it is creates opportunities for dialectical discussions. With younger students, a familiar but deceptively mundane subject—such as homework—could be the platform for investigating bigger education issues. Older students could be guided to explore controversial issues such as gun control, capital punishment, voting rights, mandated testing, and other topics that can be examined from multiple perspectives.

Regardless of the topic, the content area, or the breadth of the discussion, a fundamental first step should be to establish connectivity through prior knowledge and relevance. The classroom space should be meaningfully connected to students' real worlds—that is the role of prior knowledge. Researchers who explore the conditions under which students learn consistently point to prior knowledge as the necessary "hook" for constructing new knowledge. Helping students find that hook is the responsibility of the teacher. Relevance can be established through simple connections. For example, an English teacher launching a unit featuring native American author Louise Erdrich could activate prior knowledge by having the class share culturally specific beliefs and rituals from their own culture. A whole-class discussion board, either in traditional classroom formats or electronic format, would trigger comparison of different cultural beliefs and analysis of the underlying catalysts for those beliefs. Thus, by the time students read the Erdrich stories, they would have substantive grounding in the importance of culturally specific beliefs that inform so many of her stories.

The importance of activating prior knowledge cannot be overestimated. Even minimal prior knowledge enables learners to forge connections between their current experience and understandings and new knowledge. Teachers should strive to introduce every major lesson or unit by helping learners discover prior knowledge that can help them contextualize new knowledge within their current understandings.

Engaging instructional strategies reflect the teacher's pragmatic assessment of immediate learning situations. Lessons should be carefully crafted to include these basic components: (1) an introductory stimulus that pulls learners into the topic of the lesson; (2) a presentation that includes learner-centered activities; and (3) a conclusion that brings the lesson to a coherent close. Even the best constructed lesson, however, requires on-the-spot adjustments as the teacher gauges the learners' receptiveness and does on-the-spot evaluations of instructional effectiveness. When students are obviously disinterested in a lesson, the teacher can make automatic adjustments by shifting to a strategy that gets the learners physically involved through movement, using manipulatives, or shifting to a more interactive delivery method. When informal assessment indicates that learners did not "get" a lesson, the teacher can devise a different approach to reteaching the material. Determining instructional effectiveness is an ongoing, necessary component of implementing effective, responsive instruction.

Motivating Students

Motivation is an abstraction, but it is manifested in real behaviors in the classroom. Experts generally define motivation as a force that compels individuals to choose certain behaviors in pursuit of a goal (Eggen & Kauchak, 2012, p. 48; Burden, 2006, p. 121). In the classroom, motivation usually refers to the students' interest in learning in general and immediate interest in specific lessons. Operationally, motivated students make the classroom a joyful place for teacher, with everyone participating and everyone appearing to enjoy endeavors. Unmotivated students usually frustrate teachers because they seem to interfere with instructional goals; in the long term, unmotivated students make teachers feel like failures. Realistically, teachers cannot motivate every single student in the classroom, but instructional techniques and teaching strategies should be consciously designed to create and sustain students' motivation.

Certain teacher behaviors and attitudes promote student motivation in the classroom. First, we need to remind ourselves about the importance of creating a positive, productive learning environment, which we discussed in Domain II. If the teacher has worked to pull the class together into a cohesive learning community, the foundation for motivated students is set. A classroom climate that celebrates diversity, values the individual, promotes success, and cultivates responsibility provides a solid foundation for motivated learners. And a dynamic, enthusiastic, knowledgeable teacher is a good agent of motivation.

Teaching experts suggest that there are some things teachers can do to motivate students to participate actively and to work toward highest levels of achievement. Teachers should strive to know their students and learn about their interests. This knowledge enables teachers to construct lessons that reflect student interest. Teachers should also provide choices so that learners feel they have a real role in the learning community. Well-planned lessons created with the learner in mind (versus covering curricular topics) should generate genuine interest.

General teaching approaches conducive to high motivation levels include fostering a culture of success, devising challenging lessons that promote higher-order thinking skills, scaffolding new material with relevant examples, creating interactive lessons, and integrating authentic assessment. These approaches should be integrated into the underpinnings of the classroom environment and holistic planning.

On a day-to-day, lesson-by-lesson basis, motivation can be bolstered through strategies that support learners as they negotiate the demands of the lesson. To some extent, motivation is the result of high interest levels, which can be encouraged through the following strategies:

1. Opening the lesson with an introductory activity that engages learners immediately and personally. When new material is being introduced, this opener should activate prior knowledge.

2. Using varied delivery methods within a single lesson. Lecture, demonstration, interactive segments, discussion, group activities, informal assessment, and questioning can be integrated masterfully to keep learners' attention.

3. Pacing the lesson so it does not rush learners through important material but that does not labor so long that learner interest dissipates.

4. Making real-world connections to content knowledge. Students enjoy hearing anecdotes about the teacher's experiences and understandings of new material. They also appreciate the clarity offered through tangible examples of how course content is operationalized in the real world.

5. Making learning *fun*. Introducing elements of whimsy, surprise, and play can break up the monotony that can easily set in over the course of a long school day.

6. Scaffolding challenging material through sequenced steps, effective examples, demonstrations, and extra processing time (adapted from Burden, 2006, pp. 121–129; Eggen & Kauchak, 2012, pp. 50–54).

Motivation is sustained over the long term when learners feel their efforts will be rewarded with success. Our discussion of Competency 010 will examine in detail how feedback is integral to student success. The expectation of success significantly influences a student's motivation. While learner effort certainly plays into individual success, teacher's high expectations for all learners sustain an effective, responsive learning environment. Even when learners fail to meet minimum standards for success, teachers should strive to help them recognize what they *have* achieved and to set realistic goals for continued achievement.

Teaching English Language Learners

When English language learners are integrated into mainstream classrooms, teachers need to make adjustments and accommodations that appropriately address the students' language learning needs. In some cases, instruction must be differentiated to enable ELLs to succeed. Instructional adjustments do not mean a reduction in rigor or oversimplification of course material. ELL specialists (Reis, Quintanar, & Cabral, 2008, pp. 20–21; Ramos, 2013, p. 28) suggest best practices for making learning meaningful and productive for students who are learning content material *while* they are working on English language proficiency:

1. Building new learning on students' cultural and language background and experiences

2. Providing instructional scaffolding to guide learners through new knowledge

3. Integrating ELLs students meaningfully and fully into the learning community through cooperative learning, modeling, and authentic language-development activities

4. Integrating opportunities for learning curricular content through speaking, listening, reading, and writing

Requirements for teaching ELLs in Texas include integrating English Language Proficiency Standards (ELPS) from the Texas Essential Knowledge and Skills (TEKS) (TEA, 2013). Promoting ELLs English proficiency in accordance with ELPS means that the teacher must have a high level of familiarity with ELPS expectations in reading, writing, speaking, and listening at various proficiency and grade levels. Students designated as ELL must be tested each year to assess progress toward higher levels of English proficiency (TEA), so content-area teachers with mainstreamed ELLs in their classroom are responsible for promoting students' continuing development in general English proficiency (vocabulary, grammar, syntax, and mechanics) in the context of content-area learning.

■ Review Questions

1. A high-school English teacher is preparing a unit on Jack London's "To Build a Fire," a story set in the Yukon which ends with the main character freezing to death after refusing to follow advice about the dangers of being in super-cold temperatures. Before the students read the story, the teacher brings a small ice chest filled with ice water and asks for volunteers to submerge their hands in the water and talk about how it feels. This instructional strategy primarily addresses which of the following rationales for actively engaging students in learning?

   (A) Connecting two content areas—literature and science

   (B) Activating prior knowledge

   (C) Promoting higher-order thinking skills

   (D) Creating an interactive communicative context for discussing the story

   The correct response is **(B)**. (B) correctly recognizes the prior-knowledge strategy. The teacher is encouraging students to link their understanding of a real-world phenomenon to a key plot element in the story. (A) is incorrect because the teacher is not providing a sufficient context to consider scientific aspects of extreme cold, and the scenario does not suggest cross-curricular intentions. (C) and (D) do not reflect the instructional intent of the activity as presented in the scenario.

2.   A grade 6 science teacher assigns a project in which students work in groups to collect as many leaves as possible from their home environments, the school grounds, and other public areas they visit in a one-week period. The teacher sets up the group collection as a contest, with the students spending a few minutes each day entering their data on a class-progress chart. This project primarily addresses which of the following means of generating motivation?

   (A)   The project includes a competitive element that activates students' motivation to win by working cooperatively toward meeting a group goal

   (B)   The project provides sufficient time for overachievers and less motivated students to work comfortably

   (C)   Students will have fun doing the project

   (D)   The project integrates possibilities for parents to help students to complete the project

The correct response is **(A)**. (A) accurately identifies the components of this assignment designed to encourage students' self-motivation to participate meaningfully in this learning task. The competition adds a gamelike component to this group task, which is likely to heighten students' sense of individual responsibility and desire to complete the task effectively. (B) addresses an important part of motivation, but the time period is appropriate for all learners; the scenario does not address potential problems caused by underachievers. (C) and (D) are not presented as salient components of the project.

3.   A middle-school math teacher has several intermediate ELLs in his class. Which of the following instructional scaffolding strategies would most effectively provide accommodations for ELL students in understanding content-area instruction?

   (A)   The teacher distributes a different object to each group of students. The group writes a word problem based on the object they received.

   (B)   The teacher has the ELL students work with a native speaker "buddy" on all in-class assignments.

   (C)   The teacher has the ELL students work at the computer to translate word problems into their L1.

   (D)   The teacher creates a wall chart that identifies the typical parts of a word problem and several charts that show actual word problems color-coded according to those parts.

The correct response is (**D**). This answer offers instructional scaffolding both for ELL and native speakers, thereby promoting a class climate that values all students and accommodating ELLs' need for guidance and support without promoting a deficit view. (A) would be an appropriate content-area activity, but it does not provide the scaffolding that intermediate ELL students would need. (B) and (C) are strategies sometimes used in mainstream classes to help ELL students, but these do not provide the instructional scaffolding referenced in the scenario.

Competency 009

Competency 009

The teacher incorporates the effective use of technology to plan, organize, deliver, and evaluate instruction for all students.

Competency 009 broadly addresses the topic of **technology and teaching**. Eight descriptive statements in this competency cover the following general topics:

- Teacher's knowledge of technology

- Using technology to enhance traditional delivery methods

- TEKS Technology Applications

Competency 009 addresses teacher responsibilities in integrating technology into traditional learning venues. The underlying premise in Competency 009 is that technology can richly enhance student learning, so teachers must keep up with technology developments and work actively to use technology to move students toward higher levels of achievement. Competency 009 also reminds us that pedagogical applications of technology are far-ranging and can become an integral part of a teacher's repertoire of effective instructional strategies.

There are TEKS Technology Applications for elementary, middle school, and high school. Additionally, there are Technology Applications Standards for All Beginning Teachers. According to the TEA Approved Educator Standards web page, these technology applications are integrated in to the PPR. (TEA, 2013, Technology Applications). Notice that the cover page of these standards states that new teachers are responsible only for Standards I–V. Competency 009, Descriptive Statement F, addresses the Technology Applications TEKS, so if you do not already have a downloaded copy of this document, you should download it now and study it. Reading through this TEA document will give you specific indicators of exactly how teachers are expected to integrate technology into teaching at various grade levels.

Competency 009 Key Terms

The following key terms are integral to fully understanding the scope of Competency 009. You should consider creating flashcards to remind you of what they mean so that you can recognize the direct or implied references to these terms in the test items.

Competency 009 Key Terms		
basic technology	fair use of intellectual property	spreadsheets
databases	graphics	technology and class content
equity	inquiry and research	TEKS Technology Applications
ethical use of technology	integrating technology	user-created content
evaluation	online communication	word processing

Teacher's Knowledge of Technology

Technology has become ubiquitous—phones, televisions, microwaves, home security systems, the vehicles we drive, online banking, e-readers, increasingly sophisticated computers, etc. Technology is inextricably woven into our lives and our students' lives; thus, it makes profound sense to integrate appropriate technology into our teaching lives. For a long time, it was possible to resist bringing technology into our classrooms, but students today have been exposed to sophisticated technology from the time they were born. It makes no sense to persist exclusively in traditional delivery systems when in the real world, our students process information in technologically dependent, technologically enhanced ways. Once upon a time, the traditional blackboard was considered a major technological advancement! (Wesch, 2007; Evans, 1910).

Even if they are not as technology dependent as their students, teachers are obligated to keep up with basic developments in hardware, software, networks, and peripherals. Current technology offers teachers innovative possibilities for enhancing student learning. Juxtaposed with the discussion of student motivation in Competency 008, the integration of technology is a logical, pragmatic enhancement to traditional delivery methods. However, teachers do need to stay up-to-date with technological developments that can be meaningfully and practically used in the classroom. Even if the school district's budget does not allow for state-of-the-art hardware and software in every classroom, teachers can remain in the technology loop by reading professional articles on innovative uses of technology in the classroom. The reality is that many of our students know far more about technology than we do, but as designers of curriculum and day-to-day lessons, we are responsible for recognizing how technology can be effectively incorporated to enhance our students' learning experiences.

Knowledge of technology includes a solid understanding of legal and ethical issues. The ease of access to electronic information that changes and grows literally by the second creates another realm of instructional responsibility for teachers. The use of digital information in educational settings must reflect laws governing the appropriate and fair use of intellectual property as well as district acceptable-use policies. Instantaneous postings of photographs and "information" has blurred young people's recognition of boundaries that define privacy and fair use. When technology is incorporated into classrooms, these boundaries must be articulated and explained.

Using Technology to Enhance Instruction

Technology should not be used simply as an "add-on" to traditional instruction or as "computer-assisted" instruction. As presented in Competency 009, technology can radically change traditional approaches to teaching every subject. For example, having students produce word-processed essays is not much different from having them type them out on an "old-fashioned" typewriter *unless* the instructor sees innovative teaching possibilities in computer-produced writing. The writing process works out much more differently when the computer is used for inquiry, collaboration, planning, drafting, peer discussion, substantive revision, and publication. In many ways, the instantaneous nature of writing on a computer—you can zap a whole paragraph if you do not like it, you can do an immediate search for just the right word, you can IM (instant-message) a classmate to get feedback on a sentence or to ask a question—substantively changes students' attitudes toward the writing process. Where at one time publication of class-produced writing might have meant adding essays to the class display wall, today, publication might mean posting writing on the class web page or blog or uploading an essay to a writing site, such as the National Council of Teachers of English National Day on Writing website, or including the essay on a Facebook timeline.

In science and history classes, students can follow up on questions the second they think of them. For example, a student might be assigned a chapter that includes discussion of Darwin's experiences on the Keeling Islands where, he began to develop "Darwin's Paradox" (Johnson, 2010, pp. 1–7). The Internet makes it possible for students to pursue inquiry as far as their time and inclination allow. Technology makes it possible for students to transform their learning experiences into interactive, knowledge building quite different from the traditional approach that has for centuries put the teacher in the role as owner and dispenser of knowledge. Technology enables students to take ownership of their learning.

Technology has become almost indispensable in certain traditional academic tasks, such as conducting research. Increasingly, students can find almost anything on the Internet; databases, e-books, and interlibrary partnering position students as much more active researchers. However, teachers must teach students how to evaluate the reliability and validity of sources, how to use productive search techniques, how to store data located on the Internet, and how to make fair use of intellectual property.

As technology is integrated into content-area lessons, the learning artifacts students produce become increasingly more sophisticated and more diverse. With appropriate instruction in technological tools and procedures, students can be assigned projects that include graphics, music, video, and collaboratively created content. Technology makes it possible to expand the classroom space to include local and global contributors to even the simplest project.

In short, technology is not just a "fun" addition to class or a distraction from the dreariness of day-to-day traditional delivery methods. Technology is in itself a delivery system that changes the tenor of classroom transactions and brings exciting variety into the classroom. Digital learning products cannot be scored using traditional methods, and teachers need to adapt traditional evaluation and assessment strategies to assess adequately and fairly digital submissions, multimedia presentations, multiuser products (such as wikis and forums), and other innovative evidences of student learning.

Despite the ubiquity of technology, socioeconomic factors create an uneven field in access to technology. While some families are able to maintain up-to-date technologies in their homes, which their children can rely on for learning, other families cannot afford even basic technology. Teachers should not assume that all students have equal access to technology at home. Teachers must make necessary adjustments and accommodations to ensure all learners have equity in access to technology.

TEKS Technology Applications

TEKS Technology Applications are based on curriculum strands from the National Educational Technology Standards for Students and performance indicators from the International Society for Technology in Education (TEA, 2013, TEKS for Technology Applications). Collectively, the TEKS Technology Applications for elementary, middle school, and high school offer a comprehensive overview of diverse options for integrating technology into content-area instruction. Across all three school levels, the TEKS Technology Applications cover six broad categories of technology-related knowledge and skills that reinforce and promote learning:

1. **Creativity and Innovation:** This category addresses skills ranging from file formation to creation of original works.

2. **Communication and Collaboration:** This category lists various venues for digital communication that promotes collaboration locally and globally.

3. **Research and Information Fluency:** This category identifies skills generally associated with inquiry and research, ranging from knowing Boolean logic to evaluating resources for accuracy and validity.

4. **Critical Thinking, Problem Solving, and Decision Making:** The skills described in this section apply to projects that call for data or information collection, diverse perspectives, and transferring knowledge to technological applications.

5. **Digital Citizenship:** This category addresses ethical use of data and information acquired digitally. Additionally, it points out negative effects of inappropriate participation electronic communication (such as online bullying, personal security issues, piracy, and privacy issues).

6. **Technology Operations and Concepts:** This category covers knowledge of technology procedures, software and hardware, and general terminology and concepts.

As part of your preparation for the PPR exam, you should carefully study the TEKS Technology Applications relevant to your grade level. The descriptions provided for each category are sufficiently detailed to provide a strong indication of specific ways in which Competency 009 can be operationalized in the typical classroom.

Review Questions

1. A grade 6 English teacher and social studies teacher are team teaching a unit on the Civil War. As a culminating activity, they assign group projects designed to analyze connections between the literary depictions of Civil War situations and the historically recorded events. The teachers want to integrate Technology Applications TEKS into this culminating assignment. Which of the following instructional strategies would best address Technology Applications TEKS emphasizing collaboration and teamwork in the context of this culminating assignment?

    (A) The culminating assignment is a wiki, which students set up to invite comments from the entire class community

    (B) The culminating assignment is a research paper that must be produced from start to finish using word-processing tools

    (C) The culminating assignment is a multimedia presentation summarizing each group's analysis of the connection between the literary texts and historical events

    (D) The culminating assignment is a database that identifies historical issues and connects them to fictional resolutions in the literary texts

    The correct response is (**A**). A wiki is considered one of the best digital venues for encouraging collaborative thinking and writing through user-created content. By opening the wiki to the entire class, each group would collaborate to evaluate comments and suggested revisions of the wiki content. (B) does not provide for meaningful integration of technology and does not adequately address the teachers' goal. (C) calls for a summary, while the teachers' intention is to promote higher-order thinking through analysis. (D) does not offer the best use of technology in this scenario; the database is being used simply as a chart rather than as a technology application that genuinely engages students in using technology to promote higher levels of learning.

2. A grade 4 teacher is preparing students for the state-mandated writing exam. She wants to integrate word processing to improve students' ability to synthesize knowledge about practice prompts, to generate an essay, and to evaluate their work. Which of the following technology-based assignments would best address the teacher's instructional goal?

    (A) The students write a practice essay using paper and pencil and then transfer it to electronic format using the word-processing program on the in-class computers.

    (B) Working at the school's computer lab, the students create a practice essay under time restrictions, print it out, and revise it as homework.

    (C) Working in writing groups at the school's computer lab, students produce individual essays and then collaborate with their writing group members to help each other do on-screen revisions of their essays.

    (D) The teacher assigns a timed paper-and-pen practice essay. The next day, working in a computer lab, the teacher assigns a different timed practice essay to be completed at the computer. Then, the students discuss the differences between the two experiences.

    The correct response is (**C**). Working in writing groups in the computer setting allows students to enhance the writing process through application of word-processing tools. The writing groups setup allows students to collaborate on the discovery, planning, and peer revision parts of the writing process while providing an opportunity for students to work independently in generating individual essays. (A) and (B) do not encourage the use of task-appropriate technology and do not adequately address the teachers' goal. (D) uses word processing to create a writing-on-demand product, but it does not address the teacher's instructional goal.

3. A high-school chemistry teacher assigns a research project that integrates database and Internet site searches for research collection, requires logging in to well-known online writing center sites to learn correct documentation, and stipulates use of a plagiarism detection tool prior to final submission. This research project primarily addresses which of the following technology application goals?

    (A) Acquiring and evaluating electronic information and making fair use of intellectual property

    (B) Incorporating online research into a traditional research paper

    (C) Preventing students from plagiarizing

    (D) Providing hands-on experience with typical software applications and functions

The correct response is **(A)**. This research assignment is structured to give students hands-on experience with procedures for effectively and ethically using electronic information to create a technologically generated product. (B) does not adequately reflect the extensive use of technology called for in the scenario. (C) addresses only one aspect of the instructional goals. (D) reduces the assignment to a level far below the extent of the assignment requirements presented in the scenario.

Competency 010

Competency 010

The teacher monitors student performance and achievement; provides students with timely, high-quality feedback; and responds flexibly to promote learning for all students.

Competency 010 broadly addresses the topic of **assessment and learning**. Five descriptive statements in this competency cover the following general topics:

- Assessment and learning
- Feedback

Assessment is sometimes equated with testing, but from a more comprehensive, pedagogical view, assessment is the ongoing support that teachers provide to help students achieve instructional objectives. Classroom assessment occurs every day in forms ranging from a teacher's observation of students' demeanor during a class discussion to a more formal daily quiz at the end of the period. To understand the spirit of Competency 010, we need to let go of the assumption that assessment of student learning occurs formally through mandated annual exams. Assessing student learning is an integral part of everyday teaching. And effective assessment depends on the pedagogical foundations created by a strong classroom community, clearly articulated goals and objectives, and effective, student-centered instruction—topics which are addressed in Domain I, Domain II, and the other competencies in Domain III.

■ Competency 010 Key Terms

The following key terms are integral to fully understanding the scope of Competency 010. You should consider creating flashcards to remind you of what they mean so that you can recognize the direct or implied references to these terms in the test items.

Look through Competency 010 and mark key terms. Also, study the sections on Providing Feedback to Students and Demonstrating Flexibility and Responsiveness in the *Pedagogy and Professional Responsibility Standards EC–Grade 12*. Remember that the language of the standards can reinforce your understanding of terms and concepts in Competency 010.

Competency 010 Key Terms		
advantages	feedback	earning opportunities
assessment methods	flexibility	real-world applications
characteristics	high expectations	self-assessment
disadvantages	instructional goals	technology and assessment

■ Assessment Strategies

At the core, assessment is supposed to measure student learning. To measure learning, however, we have to start with metaphorical measuring sticks—learning outcomes. Our discussion of Competency 003 in Domain I covered the importance in establishing overall instructional goals and student learning outcomes for lessons and unit. Those stated outcomes are crucial in assessment because they enable us to determine to what degree students are meeting those outcomes.

Technically, every assessment should be linked to a specific learning outcome. For example, if a teacher administers a unit test, each item on the test should be directly linked to a specific learning outcome. Grades, which have for most of our educational history been linked to assessment, are considered inadequate assessments (Suskie, 2009,

p. 11). Let us say that Julie scores a 74 on a history unit test on pre-Revolutionary War America, and Jake scores 94. The grades themselves offer no indication of which unit objectives each student met. For example, Julie may have correctly responded to all five questions covering the role of the *Stamp Act* in fueling revolutionary spirit, while Jake may have missed all those questions. This illustrates the problem with using generic grades as assessments. By looking at the grade alone, the teacher does not know how to adjust instruction to get each student closer to meeting crucial objectives.

Various assessment methods, approaches, and strategies can be effectively used to measure student learning. Assessment can be objective, which means that there is only one correct response for each item, and the assessment can be scored without professional judgment, by machine or with a traditional answer key. Such exams include multiple-choice, true-false, or matching items (Suskie, 2009, p. 33). To determine what the results say about the students' mastery of instructional objectives, a teacher or administrator needs to examine and interpret the results based on the connection between specific test items and instructional objectives.

Subjective assessment requires that scorers make decisions about the correctness of student responses. Those decisions should be based on criteria that establish performance levels in order to determine students' mastery of learning objectives. Typically, criteria for determining performance levels are presented in a rubric, a scoring guide that lists discrete qualities and specific descriptors for each quality. Score levels in subjective assessments usually correspond to performance levels such as superior, satisfactory, unsatisfactory. In Texas, scores on the State of Texas Assessments of Academic Readiness include both objective and subjective assessment (the constructed responses for reading and writing are rubric-scored subjective assessments), but ultimately, Performance Level Descriptors are used to report students' level of mastery of the Readiness Standards for each subject area.   .

Another way to talk about assessment is on the basis of quantitative or qualitative measures. Quantitative means that results are numerical and can be statistically reported and analyzed (for example, 10 percent of test-takers scored 90 percent or above, and so on). If performance levels have been set ahead of time and items are keyed to specific learning outcomes, quantitative scores provide an indication of how effectively learning objectives are being met. In qualitative assessments, the scorer needs to determine subjectively on the basis of preset criteria what score or performance level description the test-taker should get.

Qualitative assessments are typically used for assessing performances, collaborative activities, online discussion forums, constructed responses, and other products that give the learner flexibility and some autonomy in responding and likewise allow the scorer to recognize qualities in the student response that may not be directly measured by the scoring guide. As one assessment expert puts it, "Qualitative assessments add a human dimension to an assessment effort, enhancing the dry tables and graphs that constitute many assessment reports with living voices" (Suskin, 2009, p. 33). Finally, qualitative assessment results can be reported *quantitatively*. For example, cumulative assessment results for essays scored using a rubric that provides four scoring levels (1, unsatisfactory; 2, satisfactory; 3, good; 4, excellent) can be reported quantitatively (5 percent of test-takers scored 4; 10 percent scored 3; 75 percent scored 3; and 10 percent scored 1), even though the assignment of the scores to individual essays had to occur qualitatively.

Assessment strategies must reflect the cognitive levels built into instructional goals and learning objectives. In other words, the teacher must ask himself or herself, "What do I want to measure, and how can I best measure it?" Factoring in time for setting up and carrying out the assessment is an important part of assessment decisions. The following chart compares typical assessment possibilities.

Comparison of Different Types of Assessments

Assessment	Description	Advantages	Disadvantages
Objective exam	• Multiple choice, matching, or true/false items • Only one correct response per item • Items generally measure lower-level cognitive skills although items can be constructed to measure higher-order thinking skills that call for decision making about scenarios presented in the item	• Can be scored quickly • Items can be written to reflect specific learning outcomes	• Writing good objective items is time-consuming • Students can overthink responses

(continued)

Assessment	Description	Advantages	Disadvantages
Essay or other constructed response	• "Open-ended" response with no single "correct" response • Results generally scored on the basis of predetermined criteria	• Can be used for a wide variety of content areas • Can elicit a wide variety of performance tasks (for example, writing, speeches, wikis and other technology-generated products, performances, creative works) • Allows learners to demonstrate authentically their understanding of material being tested	• Time consuming to administer and to score • Rubrics tend to be limited in scoring gradations (for example, a four-item rubric does not permit a scorer to assign a score of 3.2)
Portfolio	• Student-selected collection of learning products	• Affords learners a great deal of choice • Provides time for revision of items • Provides a comprehensive view of learner achievement	• Time-consuming to score because portfolios include several products and typically a reflective piece • As the portfolio is being compiled, students may not have any indication of how they are doing in the class because major grades are deferred until the completion of the portfolio
Performance or presentation	• Demonstration of discipline-specific skills, competencies, or creativity	• Provides opportunities for individual expression • Provides a comprehensive view of learner achievement • Collaborative performances provide ideal opportunities for student to develop cooperative working abilities	• Logistically, may be too time-consuming to require individual performances • Scoring should be based on a rubric that stipulates performance standards—creating a robust rubric is time-consuming and challenging

(continued)

Assessment	Description	Advantages	Disadvantages
Technology-based: clicker feedback	• Interactive, electronic in-class response to lesson components as they are being presented	• Instant feedback on student understanding of lesson • Instant possibilities for redirecting the class or backtracking to reiterate material that clicker responses indicate is being misunderstood	• Possibly too much data to process in a short lesson cycle • May discourage traditional interactive discussion and questions
Technology-based: initiator-contributor products	• Multiple author, user-created products (wikis, discussion threads, discussion forums)	• Provides learners a great deal of autonomy in engaging in online discussions • Provides a comprehensive view of how learners are shaping understanding	• Evaluating individual contributions is cumbersome. • Individual contributions may be minimal or superficial. • Expectations must be clearly articulated by the instructor (such as number of posts, quality of the contribution, etc.)
Real-world applications	• Assignments that simulate instances of real-world use of content-area material	• Well-constructed assessments show students the real-world value of class content • Students may be able to actually use the assessment product in real-world situations	• Assessment requirements might fail to make realistic connections between class content and real-world situations • Devising a rubric or other scoring system may be challenging
Think-aloud	• Learner talks about his or her process in working through a task	• Provides comprehensive view of learner's understanding • Offers learners opportunity to direct the product toward his or her greatest competencies	• Time-consuming • May require electronic or digital recording of data, which then needs to be processed

Understanding the role of assessment in classroom instruction is a vital component of maintaining an effective, responsive instructional environment. Assessment should be seen as an opportunity to use results to improve instruction so as to move learners toward higher levels of achievement. In daily class situations, for example, ongoing assessment can be the impetus for redirecting the lesson. Let us say, for example, that a teacher tries to have a class discussion at the end of a short lecture, but the students are not participating. In assessment terms, learners have not met instructional objectives. Instructional flexibility calls for a quick revision of the lesson; perhaps the teacher needs to offer some specific examples or explain in greater detail or have students do a hands-on activity.

Assessment that occurs at the end of longer instructional segments, like a culminating assignment in a unit, can similarly point to the need for different instructional approaches to guide students to higher levels of achievement. The bottom line with assessment strategies is that assessment should not be final. Each assessment result allows teachers to simultaneously look back at what worked in a specific learning cycle and what needs to be adjusted. Continuous improvement should be the goal of assessment.

Feedback

Feedback is a vital component of ongoing assessment. Another way of talking about assessment is defining it as *formative* or *summative*. Summative assessment is assessment that offers a final score at the conclusion of a learning cycle. State-mandated assessments, six-weeks tests, and other assessments that cannot be revisited are summative. Formative assessments are more in line with continuing assessment because the teacher offers feedback that allows the learner to adjust his or her product.

Anytime a teacher works with a student to identify strengths and weaknesses in a project (which could be an essay draft, a homework assignment, a science experiment report, or any other product) and gives the learner an opportunity to modify the project, we are looking at formative assessment. Assessment is designed to measure students' capabilities in meeting learning outcomes; thus, formative assessment should be used to enhance student learning and promote opportunities for top scores that indicate high achievement. Feedback should be constructive, specific, nonjudgmental, and directive—learners need to know specifically what they have done effectively and what they need to do to improve. Additionally, teachers need to work with students to help them become proactive and independent in applying self-assessment techniques. Students should know up front what is expected in assignments and should have access to criteria for each scoring level.

Effective feedback is a fundamental component of developing and sustaining motivation. Knowing we are on the right track on a challenging project keeps us motivated to complete the project and perhaps to complete it with distinction. Even low-achieving students need to know that they are doing *something* right, particularly if there are indications that they are genuinely trying. While it is very easy to zero in on error, teachers need to work at looking at student work with an eye for identifying and praising what has been done effectively. Formative feedback creates opportunities to show students how errors are signs of growth and how first attempts can be reworked into stronger, on-target submissions.

Teachers may resist feedback opportunities because providing written feedback is so time-consuming. However, feedback can be on-the-spot, in-class, and minimal. Possibly the most important aspect of feedback is making the learner feel recognized for his or her attempt and providing incentive to keep going.

Review Questions

1. A high-school English teacher has assigned a research paper based on educational issues. Students have read and discussed several articles on homework. Students have developed a short questionnaire, which they are supposed to administer to 10 students (not in their class) to collect data on student attitudes toward homework. This instructional activity primarily reflects which of the following assessment strategies?

   (A) The survey provides a real-world application of class content

   (B) Administering the survey will enable students to practice oral language skills

   (C) Developing the survey allows students to demonstrate critical-thinking skills

   (D) The survey items will allow the teacher to measure how effectively students understand the concepts being addressed in the unit

   The correct response is (**A**). The survey allows students to make an immediate, out-of-class application of course content. In the real world, surveys are a common means of assessing consumer response to products, determining levels of consumer participation, and gauging preferences for options (such as television programs, radio programs, phone apps, etc.). (B), (C), and (D) do not logically apply to the survey because there are no mechanisms for measuring how students are using skills mentioned in these responses.

2.   Which of the following explanations best describes how a rubric can contribute to student achievement?

   (A)   A rubric shows students how to avoid incorrect responses

   (B)   A rubric describes categories of responses so that students realize what they need to know and do to achieve scores at each scoring level

   (C)   A rubric provides examples that students can use to model their own responses to a learning task

   (D)   A rubric provides content-specific guidelines that help students interpret challenging test items

The correct response is **(B)**. When rubrics are made available prior to assessment, students can use descriptors at the various score levels to understand what is required for satisfactory and higher ratings. (A), (C), and (D) are incorrect representations of rubric-based assessment.

3.   A high-school communication teacher is preparing students for a formal speech. Which of the following instructional activities would best enable students to self-assess their speeches before the final, formal presentation?

   (A)   The teacher reviews each student's speech outline and identifies needed improvements

   (B)   The teacher distributes criteria listing what features are required in the speech

   (C)   The teacher shows clips of famous speeches and guides the class in analyzing what makes each speech effective

   (D)   The teacher has students brainstorm to produce a list of pitfalls to avoid in formal presentations

The correct response is **(C)**. This response offers the best possibility for students to move independently to higher levels of achievement. By watching a famous speech and identifying effective elements, students should be able to compare the speeches they are preparing and apply the features of effective speeches to their own efforts. (A) does not provide self-assessment opportunities. (B) and (D) create a checklist approach but do not offer students actual examples of effective speeches the way (C) does.

PART IV: DOMAIN IV

Fulfilling Professional Roles and Responsibilities

PART IV: DOMAIN IV

Fulfilling Professional Roles and Responsibilities

Domain IV covers educator responsibilities that extend beyond pedagogy. Cultivating family involvement, maintaining professional sharpness through professional development, and knowing legal and ethical requirements that impact classroom events may not directly contribute to teaching effectiveness, but these responsibilities are part of every teacher's realm of responsibilities.

Before continuing through this chapter, carefully read and annotate the three competencies and descriptive statements in Domain IV from the *Preparation Manual 160 Pedagogy and Professional Responsibilities EC–12*. Underline key terms, mark terms you do not know, and pay special attention to the terms in parenthesis because those provide very specific indicators of the parameters of the competency. Domain IV covers these three competencies:

Competency 011: The teacher understands the importance of family involvement in children's education and knows how to interact and communicate effectively with families.

Competency 012: The teacher enhances professional knowledge and skills by effectively interacting with other members of the educational community and participating in various types of professional activities.

Competency 013: The teacher understands and adheres to legal and ethical requirements for educators and is knowledgeable of the structure of education in Texas.

Standard IV of the Pedagogy and Professional Responsibilities Educator Standards applies to Domain IV; you should look over those knowledge and skills statements to reinforce your understanding of the scope of Domain IV, particularly to notice the reiteration of concepts and terms relevant to Domain IV.

Competency 011

Competency 011

The teacher understands the importance of family involvement in children's education and knows how to interact and communicate effectively with families.

Competency 011 addresses **parental/family involvement** and is explained through six descriptive statements, which cover the following general areas:

- Communication with families

- Collaboration with families

In the context of promoting student learning, family involvement enlists parents and other caregivers as collaborators in the task of helping students achieve educational goals. Initiating and maintaining family involvement is the teacher's responsibility. It ranges from perfunctory communication designed to simply notify parents about basic class information to well-considered collaboration when a young person is at risk. Family involvement matters in the scheme of education because teachers need families and parents to work as partners in educating their children.

Competency 011 Key Terms

The following key terms are integral to fully understanding the scope of Competency 011. You should consider creating flashcards to remind you of what they mean so that you can recognize the direct or implied references to these terms in the test items. Also make sure to review the "Interacting and Communicating with Families" section of Standard IV of the *Pedagogy and Professional Responsibilities Standards EC–Grade 12.*

Competency 011 Key Terms		
communicating with families	conferences	family involvement
community resources	electronic communication	regular communication

Communication with Families

There are numerous general reasons for establishing communication, but the overriding purpose for all types of communication with families is to set a foundation for collaboration in helping students meet academic goals.

The following five guidelines define generally accepted approaches for communicating with parents (Burden, 2006, pp. 65–66; Jacobson, Eggen, & Kauchak, 2006, pp. 307–309):

1. Communication should be initiated early in the school year. Teachers can send introductory letters to families primarily aimed at establishing initial contact. The teacher might simply introduce himself or herself to parents via this letter, offering general information about the class. Sometimes, this initial contact can include information about class procedures, needed supplies, class rules, and other class information. It is important that the initial contact with parents occur early in the school year, as early as the first two weeks of school. Additionally, teachers need to ensure that parents understand that the communication is two way; in other words, parents must feel that they can contact the teacher with questions, suggestions, concerns, etc.

2. Communication should foster positive, friendly relations. Communication with parents should make parents feel positive about the contact so that, as the year progresses, parents feel good about working with the teacher to promote their children's academic growth and feel comfortable about approaching the teacher should problems occur.

3. Families should be informed about class procedures, including rules, homework schedule, and major events. Sometimes, the initial contact letter can include procedural information. Regardless of how it is conveyed to parents, this information needs to be passed on to ensure that families are aware of what is expected of children.

4. Teachers should invite parents to volunteer in class events such as field trips but also daily class activities. School events would be difficult to carry out without family assistance, so teachers need to help parents feel that they belong to the class community. When parents participate as sponsors or chaperones in class events, they are teaming with the teacher to maintain a safe, supportive class climate. When parents visit the classroom to volunteer or simply observe, they are provided insight into their children's school life.

5. Teachers should strive to maintain ongoing communication with families. Operationally, ongoing communication with families can take the form of traditional notes or letters that follow up and update the initial contact made early in the year. Some teachers have class newsletters that might be created by the class. Electronic communication, such as email, class web pages, or class blogs can provide interactive communication venues. Traditional phone calls provide a viable means of keeping parents up-to-date on their children's school activities.

One high-school teacher's story about Rudy, a student in her creative writing class, conveys the power of personal contact through a phone call. The teacher took time to call a parent to praise his daughter's much-improved attitude, participation, and progress after a period of problematic behavior. In telling this story, the teacher explained, "The next day at school, Rudy thanked me... She said her dad let her know how much it meant to him. She added that it was very important to her that he know how much she had truly changed" (Burden, 2006, p. 76). This phone-call story also underscores another aspect of ongoing communication with families: what goes on at home and at school might be related, and knowing how a child is functioning at school could offer insights into home behavior and vice versa.

Communication with parents should not be intrusive. In other words, teachers should not pry into family or home life (although our discussion of Competency 013 addresses realities that teachers need to be aware of and are legally obligated to act on). However, if the foundations of positive, open communication have been established from the beginning of the year, the expectation is that parents and teachers can work together to do what is necessary to promote their children's well-being and success in school.

A few special circumstances should be addressed in discussion of communication with parents.

First, technology vastly extends the possibilities for communicating with families. The teacher can create a mailing group and automatically send updates of class activities to all parents. Similarly, the teacher can send emails to individual parents as called for by specific circumstances. However, the same pitfalls that apply to email in general apply to using email to communicate with parents. Busy individuals sometimes ignore email when it arrives and then forget about it altogether. As communication becomes instantaneous through texting and Twitter, email has become almost as antiquated as "snail mail." For families with socioeconomic problems that prohibit up-to-date technology, email and other electronic formats are not the best means of maintaining communications. In those cases, teachers might want to print out copies of email messages for students with no Internet access to take home.

Communication via class web pages, blogs, and other digital formats achieves two purposes: (1) the teacher maintains ongoing communication with parents; and (2) this option offers a real-world application of technology (which we discussed in Competency 009).

Family diversity also enters into the communication arena. English language learners may come from families whose parents are not sufficiently proficient in English to understand communications from teachers. In those cases, teachers can work with students to either translate communications into the family's home language or to help the students explain information to parents (although making the child consistently the intermediary detracts from the spirit of teacher-parent communication).

Families from underrepresented groups and/or low socioeconomic backgrounds may not be able to offer substantive support to their children in managing school responsibilities. A young person who is expected to babysit younger siblings while parents work will not have discretionary after-school time for homework, extracurricular activities, or supplementary activities such as visiting the library. Families with low educational backgrounds may not be able to establish and sustain a culture of academic success in the family environment. In these cases, teachers can proactively suggest ways that parents can support their children's academic achievement. For example, simple things such as suggesting that parents invite their children to talk about the school day, provide a quiet place to study, limit TV viewing and gaming time, and ask to see school work can help families support their children's academic efforts (Jacobsen, Eggen, & Kauchak, 2006, pp. 310–311).

Teachers can also help families take advantage of community resources that support young people's education. Teachers can be advocates for children who need quality after-school programs by informing parents of applicable programs. Families with special needs children or with holistic needs (such as military families) can also be encouraged to seek out community support groups that are frequently funded through federal programs.

Parental involvement is widely recognized as a key factor in sustained student success, in maintaining a positive attitude about school, and in promoting high attendance. Parents provide important affective support by maintaining high expectations for their children and by supporting current academic efforts that promote children's desire for higher education. Parental attitudes also shape their children's social and behavioral patterns in school (Patrikakou, 2008, p. 1–2, 6). Even though schools may have well-developed parental involvement initiatives, ultimately, the teacher is the most powerful representative and advocate in creating parent-teacher relationships that enable a young person to thrive academically: "What draws parents' attention is specific information about their own child. Teachers who provide parents with specific, concrete examples of their child's strengths and weaknesses achieve higher levels of collaboration, maximizing the benefits for the child" (Patrikakou, 2008, p. 6).

■ Conferencing with Parents

Establishing and sustaining positive communication with families creates a good foundation for productive parent-teacher conferences. Teachers should make sure parents understand that conferences can be requested by parents and that they do not have to be triggered by problems. From the teacher's perspective, a parent-initiated conference shows that the parent is genuinely involved in the child's education experiences and wants to improve those experiences. From the parents' perspective, conferences they have initiated put them in the role of advocate for their children's educational well-being and success.

However, conferences triggered by behavioral or academic problems are a reality of the teacher's experience. The five guidelines below should keep such conferences from taking on a negative tone (Burden, 2006, pp. 79–80):

1. The teacher should make sure there is a comfortable site either in the class-room or in another part of the school to talk privately with parents.

2. The teacher should have all necessary materials (the student's folder or relevant classwork, documentation of infractions, grade book, and other artifacts of the student's class work).

3. The teacher should maintain a positive tone even if the conference is to deal with an apparently unpleasant situation. The teacher should praise the child's accomplishments and ensure that the parents know the child's academic strong points. The teacher can also refer to the child's contribution to the class community.

4. The teacher should invite parents to suggest ways of dealing with behavioral or academic issues. Additionally, the parents need to understand that they can be partners with the teacher in helping a child get back on an even footing.

5. The teacher should work at ending the conference with parents and teacher feeling that they have made progress in addressing the problem that triggered the conference.

Conferences with parents are an important part of maintaining a productive class climate. Ongoing communication designed to keep parents informed about their children's progress, about class events, and about day-to-day school activities can make parents feel like participants in their children's educational experiences. Conferences, although they are necessary to correct or prevent problems, can be a vital part of helping parents and children stay highly engaged in educational endeavors.

Review Questions

1. A grade 4 teacher, who teaches in a school where 90 percent of the children are categorized as low SES and/or ELL, wants to encourage family involvement at a Demo Morning her class is having in one week. Children will demonstrate what they are proudest of having achieved in the past few weeks. Which of the following communication strategies most effectively addresses the teacher's goal to promote family involvement in this school activity?

    (A) The teacher has students create personalized invitations for their families that include a brief "teaser" about what the child will present.

    (B) The teacher purchases a set of blank invitations and has children copy a message about the event onto the card.

(C)   The teacher creates a flyer with all the information but leaves one of the panels blank so that all the children can sign their names. The teacher duplicates the flyer and has each child take one home.

(D)   The teacher calls each family to personally invite them to the Demo Morning.

The correct response is (A). The personalized invitations will create a meaningful connection between the child's school experience and the family and will most effectively address the teacher's goal to encourage the parents' attendance. (B) and (C) are generic communications and not likely to convey the personal connection created in (A). (D) is an impractical option given the possibilities that the families might not speak English or might not be home when the teacher can call; additionally, calling each family would require a major time expenditure on the part of the teacher.

2.   Which of the following guidelines best explains how a teacher should start a parent-teacher conference?

(A)   The teacher gives the family representative a letter written on school stationery listing the date, time, and reason for the conference

(B)   The teacher shows the family representative the student's latest tests, homework, and worksheets

(C)   The teacher tells the family representative about the student's latest academic and/or social accomplishments in class

(D)   The teacher asks the family representative to describe what the student is like at home

The correct response is (C). (C) is considered the best strategy for starting a parent-teacher conference. By praising the student's accomplishments, the teacher demonstrates evenness in assessing the student's capabilities, particularly if the conference is triggered by behavioral or academic infractions. (A) creates an unnecessary level of formality, although the teacher is likely to keep correct records of the date, time, and reason for the conference. (B) is not necessary unless the parent wants to review the child's records. However, the teacher should have these records readily available and updated before the conference in case the parent wants to see them. (D) is irrelevant and could be construed as being intrusive.

3.   Students in a middle-school math class are not completing their homework. Students are either failing to do it altogether or are bringing in partially completed work even after the teacher reduced the number of problems being assigned on homework days.

Which of the following additional strategies would most effectively promote family involvement in helping students complete their homework?

(A)   The teacher sends home a short note reminding parents to help their children set aside time for homework and suggesting that parents monitor their children's TV viewing and recreational time

(B)   The teacher tells students to have their parents check off every completed problem and sign the homework page

(C)   The teacher creates homework assignments that require help from parents or older siblings

(D)   The teacher sends home a note asking parents for permission to keep their children after school for 30 minutes so that they can complete their homework before going home

The correct response is (A). This answer offers friendly suggestions for parents regarding the importance of setting aside time for homework without expecting parents to actually participate in the completion of the assignment. (B) gives parents a policing responsibility and does not promote student responsibility for homework completion. (C) assumes that families have the time and expertise to spend on the child's homework. Teachers should not assign homework that students cannot complete on their own. (D) might be a possible solution in some circumstances, but without evidence about the cause of the students' failure to complete homework, the after-school extension appropriates time from both the teacher's and the families' day.

Competency 012

Competency 012

The teacher enhances professional knowledge and skills by effectively interacting with other members of the educational community and participating in various types of professional activities.

The broad area addressed by Competency 012 is **professional development**. Nine descriptive statements in this competency cover the following general topics:

- Being a member of the educational community

- Continuing professional development

One of the most professionally satisfying aspects of being a teacher is the continual growth that occurs simply as a result of being in the classroom and around colleagues every day. Even longtime teachers will happily admit that they learn something new from their students every day. Competency 012 identifies basic opportunities that enable new teachers to keep growing professionally.

Competency 012 Key Terms

The following key terms are integral to fully understanding the scope of Competency 012. You should consider creating flashcards to remind you of what they mean so that you can recognize the direct or implied references to these terms in the test items.

Test-taking tip: Pay close attention to specific terms embedded in the descriptive statements and especially those included in parenthesis. Connecting those specific terms to Competency 012 will provide necessary clues in responding correctly to test items that target this competency. Study strategy: Make note cards to help you associate these terms with Competency 012. Reinforcement: Two sections of Standard IV of the *Pedagogy and Professional Responsibilities Standards EC–Grade 12* apply to Competency 012: Interacting with Other Educators and Contributing to the School and District and Continuing Professional Development.

Competency 012 Key Terms		
being a team player	district hierarchy	resources
collaboration with colleagues	mentoring from experienced educators	support systems
cooperation to achieve goals	professional development resources	teacher appraisal

Being a Member of the Educational Community

When you become a teacher, you join an educational community that includes 3.1 million educators (U.S. Department of Education, NCES, 2013, Digest of Educational Statistics, Table 92). In Texas, you are joining a community that includes 335,000 fellow educators (U.S. Department of Education, NCES, 2013, Digest of Educational Statistics, Table 95). Locally, you will be working directly with a much smaller group of colleagues, but you are all a part of an extensive professional community. Keeping that community vibrant, up-to-date, and effective is what Competency 012 is about.

Being an active member of the teaching community includes the following three fundamentals:

1. Knowing all TEKS relevant to your discipline and knowing associated TEKS, such as Technology and ESL TEKS. Remember that TEKS are described by the Texas Education Agency as "state standards for what students should

know and be able to do" (2013). From your perspective as an educator, TEKS should be in immense help in creating your long-term and short-term instructional goals and in determining what areas of your educator preparation need bolstering. (We will discuss other specialized knowledge in Competency 013.)

2. Forging cooperative relationships with colleagues. As a member of your teaching community, you are a player in meeting the district's goals and a valuable member of your campus group. Professional colleagues provide an entrée into the culture of the campus and help novice teachers operationalize pedagogical strategies in real classroom situations. New teachers should make sure to ask questions about campus goals and practices and to rely on advice and guidance from experienced teachers. Vertical teams, horizontal teams, and team-teaching provide opportunities for collaboration and innovation in meeting instructional goals. New teachers are sometimes assigned mentors to help them transition into the profession, but informal mentoring that occurs as a result of daily interactions with colleagues is as valuable as formal mentoring.

   An exciting part of being a teacher is the continuing (and apparently unending) opportunity for participation in initiatives that pull students and teachers together in school-wide events. Serving on committees gives teachers a voice in decision making; working on cross-disciplinary committees expands the teacher's view of the campus community and broadens disciplinary perspectives.

3. Utilizing administrative and staff support. The administrative hierarchy within a campus can help a new teacher position himself or herself holistically within the school. Administrators see "the big picture," and knowing where you fit and how you can contribute to that picture is important as new teachers position themselves in the profession and in the immediate campus environment. Additionally, administrators and specialists (principals, department heads, curriculum specialists, and designated specialists) have an amazing breadth of knowledge regarding the school, the district, and state educational environments. New teachers should rely on these experts to troubleshoot but also in proactive growth.

Continuing Professional Development

Professional development is, partially, a daily outcome as teachers evaluate the effectiveness of lessons and specific strategies. Our discussion in the chapter on Competency 010 addressed instructional flexibility in assessing the effectiveness of instructional strategies. Professional growth calls for reflectiveness as well. Although there are formal venues for assessing teacher performance, teachers should continually self-assess to identify what is working and what needs to be adjusted in teaching. Formal appraisal systems are designed to offer feedback to teachers in improving instructional skills; continual professional growth is an important outcome of mandated appraisals.

In Texas, teacher appraisal is mandated by the Texas Education Code (TEC) (Texas Constitution and Statutes, 2011). In response to that mandate, the state has developed a comprehensive teacher appraisal system—the Professional Development and Appraisal System (PDAS)—but TEC allows districts to develop their own system. PDAS is designed to "improve student performance through the professional development of teachers." (TEA, 2005, p. 16) The domains and criteria in this appraisal system correlate closely with PPR Competencies and Standards, thereby underscoring the articulated link between student learning and teacher professional development.

In the arena of day-to-day teaching, authentic assessment practices allow teachers to self-assess instructional effectiveness and make adjustments almost immediately. Formal appraisal systems operate on a similar need to work toward continuous improvement of teaching. New teachers need to recognize that to be prepared for a required appraisal, they need to be working constantly to improve their teaching.

In addition to networking with local colleagues, teachers should join professional organizations that publish research and practice reports that can be used to enhance all aspects of teaching. Each discipline has a major national organization, like the National Council of Teachers of English (NCTE), the International Reading Association (IRA), the National Science Teachers Association (NSTA), the National Council of Teachers of Mathematics (NCTM), and the National Council for the Social Studies (NCSS). These organizations have websites that offer an abundance of resources, some of which can be accessed even without membership. For example, NCTE offers readthinkwrite, a resource that allows teachers to search for lessons on specific topics. NCTM, NSTA, and NCSS websites show lessons and resources in specific content-area topics at elementary, middle, and high-school levels. Additionally, these organizations stay up-to-date on pedagogical, social, and content information that impacts instruction in these areas. Most professional organization websites also offer sample articles from their journals. These journals are a rich resource for continual professional development. For example, the NSTA website shows that the September 2013 issue of *Science and Children* includes the following articles, all of which are directly linked to key content area and pedagogy (National Science Teachers Association, 2013):

- Teaching Through Tradebooks—using children's literature to teach the diversity of animal habitats

- What Does Culture Have to Do with Teaching Science?—teaching plant growth from an Asian-Hindu lens

- Science as a Second Language—integrating science and vocabulary instruction for English language learners

Additionally, these organizations have regional, state, and local affiliates that are able to connect more directly with teachers in that discipline. Such organizations allow teachers to collaborate by sharing teaching innovations and discussing common problems with a view toward improving professional satisfaction and promoting student learning.

Regional service centers offer resources and support staff to help region teachers work on instructional and development. Texas school districts are served by 20 regional Education Service Centers (TEA, 2013, Texas Education Service Centers). Service centers also publish updates on issues that impact all teachers, such as changes in mandated state assessments or federal regulations on special teaching situations such as ELL or special education. Service centers also promote teaching excellence by provide workshops to help teachers navigate PDAS requirements. As part of your PPR preparation, you should take a few minutes to navigate through the Service Center website for your region.

Additionally, many universities have public-school teaching initiatives that create partnerships between university faculty and in-service and pre-service teachers. Sometimes, resources from such initiatives are posted on the institution's College of Education website and are available for teachers who visit the website. Online seminars and webinars, many of which are available at no cost, also allow teachers to be continually involved in professional growth.

Teachers never stop being students. Teachers should start each teaching day expecting to learn something new about teaching that day. Networking with local and national colleagues, either in person or online, can help teachers construct new teaching knowledge out of everyday classroom experiences. Networking also makes teaching a never-ending journey toward professional improvement that supports and enhances student learning.

Review Questions

1. An English teacher is interested in incorporating technology into teaching literature and writing. The teacher feels competent in using word processing to enhance students' writing processes, but he wants to incorporate other types of technology to help students appreciate literature more fully. Which of the following options would most effectively address the teacher's professional developmental goal?

   (A) Requesting funding for additional hardware in the classroom

   (B) Reading professional journal articles on the impact of technology on student learning

   (C) Talking with English colleagues about how they incorporate technology in their teaching

   (D) Working with the campus technology specialist to identify what hardware and software is available to meet his targeted instructional goals

   The correct response is (D). This answer correctly recognizes the expertise of the campus technology specialist in helping teachers match instructional goals to available technology. (A) is incorrect and illogical because the scenario suggests that the teacher does not know what technology might fit his needs. (B) is an appropriate later step, but first, the teacher needs to find out how available technology can help him meet his instructional goals. (C) would be a good option if the teacher were looking for general advice on incorporating technology; the scenario suggests that he has specific goals in mind and is ready to seek the support of a specialist.

2. A grade 3 math teacher wants to improve his students' understanding of fractions. He has already observed several colleagues conducting lessons on fractions and has asked the department chair for advice and has made several instructional improvements. Which of the following additional professional development resources would best address this teacher's instructional improvement goal?

   (A) Consulting the website of the National Council of Teacher of Mathematics to find lessons and materials on teaching fractions

   (B) Enrolling in an undergraduate course on elementary math methods at the local university

   (C) Doing a Google search on "teaching fractions to children"

   (D) Reviewing textbooks on teaching methods for elementary school children

The correct response is (A). (A) is a logical and practical next step in this scenario. A professional organization will offer highly vetted, easy-to-access resources for content-area teaching. (B) is an impractical solution to the teacher's problem. A course would very likely refresh the teacher's pedagogical knowledge in math, but it would not provide a timely step to address the teacher's immediate concern. (C) is a common approach but should not be promoted as a means of solving classroom instructional problems. An Internet search of this sort offers no filter for identifying legitimate postings or for contextualizing the search within best content-area practices. (D) is not likely to offer content-specific teaching strategies.

3. Which of the following statements best describes the overarching goal of teacher appraisal systems?

    (A) To ensure teachers are adequately preparing students for success on state-mandated exams

    (B) To encourage teachers to continually integrate innovative teaching strategies into their lessons

    (C) To determine whether teachers are aligning lesson plans to state curricular standards

    (D) To promote improved student learning through teachers' professional development

The correct response is (D). (D) accurately presents the major intention of teacher appraisal: to improve student learning. (A), (B), and (C) are integrated into teacher appraisal indirectly through criteria and general evaluation categories but individually do not represent the overall goals of teacher appraisal.

Competency 013

Competency 013

The teacher understands and adheres to legal and ethical requirements for educators and is knowledgeable of the structure of education in Texas.

Competency 013 covers **legal and ethical requirements that impact teaching**. Seven descriptive statements in this competency cover these general topics:

- Legal requirements generated by federal laws
- Ethical requirements
- The Texas education system

Teachers in Texas have an excellent resource for staying informed on all issues that impact educators: the Texas Education Agency. In additional to offering information about Texas-specific educational issues, such as the state's assessment system, the TEA website (*www.tea.state.tx.us*) is updated constantly and offers directions, general information, and resources on how federal legislation impacts teachers and school districts. Articles and news releases reporting changes to Texas education structures are posted daily on the home page. The TEA website should be on every Texas teacher's favorites list and should be checked routinely. Sometimes changes happen quite quickly; other times, changes occur over a long period, involving revisions to documents and reports from committees. The TEA website also makes available PowerPoint presentations that TEA members make at professional meetings. In short, the TEA website allows teachers to fulfill the expectations of Competency 013.

Competency 013 Key Terms

The following key terms are integral to fully understanding the scope of Competency 013. You should consider creating flashcards to remind you of what they mean so that you can recognize the direct or implied references to these terms in the test items.

Competency 013 Key Terms		
acceptable use	equity	special education
advocacy	ethical use of resources	state assessment system
child abuse	ethical use of technology	state educational system
data security	fair use	student and family rights
Educators' Code of Ethics	legal requirements	student records

Legal and Ethical Requirements

In addition to instructional strategies aimed at promoting student learning, educators must abide by and enforce what seems to be an ever-growing array of federal regulations for ensuring the safety and welfare of students. While sometimes federal regulations may seem intrusive, teachers need to remember that those regulations are in place to protect the children we teach and to ensure that the educational environment is safe and equitable. These regulations are vast in scope, covering legal areas that may seem to be beyond the understanding of average educators. That is why most districts offer workshops on observing and implementing federal legislation in school and classroom environments. Nonetheless, it is important to underscore the language of Competency 013: "The teacher understands and adheres to legal and ethical requirements for educators..."

The following list offers a summary of the basic legal requirements that impact educators. As you read through the succinct summary of salient legislation, you should visit the TEA and U.S. Department of Education web pages for each bullet below.

- **No Child Left Behind (NCLB):** NCLB is the 2001 reauthorization of the 1968 Elementary and Secondary Education Act. In its latest form, NCLB is the impetus for programs that ensure educational equity for Limited English Proficient students (also categorized as English language learners) and for low socioeconomic status (SES) students. Operating under the broad goal to close achievement gaps among students with uneven educational opportunities, NCLB addresses issues of accountability (responsibility for helping students meet challenging educational objectives), teacher quality, educational equity, and federal funding to promote those initiatives. According to TEA, almost every school district in Texas is impacted by NCLB (TEA, 2013, No Child Left Behind/Elementary and Secondary Education Act). REA's *TExES English as a Second Language Supplemental (154)* guide is an excellent resource in understanding teacher responsibilities in the areas addressed by NCLB and court decisions that impact equity issues in public education.

- *The Family Educational Rights and Privacy Act* **(FERPA):** This federal act protects privacy of student records by stipulating who has access to student records and under what circumstances those records can be made available (U.S. Department of Education, 2013, *Family Educational Rights and Privacy Act*). This law gives parents the right to request and examine school records of their children under 18, to request corrections in the records, and to provide or deny consent for the release of "directory" information about their children. This act also gives schools the right to share student records to appropriate entities, such as a school the student is transferring to.

- *The Individuals with Disabilities Education Act* **(IDEA):** This law ensures services to children with disabilities and regulates intervention, special education, and related services. For teachers, this act has direct bearing on how students with disabilities are integrated into their classes. IDEA provides stipulations for the development of each student's Individualized Education Program, which addresses the adjustments necessary to integrate the impacted child meaningfully into the school environment. In Texas, IDEA is implemented and enforced through the Admission, Review, and Dismissal process, described in detail in *A Guide to the Admission, Review, and Dismissal Process* (TEA, 2012).

  IDEA covers a vast array of regulations regarding evaluation, placement, and education of children with disabilities. A few key points addressed in the ARD guide include supporting parents who request a Full and Individual Evaluation for special education services, annual review of progress by the ARD, recommendations for level of participation in the state-assessment system, reevaluation, and numerous other circumstances. REA's *TExES Special Education and Supplemental for EC–12 (161)* guide is an excellent resource in understanding teacher responsibilities in the areas addressed by IDEA.

- **The Texas Education Code:** This includes Chapter 37, Discipline: Law and Order (2011). It addresses each school district's responsibility to establish a student code of conduct and identifies conditions under which students may be removed from a classroom, campus, or disciplinary alternative education program. Guidelines on expulsion and suspension are also included. Chapter 37 details school responsibilities in areas including the following: circumstances that may call for a student's removal from class, such as documented disruptions, interference with the teacher's ability to communicate with all students; bullying and harassment; corporal punishment; disciplinary actions involving students with disabilities; and restraint of students. The TEA web page Chapter 37, Safe Schools, provides bullet points relevant to discipline in schools and provides links to sections of the Texas Education Code that cover this topic (TEA, 2013, Chapter 37, Safe Schools).

- **Child Abuse and Neglect Reporting Requirements:** This is the TEA web page that addresses mandatory responsibilities in reporting abuse or neglect. The information is presented via a detailed letter from the Commissioner of Education. While there are many aspects to dealing with suspected child abuse or neglect, on this topic, TEA stipulates the individual educator's responsibility as follows:

> Any suspicion of abuse and neglect must be reported within 48 hours, or less as determined by the local school board, by the person(s) who observed the suspected abuse and neglect. School personnel may not rely on another person or administrator within the school district to report suspected child abuse or neglect for them.

The seriousness of this responsibility is further emphasized by the inclusion of information on a child-abuse hotline to report non-emergency situations and the reminder that if a child is in immediate danger, the individual should dial 911 or contact local police as a first response (TEA, 2013, Child Abuse and Neglect Reporting and Requirements).

- **Legal and Ethical Responsibilities:** Educators have legal and ethical responsibilities in the use of educational resources and technologies. A comprehensive overview of these responsibilities is integrated into the Technology TEKS (TEA, 2013, Chapter 126) in the section on Digital Citizenship as shown in the excerpt below from the middle-school technology TEKS:

  > Digital citizenship. The student practices safe, responsible, legal, and ethical behavior while using technology tools and resources. The student is expected to:
  >
  > (A) understand copyright principles, including current laws, fair use guidelines, creative commons, open source, and public domain;
  >
  > (B) practice ethical acquisition of information and standard methods for citing sources;
  >
  > (C) practice safe and appropriate online behavior, personal security guidelines, digital identity, digital etiquette, and acceptable use of technology; and
  >
  > (D) understand the negative impact of inappropriate technology use, including online bullying and harassment, hacking, intentional virus setting, invasion of privacy, and piracy such as software, music, video, and other media. (TEA, 2013)

To be able to promote these student expectations, educators must have a clear understanding of principles regarding fair use of intellectual property, copyright laws, and acceptable-use policies. Acceptable-use policies are established by the district and generally posted on the district's website. These policies govern the way technology networks and resources are used by participants in the group, in this case, by teachers, staff, administrators, and students in a school district. Acceptable-use policies generally integrate copyright and fair-use information intended to promote the appropriate use of intellectual property and to safeguard privacy and individual safety for users.

Educators need to be aware of copyright and fair-use laws related to the copying and distributing copyrighted materials *for educational purposes*. The laws are actually quite detailed, but, in general, duplicating materials for immediate, limited educational purposes is considered fair use of intellectual property (U.S. Copyright Office, 2009). Fair-use and acceptable-use policies are particularly important in ensuring that materials are appropriately used in digital settings. If teachers are unclear about fair use of specific materials, they should consult administrators, department chairs, campus technology specialists, and the district's informational technology department.

TEA makes extensive resources and links available on its Internet Safety: Communication web page (TEA, 2013) designed to guide students and teachers in using and publishing information in digital formats safely and responsibly.

Purpose and Scope of the Code of Ethics and Standard Practices

The State Board for Educator Certification, in compliance with the Texas Administrative Code, developed a Code of Ethics and Standard Practices that defines expected conduct as educators interact with colleagues, parents, and students. These guidelines cover areas of personal integrity, moral character, safety, respect, and equity designed to maintain the dignity of the profession (Texas Secretary of State, 2013, §247.1). As part of your PPR preparation, you should access this code from the link provided on the TEA web page titled Educators' Code of Ethics (*www.tea.state.tx.us*).

The Code of Ethics covers three areas, each of which is defined by a list of standards that specify behaviors that educators should refrain from or adhere to. The three areas are (1) professional ethical conduct, practices, and performance; (2) ethical conduct toward professional colleagues; and (3) ethical conduct toward students. Most of the standards are succinct statements of behaviors that promote dignity in the profession. The following excerpts from the Code of Ethics provide an indication of the tenor and substance of the standards:

Standard 1.1: The educator shall not intentionally, knowingly, or recklessly engage in deceptive practices regarding official policies of the school district, educational institution, educator preparation program, the Texas Education Agency, or the State Board for Educator Certification (SBEC) and its certification process.

Standard 1.2: The educator shall not knowingly misappropriate, divert, or use monies, personnel, property, or equipment committed to his or her charge for personal gain or advantage.

Standard 2.1: The educator shall not reveal confidential health or personnel information concerning colleagues unless disclosure serves lawful professional purposes or is required by law.

Standard 2.5: The educator shall not discriminate against or coerce a colleague on the basis of race, color, religion, national origin, age, gender, disability, family status, or sexual orientation.

Standard 3.1: The educator shall not reveal confidential information concerning students unless disclosure serves lawful professional purposes or is required by law.

Standard 3.2: The educator shall not intentionally, knowingly, or recklessly treat a student or minor in a manner that adversely affects or endangers the learning, physical health, mental health, or safety of the student or minor.

Standard 3.9: The educator shall refrain from inappropriate communication with a student or minor, including, but not limited to, electronic communication such as cell phone, text messaging, email, instant messaging, blogging, or other social network communication.

(excerpted from the Texas Administrative Code, Rule §247.2)

The State System of Education

Once you become a teacher in Texas, you join a vast network that includes students, colleagues, administrators, and staff members operating under guidelines and rules of the Texas Education Agency, the State Board for Educator Certification, and the Texas Education Code. Teacher responsibilities extend to all the federal and state regulations covered in the section above, but as individuals, teachers have responsibilities in the following areas of professional responsibilities: student records, understanding the state-mandated assessment system, and advocacy.

Student Records

Teachers need to keep accurate, well-documented records of student attendance and excused absences. Data reflecting student course work, test scores, project participation, and other evidences of the students' learning accomplishments should be accurate and readily accessible. Teachers need to remember that according to FERPA rules, parents can request access to their minor children's academic records. Additionally, periodic evaluations mandated through IDEA, NCLB, TELPAS, and other assessments rely on teacher's classroom observations and records; thus, maintaining student records extends to areas far beyond keeping a neat grade book.

Understanding the State-Mandated Assessment System

In 2012, the State of Texas Assessments of Academic Readiness (STAAR) replaced the Texas Assessment of Knowledge and Skills (TAKS). STAAR is a component of the state's College and Career Readiness Initiative, not just an assessment of elementary and secondary academic knowledge and skills. In grades 3–8, students are tested annually in reading and mathematics. In grades 4 and 7, writing is also assessed, science in grades 5 and 8, and social studies in grade 8. In high school, exams in English I, English II, Algebra I, biology and U.S history are considered end-of-course exams (EOC). STAAR exams are based on *readiness standards* and *supporting standards* identified from TEKS. Readiness standards are tested at the designated grade level, but supporting standards cross into subsequent grades until they become readiness standards (TEA, 2013, STAAR Resources). Thus, STAAR creates an ongoing vertical alignment of instructional approaches from elementary through high-school grades.

TEA is an invaluable resource on STAAR readiness. TEA materials include official updates on the STAAR program; PowerPoints presented by TEA officials; and test blueprints, assessed standards, rubrics, scoring guides, and released tests (Texas Education Agency, 2013, STAAR Resources). While campuses and school districts offer workshops and orientations on STAAR, it is the individual teacher's responsibility to be fully knowledgeable about the mandated state-assessment system because such knowledge translates into effectively targeted instruction that prepares students for success on these high-stakes exams.

Advocacy

A teacher should be a self-advocate in integrating himself or herself into the state education system. To an outsider (a person who is not a pre-service or in-service educator), the breadth of knowledge, the quality of skills, the expected ongoing professional development, and understanding of legal requirements that teachers are responsible for probably seem overwhelming. Self-advocacy means that teachers know how to stay in the loop and how to negotiate all the demands. It could seem that the joy of being in the classroom in front of students could easily be obscured by simply keeping up with all requirements. Despite the fact that campuses and districts do disseminate needed information to teachers, the teacher himself or herself is the best agent for continual "withitness"—knowing what is happening, why it is happening, and how you fit into the big picture. Staying in tune with the Texas Education Agency and keeping up with the profession (as discussed in Competency 012) are vital routines for continued success and intellectual well-being as an educator.

Teachers are also the best advocates for their students. Many educators say that they were drawn into teaching because they want to share their love of learning with students or because they want to help or work with young people. Educators are nurturers, role models, and, in some cases, the individuals who have the best understanding of what their students are capable of achieving. Advocacy of students is yet another responsibility, but it is one that most educators embrace. The students in our classes are headed toward careers and college interests that may have been sparked by a lesson in our classes. Advocacy extends to working with parents, to promoting community literacy, to guiding underrepresented groups into STEM interests, to sharing our successes with local, state, and national colleagues, to starting each teaching day realizing that we never know what wonderful things will transpire in the course of the eight hours we share with our students and colleagues.

■ Review Questions

1. Which of the following correctly identifies the state-mandated assessment system in Texas?

    (A) Texas Assessment of Knowledge and Skills

    (B) Texas Essential Knowledge and Skills

    (C) State of Texas Assessments of Academic Readiness

    (D) Texas College and Career Readiness

    The correct response is (**C**). Since 2012, STAAR is the state assessment program administered in Texas elementary and secondary public schools. (A) is the system that was replaced by STAAR. (B) and (D) are not assessment systems.

2. The parent of a grade 6 student wants to see and discuss his child's grades for the fall semester. Which of the following responses correctly describes the parent's and student's rights under FERPA?

(A) The parent must obtain the student's approval in order to get access to the records

(B) The parent is entitled to inspect and review the child's school records

(C) The parent must explain in writing why he wants to see the records

(D) The parent does not have access to the records unless the teacher of record initiates a request.

The correct response is (B). FERPA gives parents or guardians the right to request and review their minor children's school records. (A), (C), and (D) are inaccurate representations of FERPA.

3. A high-school history class is working on research presentations primarily using digital sources. A group writing about British imperialism finds a picture of George Orwell they want to include in their presentation, but they are unable to copy the image because the website says the photograph is copyright protected. Which of the following teacher actions best adheres to legal requirements on fair use of intellectual property?

(A) The teacher suggests that the students take a screen shot of the web page and integrate it that way, making sure the website is correctly documented.

(B) The teacher advises students to print out the web page, cut out the photograph, and make a PDF of the image, which they document correctly.

(C) The teacher helps the students search for an image that can be integrated based on fair-use guidelines that allow the use of intellectual property for educational purposes.

(D) The teacher revises the assignment to stipulate that illustrations in the presentation must be original.

). Using copyrighted materials for educational purposes ght infringement. (A) and (B) represent unethical uses n though the teacher advises students to document the lem and misses the opportunity to help students under- of intellectual property.

PRACTICE TEST 1

TExES Pedagogy and Professional Responsibilities EC–12 (160)

Also available at the REA Study Center (*www.rea.com/studycenter*)

This practice test is also offered online at the REA Study Center.
We recommend that you take the online version of the test to simulate
test-day conditions and to receive these added benefits:

- **Timed testing conditions**—helps you gauge how much time you
  can spend on each question

- **Automatic scoring**—find out how you did on the test, instantly

- **On-screen detailed explanations of answers**—gives you the
  correct answer and explains why the other answer choices are wrong

- **Diagnostic score reports**—pinpoint where you're strongest and
  where you need to focus your study

TIME: 5 Hours
90 Multiple-choice questions

In this section, you will find examples of test questions similar to those you are likely to encounter on the TExES Pedagogy and Professional Responsibilities (160) Exam. Read each question carefully and chose the best answer from the four possible choices. Mark your responses on the answer sheet provided on page 239.

Use the information below to answer questions 1 to 5.

A grade 6 history teacher is beginning a unit on Native American history; each group will identify a specific tribe on which to concentrate. The unit will integrate a variety of instructional approaches, including Internet research and a culminating presentation. The teacher wants to use this unit to help develop students' independence as learners and to engage in learning activities that promote high levels of understanding of the history content.

1. The teacher starts the unit by having each group formulate questions they have about Native American history and culture. This activity primarily addresses which of the following instructional strategies for actively engaging students in learning?

   (A) Focusing on factual content since this is a history unit
   (B) Higher-order thinking skills
   (C) Activating prior knowledge
   (D) Identifying weaknesses in the students' content-area knowledge

2. After all the groups present their questions, the teacher compiles a master list of all the questions. Which of the following strategies is most likely to promote students' motivation as they work on the project?

   (A) The teacher distributes the questions evenly among all the groups so that all the questions are covered
   (B) The teacher allows each group to select questions they want to explore
   (C) The teacher selects five questions and assigns them to all the groups so that everyone is equitably addressing the same topics
   (D) The teacher scratches out questions that seem too easy or are repetitive and creates new questions for the groups to consider

3. Which of the following delivery methods best describes the teacher's approach in teaching the Native American history and culture unit?

   (A) Direct instruction
   (B) Role playing and simulation
   (C) Lecture, whole-class, and group discussion
   (D) Inquiry and problem solving

4. The teacher gives students the following guidelines about preparing the final presentation of their Native American history and culture research:

> The projects should be multimedia projects incorporating visuals, appropriate music, and text. Group members should work cooperatively to make sure each individual contributes meaningfully and equitably to the team product. I will work with each group to help you assign production tasks to each member. We will have two days in the computer lab to produce your projects once you compile your research.

This culminating activity primarily addresses which of the following instructional goals?

(A) To integrate technology to help students synthesize knowledge and publish the results of their research
(B) To teach students how to work productively in groups
(C) To address higher levels of Bloom's Taxonomy
(D) To create a learner-centered project that maintains students' motivation

5. Which of the following assessment strategies would most appropriately address the instructional objectives for this unit?

(A) A critical essay in which each student discusses the quality of each group presentation
(B) An objective test that covers general information pertinent to all the groups' selected tribes
(C) A reflective essay that allows each individual student to explain how participating in the project developed his/her understanding of Native American history and culture
(D) A short-answer essay exam that includes one question based on each group's tribe

6. On the first day of class, a high-school teacher begins the class by asking students to do this activity:

> Pull your chairs together into groups of four. Take five minutes to introduce each other by completing this sentence: "Hi, my name is _____; five years from now, I would like to be _____." Be ready to introduce one of your group members to the whole class.

This activity primarily addresses which of the following instructional goals?

(A) It demonstrates that the teacher values oral language in this class
(B) It begins to create a nurturing, inclusive classroom community
(C) It focuses students' attention on career choices
(D) It introduces the students to a collaborative class environment

7. A grade 4 teacher has several beginning level ELL students in his science class. The students rarely speak in class, one communicates using monosyllables in English and by pointing, and another speaks only in Spanish. Which of the following instructional adaptations would best promote the students' proficiency in English?

    (A) Giving the ELL students flashcards of high-frequency English words and content-area vocabulary
    (B) Having the ELL students practice letter/sound associations for the English alphabet
    (C) Doing teacher read-alouds of books on concepts the class is covering and integrating oral language activities that invite the ELL students to participate in class discussions
    (D) Having the ELL students write words lists of science vocabulary words and matching them to illustrations of the concept

8. Which of the following scenarios correctly describes a teacher's responsibility in integrating a special education student into a mainstream classroom?

    (A) The teacher meets with the ARD committee to specify assistance and resources needed to meet the student's educational needs
    (B) The teacher is responsible for meeting the instructional requirements specified in the student's IEP
    (C) The teacher is responsible for initially assessing the student's content-area abilities and implementing developmentally appropriate instruction
    (D) The teacher is expected to make minimal adjustments to content-area instruction but is required to offer differentiated instruction for the special education student

9. While shopping at the grocery store, a grade 5 teacher runs into one of his students' parents. The parent brings up a playground incident in which her son, Adrian, was sent to detention but the other boy received no disciplinary action. The mother tells the teacher that this is unfair and asks the teacher to do something about it. The teacher tells the parent that he was not present at the incident and does not know the specifics. Which of the following actions would best address the teacher's professional responsibilities while responding to the parent's concerns?

    (A) The teacher suggests that the parent come in for a parent-teacher conference when they can discuss the situation with more evidence
    (B) The teacher agrees to schedule a conference with Adrian's parents and the parents of the other child involved
    (C) The teacher suggests that the parent contact the school principal to get clarification on the incident
    (D) The teacher suggests that the parent call the other boy's family to find out what happened

10. A high-school biology teacher assigns a collaborative research project; students will be working in groups of five to integrate their research into a poster presentation. Which of the following teaching strategies would most effectively promote active, productive engagement by all members of each group?

    (A) The teacher suggests that each group member complete the research project independently and then the group comes together to pool the information into the group project.
    (B) The teacher shows students scenes from several movies showing characters collaborating to solve a problem. The teacher leads a discussion in which students identify key behaviors needed for effective collaborative work.
    (C) The teacher breaks up the assignment into major tasks and has each group assign a member to be responsible for each major task.
    (D) The teacher breaks up the assignment into sequenced steps and clearly explains individual and group expectations for effective completion of each step.

11. A high-school algebra teacher wants to develop his students' abilities to complete proofs effectively. Which of the following instructional strategies would most effectively target students' abilities to self-assess their work?

    (A) The teacher has students work in groups to complete difficult algebra proofs
    (B) The teacher demonstrates a proof and leaves the work on the board while students work on new problems
    (C) The teacher has students do one proof and then exchange papers to check each other's procedures and answers
    (D) The teacher creates a checklist that reminds students of basic procedures in completing algebra proofs effectively

12. Which of the following scenarios best represents an individual teacher's responsibilities in adhering to procedures for administering state-mandated exams?

    (A) The teacher needs to follow all rules and regulations prior to the exam date, such as administering benchmarks, going over practice materials, and preparing the classroom area as designated by state and district policies
    (B) Because TEKS are reflected in the readiness standards, the teacher should proceed with the scheduled curriculum and lesson plans
    (C) The teacher should conduct Internet searches for materials relevant to Common Core State Standards and integrate these materials into exam preparation
    (D) The teacher should make sure students understand that their grades will be impacted by their performance on the state-mandated exam

13. In Texas, students are designated Limited English Proficient (English Language Learner) if

    (A) on the basis of an English language arts teacher's recommendation, the student is believed to be unable to understand English sufficiently to succeed academically.
    (B) parents request in writing that the child be placed in a bilingual education program.
    (C) the mandatory home language survey shows that a language other than English is spoken at home and state-approved tests show that the student's current level of English proficiency does not support academic success.
    (D) the student's teachers meet to discuss the student's proficiency in listening, speaking, reading, writing, and general academic readiness and they determine that the child will benefit from a special language program.

14. In working with mainstreamed ELL students, which of the following strategies would enable a grade 3 teacher to adapt lessons to promote higher levels of English proficiency as described by ELPS?

    (A) The teacher schedules a meeting with an ESL teacher to ask for handouts and worksheets in basic areas of grammar
    (B) The teacher uses formal and informal assessments to determine ELL students' competency based on their performance and to adjust instruction to meet students' instructional needs
    (C) The teacher schedules a parent-teacher conference to give parents guidelines for integrating English into the home environment
    (D) The teacher asks the ELL students to stay in during lunch and recess for tutoring and for correcting problems in homework and class assignments

15. A grade 9 teacher whose ELL students are not meeting satisfactory standards on the campus benchmarks is concerned that these low achievement levels will have a negative impact on the students' persistence in developing higher levels of English proficiency. The teacher's concern demonstrates awareness of

    (A) the connection between the belief that success is possible and the motivation to learn.
    (B) the difficulty of promoting English proficiency in students who lack basic language abilities.
    (C) the lack of correlation between ELPS and day-to-day classroom activities.
    (D) the reality that ELLs need long-term bilingual education in order to sustain academic progress.

16. A grade 6 teacher is planning a unit on water and related concepts of conservation, ecology, and human needs. The teacher wants to stimulate reflection, critical thinking, and inquiry among the students. Which of the following initial learning activities would most effectively engage students in the instructional goals?

    (A) The teacher shows students the famous scene in the film adaptation of Helen Keller's life where the young Helen realizes that words are signifiers as she feels water running over her hands
    (B) The teacher asks students to brainstorm about the importance of water in their lives
    (C) The teacher has students work in groups to create a diary of water-related events that impact them in a single day and rate each event as (1) essential, (2) important, or (3) unnecessary
    (D) The teacher has students do Internet research on drought-stricken areas in the United States

17. A third-grade class includes a large number of ELL students, many of whom are reading significantly below grade level. The teacher is compiling a class library to use during sustained silent-reading and free-reading times. Additionally, she wants to ensure that the books support ELL students content-area knowledge as well as basic English proficiency. Which of the following considerations should the teacher keep in mind in selecting books for the library?

   (A) The books should have reading levels that match the ranges of student reading levels in the classroom
   (B) Because they will be used for reading beyond curricular requirements, the books should be at challenging reading levels
   (C) The books should focus on unit topics that the teacher is covering in science and social studies
   (D) The books should include books in the students' L1 to make sure that even the low-level readers are able to enjoy the discretionary reading periods

18. A grade 7 science teacher creates interest centers throughout the classroom that include short videos, pamphlets, testimonials, magazine articles, and good websites in a wide variety of careers. After the students have a chance to visit several centers, the teacher pulls the class together into a discussion circle and invites students to talk about which centers interested them most and why. This strategy reflects the teacher's understanding that the students are in which of Erikson's stages of psychosocial development?

   (A) Trust versus mistrust
   (B) Integrity versus despair
   (C) Industry versus inferiority
   (D) Identity versus role confusion

19. A grade 6 class has just completed a reading circles project based on books that each group self-selected with some guidance from the teacher. In preparation for parents' night, the teacher asks students to pick a book from the reading circle projects that they would like to share with their family. On parents' night, the teacher talks to parents about trying to start a family reading time, about helping their children keep at-home reading logs, and about reinforcing at-home reading efforts with minor rewards. The teacher's activities address which of the following areas of teaching responsibilities?

   (A) Promoting community literacy
   (B) Engaging families in their children's educational experiences
   (C) Encouraging families to create at-home libraries
   (D) Facilitating parents' participation in homework assignments

20. A teacher creates a World Holidays and Celebrations Calendar in her grade 3 class. Each month, she picks one holiday, and the children prepare decorations, learn songs, read stories, and learn the history of the cultural or national significance of the holiday. This activity primarily addresses which of the following instructional goals?

   (A) To promote students' appreciation of cultural and national diversity
   (B) To address community-based efforts to make the curriculum more culturally diverse
   (C) To provide content-area instruction in a variety of delivery methods
   (D) To help students connect school discussions of culture to their own families' experiences

Use the information below to answer questions 21 to 23.

Marcus, a student in Mr. Pruitt's grade 5 class, is having trouble working math word problems independently. Mr. Pruitt uses a variety of learner-centered activities including modeling, group work, minilessons, and manipulatives to provide guided practice and to prepare students for independent work on homework.

21. Although Marcus participates actively and successfully in class, he routinely turns in incomplete homework. Which of the following actions should the teacher take to support Marcus's learning?

    (A) The teacher should restrict Marcus's recess time so that he can complete his homework before he goes home
    (B) The teacher should send Marcus to the counselor to talk about problems he may be having at home
    (C) The teacher should request a parent conference to discuss ways the parents can help Marcus develop independent study habits at home
    (D) The teacher should reduce the amount of homework Marcus is getting

22. A few weeks later, while the class is working in groups on a challenging word problem, Mr. Pruitt is reviewing homework from the previous night. When he checks Marcus's homework, Mr. Pruitt marks all the problems as complete and correct. He says, "Marcus, eyes up, please," and he smiles and gives Marcus two thumbs up. The teacher's response to Marcus's homework primarily demonstrates which of the following strategies for promoting student learning?

    (A) Providing a break from a challenging class activity to allow students to reenergize themselves
    (B) Making sure students see the connection between doing class assignments and pleasing the instructor
    (C) Integrating a controlled distractor to make sure students can stay on task during challenging class activities
    (D) Using verbal and nonverbal interpersonal skills to communicate effectively with students about class goals

23. Mr. Pruitt recognizes the problems with Marcus as an opportunity to clarify expectations about the role of homework in overall class achievement. Mr. Pruitt plans a whole-class and small-group discussion starting with open-ended questions about what homework is for and moving into student-generated questions and answers about how teachers can make homework a better learning experience. This activity primarily targets which of the following principles of responsive instruction?

    (A) Using skilled questioning and class discussion strategies to promote inquiry
    (B) Providing an opportunity for students to see real-world applications of course content
    (C) Convincing students that all components of instruction are vital to success
    (D) Giving students a chance to voice objections to a traditional aspect of the learning environment

Use the information below to answer questions 24 to 26.

> The reading teachers at a middle-school campus meet to discuss ways to promote struggling readers' progress toward higher reading levels. At the next district-wide professional development day, the reading teachers bring up the problem during a whole-group Q and A. The middle-school teachers talk about their students' reading resistance and reluctance. A kindergarten teacher says, "Maybe your sixth graders could come and read story books to our emergent readers." The K and middle-school teachers work with the district curriculum director to iron out details.

24. This K to middle-school collaboration primarily exemplifies which of the following educator professional responsibilities?

   (A) Using outside resources to address student learning problems
   (B) Maintaining cooperative relationships with colleagues to support students' learning
   (C) Devising entertaining ways for students to complete difficult tasks
   (D) Fulfilling requirements of the state teacher appraisal system by participating in horizontal teaming

25. Pairing middle-school struggling readers with emergent readers will primarily promote both sets of students' engagement with reading in which of the following ways?

   (A) Students will be reading simple texts that are easy for both the middle-schoolers and kindergartners to understand.
   (B) Students will recognize that reading is a social activity that involves interaction between the reader and the text and among readers as they respond to the text.
   (C) Both sets of students will develop metacognitive reading strategies as they decode the texts.
   (D) Students will boost their reading levels by reading below grade level texts. Kindergartners will learn new vocabulary by listening to middle-school students explain unfamiliar words in the story books.

26. The middle-school and kindergarten teachers hold a debriefing meeting six weeks after the reading collaborative is launched. Which of the following meeting activities would most effectively enhance the teachers' professional development as they continue the collaborative?

   (A) A video of two of the students in the collaborative. The teachers discuss vocabulary exercises to ensure the middle-schoolers pronounce words correctly.
   (B) A short talk by the teacher appraisal coordinator advising teachers on how to document collaborative activities in their annual teaching portfolio.
   (C) A panel on promoting literacy skills in reluctant readers drawing information and classroom activities from *The Reading Teacher,* a publication of the International Reading Association.
   (D) Statistics showing the impact of the collaborative on students' reading levels.

Use the information below to answer questions 27 to 29.

Ms. Eliot, a grade 10 science teacher, stops every class lesson five minutes before the bell rings to give students time to fill out a Daily Learning Log sheet. Ms. Eliot has students write their name and date at the top of an index-card-sized sheet of scratch paper and write a short comment about their "take-away" from the day's class or a question or just a comment about the class.

27. This activity primarily reflects which of the following principles of effective instructional design?

    (A) Providing cooling down time at the end of a lesson
    (B) Accommodating end-of-class necessities such as collecting books and repacking backpacks during a low-level instructional activity
    (C) Giving students time to ask questions about things they did not understand
    (D) Allocating time for reflection and closure at the end of a lesson

28. At the beginning of each class, Ms. Eliot takes about five minutes to respond to comments and questions from the previous day's Daily Learning Log sheets, inviting students to comment more fully on what they wrote and to assure students that she reads the logs each day. By integrating this daily activity into each lesson, the teacher is

    (A) using interpersonal communication skills to support students' individual and collective response to each lesson.
    (B) promoting students' active listening skills.
    (C) encouraging students to be more specific in their Daily Learning Log responses.
    (D) using students' questions from the Daily Learning Log as indicators that they are not paying attention.

29. Ms. Eliot wants to integrate authentic assessment into her Daily Learning Log activity and to offer timely feedback. Which of the following uses of the Daily Learning Log responses would best enable the teacher to meet her instructional goal?

    (A) Creating pop quizzes based on the students' comments from the previous day's learning log
    (B) Using the students' comments to respond flexibly and adjust instruction to promote students' understanding of class content
    (C) Integrating a short-response question based on the lesson into each Daily Learning Log
    (D) Using a Likert scale that allows students to rate their daily learning experience from 1 (didn't learn anything today) to 5 (learned a lot today)

30. A grade 9 history teacher assigns a research unit to be completed in three weeks. Which of the following instructional plans would most effectively support the students' learning process in this research unit?

    (A) Having students select the research topic they want to explore
    (B) Having the school librarian demonstrate Internet research strategies
    (C) Breaking the research process into sequential step and setting deadlines and checkpoints for completion of each step
    (D) Analyzing a research paper from a previous class and pointing out all the problems that should be avoided

31. A grade 11 teacher plans a thematic unit on the Vietnam War. The unit will be anchored on Tim O'Brien's book *The Things They Carried* but will also include music from the war years, analysis of contemporary news coverage of the war, consideration of attitudes about the war, and a panel of Vietnam veterans from the community. This unit most effectively demonstrates which of the following features of well-constructed thematic approaches?

  (A) Integration of different disciplines to enable students to consider a topic from varied perspectives
  (B) Exploration a historical topic in a contemporary setting
  (C) Comparison of fictional and historical accounts of an event
  (D) Structuring a lesson on a topic that students will find relevant to their own lives

32. A high-school history teacher has assigned an essay as the culminating assignment in a unit on the industrial revolution in America. He has created a rubric for scoring the essay but he goes over it during the students' writing workshop days, explaining the performance-level descriptors. The teacher's discussion of the rubric primarily addresses which of the following assessment goals?

  (A) Ensuring that students follow directions closely
  (B) Giving students an opportunity to participate in creating scoring guidelines
  (C) Using the discipline of writing to promote students' higher order thinking skills
  (D) Promoting students' ability to self-assess so as to enhance the quality of their final product

33. A grade 10 teacher English teacher recognizes that group work promotes students' ability to expand their perspectives on a topic. However, the students tend to stray off-task and start chatting and eventually do not complete the assigned group task. Which of the following strategies would best promote the teacher's goal to use group work to create a productive learning environment?

  (A) Using a fishbowl demonstration to remind students of how to work together cooperatively
  (B) Creating a time limit for each component of the group task and using a timer to help students stay on-task
  (C) Stopping the group work each time students are clearly off-task and reviewing the goals for the group activity
  (D) Basing the group grade on the students' ability to stay on-task

34. A middle-school teacher has assigned a field research project in her social studies class. Students have designed a five-item interview on the topic of homework and are supposed to interview two students each. The interview includes two Likert scale questions and open-ended questions. Which of the following technology applications would best enable students to record, synthesize, and analyze their results?

  (A) Creating a spreadsheet to quantify the interview results and regroup results according to categories
  (B) Using word processing to transcribe interview results from the students' field research notes
  (C) Videotaping student groups as they work to compile the results of the interviews
  (D) Creating a class blog in which students comment on what they learned in doing the interviews

35. At the beginning of the school year, a grade 4 teacher creates these posters, decorates them using clip art, and places them around the room.

There is no such thing as a wrong answer.	It takes a lot of wrong answers to get to the right one.	Questions show you're thinking.	Mistakes are evidence that you're learning something new.	If you don't understand, just ask.

These posters primarily address which of the following instructional strategies?

(A) Creating a class environment that gives learners a great deal of responsibility for their own learning
(B) Ensuring that learners understand that the teacher is the instructional authority and the source of correct answers
(C) Creating a class climate that emphasizes supportive interactions and promotes learners' active engagement
(D) Creating a class environment that promotes oral language as a building block of increased cognitive growth

36. Which of the following descriptions best explains the significance of TEKS in determining instructional goals and objectives?

(A) TEKS mandate content for core courses in Texas public schools
(B) TEKS are the state standards for what students should know and be able to do
(C) TEKS identify recommended instructional delivery methods designed to promote students' achievement in basic content areas
(D) TEKS provide templates for daily lessons, six weeks units, and semester syllabi to ensure consistency in delivery of instruction throughout the state

37. Teacher appraisal is mandated by which of the following?

(A) The Texas Education Code
(B) The Texas Education Agency
(C) The *No Child Left Behind Act*
(D) The National Education Association

38. A grade 2 teacher wants to help her students learn to function effectively in groups. Which of the following group activities is most developmentally appropriate for promoting these young students' ability to collaborate with others?

   (A) Giving each group a box of crayons, one pair of scissors, one tube of glue, one sheet of construction paper, a few craft sticks, and other crafts materials and telling students they need to share these materials to create individual products
   (B) Giving each group a group task to complete and designating a specific task, such as gluing, coloring, cutting, folding, displaying, etc., to each group member
   (C) Giving each group a single set of crayons and timing each student's turn in using a particular color
   (D) Giving each group a piece of construction paper and having the group complete this sentence to create a class collaboration chart: "A good group member is _____"

39. A high-school math teacher has assigned individual research projects on important figures in mathematics. The teacher is requiring that all research be conducted using electronic sources. Which of the following guidelines should the teacher use to help students learn how to evaluate electronic sources for accuracy and validity?

   (A) If you find information on the Internet, you automatically know that it is correct and up-to-date
   (B) A website should be sponsored by a legitimate organization or individual with relevant credentials and should have a date of last update
   (C) Limit your research sources to generic websites that permit user-created updates
   (D) If a website has a high number of hits, it is very likely a good source of reliable information

40. Which of the following descriptions offers the best explanation of the primary intent of the state assessment system used in Texas public school education?

   (A) The state assessment system provides quantifiable data on the effectiveness of individual teacher's instructional efforts
   (B) The state assessment system generates data that is used to secure funding from the U.S. Department of Education for special programs in Texas
   (C) The state assessment system is used to correlate course grades assigned by teachers to results of state assessments
   (D) The state assessment system provides accountability and promotes instruction that prepares students for success in college and career

41. A classroom with desks arranged in rows and the teacher's desk at the front is the typical configuration of classroom space. Frequently, however, teachers rearrange the rows into clusters of desks where students face each other. This configuration of classroom space is primarily intended to impact classroom climate in which of the following ways:

    (A) To create a classroom space that emphasizes collaboration and facilitates opportunities for learning in a variety of delivery contexts
    (B) To create a room arrangement that gives the teacher a clear view of every student in the room to facilitate monitoring of students' learning needs
    (C) To create a classroom space that replaces the teacher's authority with a democratic environment that promotes learners' autonomy
    (D) To create a classroom space that enables the teacher to group students on the basis of academic abilities

Use the information below to answer questions 42 to 49.

   Ms. Rosas, a grade 8 social studies teacher, has designed a three-week unit focusing on local history in Texas communities. In the first week, students will work in groups to explore a historical event in the county in which the school district is located and give the class a preliminary presentation on their findings. In week 2, the class will take a field trip to the county historical museum. Ms. Rosas has asked the museum curator to do a lecture/demonstration on particularly interesting historical events connected to Texas communities. In week 3, all the groups will collaborate to create a single presentation synthesizing the results of their research in a multimedia presentation that will be shown to all the high-school history classes in a special assembly.

42. On the day Ms. Rosas launches the unit, she has students work in groups to answer these questions:

What are some basic facts about our county?	What are some anecdotes or historical tales associated with our county?

    Students are supposed to complete question 1 doing computer research in class but are supposed to do community field work to find answers to question 2. This introductory assignment primarily demonstrates which of the following strategies for promoting student learning?

    (A) Activating prior knowledge
    (B) Promoting development of students' research skills
    (C) Connecting history to current events
    (D) Integrating computer skills into content-area lessons

43. Following their field research, each group will prepare and present a five-minute slide show reporting what they discovered. Which of the following guidelines should Ms. Rosas use to effectively guide students in using technology to produce a slide show that communicates the required information effectively?

   (A) The teacher should have students watch several videos posted on history websites to see how information is presented in multimedia presentation
   (B) The teacher should go over the Technology TEKS that address creativity and innovation
   (C) The teacher should explain and demonstrate how to use text, visuals, and layout to communicate information in an interesting, audience-oriented manner
   (D) The teacher should find a website on creating and delivering effective presentations and have students watch it before completing their presentation

44. One group has discovered a website created and maintained by members of one of the most historically prominent families in the county. The students want to use photographs posted on this website in their group presentation, and they ask Ms. Rosas if that is okay. Which of the following responses should Ms. Rosas offer in order to guide students in legal and ethical use of digital information?

   (A) The students should contact the family to get permission to use the photographs in their presentation
   (B) Because the photographs are already available on the family's website, it is considered fair use to copy it and use it in creating a new information product
   (C) Photographs do not fall under intellectual property restrictions, so the students can use the photographs freely in their presentation
   (D) If the photographs are going to be used only in the class presentation and will not be published elsewhere, the students can integrate the photographs, making sure to correctly document the family's website as the source

45. Quite a few students have older family members who have first-hand stories of the county's history. When the students make their initial presentations, Ms. Rosas decides to integrate another activity into the county history unit: working with the students, she puts together a panel of family members who can talk about important county events. In creating the panel on the basis of student response to the project, Ms. Rosas primarily exemplifies which of the following principles of effective, responsive instruction?

   (A) Recognition of an unanticipated learning opportunity
   (B) Integrating a variety of delivery methods into the unit
   (C) Relying on students' funds of knowledge to enrich students' classroom activities
   (D) Promoting students' motivation to see a school project as a meaningful event

46. Although the panel idea was triggered by student engagement in the project, the teacher's willingness to adjust the project to include community participants reflects which of the following instructor roles and responsibilities?

   (A) Giving students greater responsibility for their own learning
   (B) Using a real-world format to present content-area instruction
   (C) Engaging family members in the educational program
   (D) Creating ongoing communication with family members

47. Ms. Rosas wants to make sure students are prepared to be active participants on the day the panelists visit the class. Which of the following strategies offers the best approach to preparing students to be actively engaged during the panel presentation?

    (A) Having a mock panel several days before the real panel to promote students' understanding of active listening and questioning skills
    (B) Brainstorming questions that students can ask the panelists
    (C) Having students watch a video of a panel discussion and then asking students to discuss what they think happens during a panel presentation
    (D) Asking students whose family members are on the panel to create biographical sketches of those family members to share with the class

48. Prior to the visit to the county historical museum, Ms. Rosas meets with the curator to share copies of the students' presentations and to summarize the stories the panelists told. A few days before the field trip, Ms. Rosas explains what a museum curator does and tells the students that the curator will have information that they did not uncover during their research. Which of the following additional instructional strategies will most effectively prepare the students to be active participants during the curator's talk?

    (A) The teacher has students do Internet research on the roles and responsibilities of museum curators
    (B) The teacher has students work in groups to create questions they want to ask the curator
    (C) The teacher schedules a class visit to the school library to have students find more information on county history
    (D) The teacher quizzes the students on the information the class as a whole has compiled thus far in this research project

49. The culminating multimedia presentation that will be shown to all the social studies classes primarily addresses Technology TEKS by

    (A) introducing students to technology as a means of enhancing learning.
    (B) focusing on technology as a means of making content-area material more interesting.
    (C) using technology applications to assess student learning.
    (D) using a variety of technology applications to create and present a collaborative work that integrates student effort and community contribution.

50. A second-grade teacher maintains a chart entitled, Trying All the Time. Each time a student attempts sometime new or risky—like trying to pronounce a difficult new word during read-alouds or volunteering to solve a math problem on the board—the student gets to put a red star on his or her row on the chart. This strategy primarily demonstrates the teacher's awareness of the students' developmental needs and characteristics by

    (A) showing students that failure does not matter.
    (B) rewarding students for attempting things that are within their current abilities.
    (C) creating a culture of high expectations in a developmentally appropriate context.
    (D) showing students that grades are not the only way to measure achievement.

51. A grade 3 teacher is having his students study missions in Texas. Working in groups at the computer stations in the classroom, they are supposed to produce a multimedia presentation that incorporates visuals and text using the software available on the school computers. The teacher distributes a rubric that includes categories for research effort, writing quality, visual creativity, and general presentation. Each category has box that can be checked. Which additional teacher action would most effectively provide formative assessment as students work on their projects?

    (A) The teacher helps each group determine which areas of the rubric they need to address
    (B) The teacher takes all the projects home each day and gives each group detailed feedback on what they are doing right and wrong
    (C) The teacher works in a peer assessment day so that the groups can give each other feedback on their projects
    (D) The teacher asks students to fill out a plusses and minuses chart at the end of each group work session to determine how the groups feel about the progress they are making

52. The school media specialist collaborates with the language arts teachers in an elementary school to set up a reading program that will reward students for out-of-class reading. The specialist installs software containing comprehension questions for 500 books. As students complete a book, they can go to the library during free time and take the comprehension quiz as many times as they need to until they score 80 percent correct. This technology-supported reading program primarily demonstrates which of the following principles of effective, responsive instruction?

    (A) Providing extrinsic rewards for students to boost motivation in completing self-selected reading
    (B) Assessing students' reading practices in a nonacademic environment
    (C) Creating high expectations for students by allowing them to retake the reading quizzes as many times as they need to
    (D) Collaboration between the media specialist and content-area teachers to create an opportunity that integrates technology to enhance student learning

53. In a grade 2 class, which of the following measures would most effectively convey expectations for behavior and procedures for walking down school hallways?

    (A) The teacher tells the students that the principal expects them to be quiet because other students are trying to learn
    (B) The teacher tells students in clear, simple terms what is expected, models the desired behavior, and gives students the opportunity to practice the behavior
    (C) The teacher has students make behavior posters using original artwork showing examples of students observing and violating the procedures
    (D) The teacher watches the students passing through the halls and corrects their behavior

54. Ms. Bensen, a grade 11 English teacher notices that Joel has been arriving late each day, is nonparticipatory, and is failing his daily work. Several days a week, the students write in their journals. If they want to share what they have written with Ms. Bensen, they put the journals in her inbox. Joel submits an entry in which he writes about how depressed he is because his girlfriend broke up with him. The behavior Ms. Bensen has observed fits which of Erikson's stages of psychosocial development?

    (A) Initiative versus guilt
    (B) Identity versus role confusion
    (C) Intimacy versus isolation
    (D) Integrity versus despair

55. Which of the following descriptions best explains teachers' cross-curricular responsibilities in helping ELLs meet academic expectations?

    (A) Instruction for ELLs must be linguistically accommodated commensurate with the student's current English language proficiency
    (B) Instruction for ELLs must be delivered through a pull-out model that focuses on language enrichment
    (C) Content-area instruction for ELLs must delivered in the students' L1
    (D) Content-area teachers with ELL students in their classes team-teach with ESL teachers to ensure that all students' language needs are effectively addressed

56. A middle-school teacher keeps a birthday calendar prominently displayed in the classroom. When a student has a birthday, the teacher gives the birthday child a hand-decorated paper bag that includes a "happy birthday" pencil, miscellaneous school supplies, and a candy bar, and the student gets to wear a "star of the day" ribbon. The teacher's actions primarily support which of the following instructional goals?

    (A) Making sure that students see connections between home and school
    (B) Creating a nurturing, inclusive classroom environment that addresses students' emotional needs
    (C) Ensuring that students see the classroom as a place where they can have fun
    (D) Promoting intrinsic motivation so that students will work diligently on class content

Use the information below to answer questions 57 and 58.

A grade 9 science teacher has assigned a short collaborative lesson on pollution problems in the school. After a whole-class discussion during which students identify tangible pollution problems in the school, they work in heterogeneous groups to identify possible solutions.

57. By dividing the class into heterogeneous groups after the whole-class discussion, the teacher is primarily implementing which of the following means of promoting student engagement?

    (A) Using developmentally appropriate approaches to complete the learning task
    (B) Creating an opportunity to informally assess the students as they work in groups
    (C) Using a variety of instructional strategies to actively involve students in learning
    (D) Controlling the social/emotional atmosphere of the classroom

58. As the students work in their groups, the teacher mingles with them, sitting in on their discussion, listening, reiterating, and encouraging the students. This teacher behavior best demonstrates which of the following principles of effective, responsive instruction?

    (A) Promoting student autonomy by giving them unstructured tasks
    (B) Assuring all students of success through nondemanding small group activities
    (C) Modeling effective communication strategies of reflective listening, simplifying, and restating
    (D) Activating students' prior knowledge by asking them questions when the teacher sits in on each group

59. A grade 3 teacher wants to develop students' motivation to read independently. The teacher creates a list of grade-appropriate books from which students select what they want to read during free reading time. Which of the following additional strategies would most effectively promote the students' desire to set and complete reading goals?

    (A) Each time a student completes a book, the teacher puts a book decal on the student's in-class work chart on the wall.
    (B) The teacher brings three games and toys she knows the students like. She creates a competition with first, second, and third prizes based on the number of books that the students read in the six-week period.
    (C) Each time a student completes a book, he/she gets to pick a prize out of the surprise box.
    (D) The teacher promises the class a pizza party if collectively the class reads 100 books in the six-week period.

60. Scaffolding is considered a best practice in working with ELLs. Which of the following descriptions best explains how scaffolding promotes learning?

    (A) Scaffolding offers temporary support, for example, through visuals, realia, simplified instructions, or examples, to provide the guidance learners need to move toward independence
    (B) Scaffolding provides instruction that is slightly below the learner's current proficiency level and thus promotes feelings of accomplishment when the learner successfully completes the task
    (C) Scaffolding offers side-by-side materials in L1 and L2 to help the learner move at his or her own pace through challenging material
    (D) Scaffolding pairs ELLs with native speakers in all class situations to ensure that the ELLs always are able to participate fully and meaningfully in class activities

61. It is the beginning of the school year, and a grade 5 teacher wants to establish productive communication with families. Which of the following contact efforts would most effectively initiate effective communication with parents and other caregivers?

    (A) Writing a letter in which the teacher introduces herself, says a bit about her background, tells parents basic classroom expectations, and invites parents to visit the classroom
    (B) Having students compose individual letters in which they tell their parents what they have done in the first few days of class
    (C) Creating a checklist of class policies and sending a copy home with each student for parents to sign and return
    (D) Calling each family and telling them the basic classroom expectations

Use the information below to answer questions 62 to 65.

Ms. McRae, a middle-school history teacher attends a professional development workshop sponsored by the Regional Education Service Center. The focus of the workshop is training and practice in using Bloom's Taxonomy to plan effective, coherent instruction. As part of the workshop, teachers draft a unit in their discipline, share it with colleagues at the workshop, and get feedback from the presenter. For her unit, Ms. McRae creates a unit on the U.S. presidents. Her overall instructional goal for the unit is to enhance students' understanding of the historical contribution of each president.

62. This workshop primarily meets which of the following teacher roles and responsibilities?

   (A) Socializing with colleagues in the same discipline to create a collaborative environment
   (B) Mentoring colleagues by modeling effective pedagogical strategies
   (C) Planning teaching activities that will meet the proficient rating level in the teacher appraisal rubric
   (D) Using professional development resources to enhance pedagogical skills

63. Ms. McRae's unit includes a few lessons modeled on a strategy she saw demonstrated at another workshop: teaching the students a rap-like song with a few lines about each president. To assess her students' knowledge of the roster of U.S. presidents, she plans a simple quiz for which students list all 44 presidents. The quiz addresses which of the following Bloom's Taxonomy levels?

   (A) Creating
   (B) Applying
   (C) Remembering
   (D) Understanding

64. Another activity Ms. McRae has included is a poster project. Students pick their favorite president, do Internet research starting with the *www.whitehouse.gov* website, and create a poster using text and illustrations. Each student will give a three-minute informal speech about his/her president, using the poster as visual support. This activity addresses which of the following Bloom's Taxonomy levels?

   (A) Understanding
   (B) Analyzing
   (C) Creating
   (D) Evaluating

65. Which of the following assessment strategies would most effectively address Ms. McRae's unit goal?

   (A) An exam that includes short answers and objective items based on the presentations
   (B) An essay in which each student reflects on what he or she has learned about U.S. history from the project and listening to classmates' reports
   (C) A multiple-choice exam that focuses on dates, names, and achievements associated with the presidents
   (D) A panel in which student panelists present arguments about the most historically influential presidents

66. A high-school science teacher is starting a unit on local grasses. After a short introductory lecture, he takes students outside to study the different types of grasses and has them write a short paragraph describing their observations. One of the ELL students mainstreamed into his class submits this paragraph:

> Is importance to notice the different kinds of grasses because of the sunshine. The thick grass it grew in the shade and also in the sun. Because it tolerates. Very thin grass it grow mostly in the sun. Is so interesting that you could see where the students walk all the times because is not grass there.

This passage primarily shows features of which ELPS proficiency level?

   (A) Beginning
   (B) Intermediate
   (C) Advanced
   (D) Advanced high

67. A grade 4 social studies teacher is starting a geographies of the world unit. ELLs make up about one third of the class. To ensure that the ELLs understand concepts such as *terrain*, *canyon*, *plateau*, *isthmus*, *gulf* and many other terms included in the unit, the teacher posts photographs and illustrations around the room. Additionally, he uses manipulatives to explain and illustrate some of the concepts, like *peaks* and *valleys*. The teacher's strategies primarily illustrate which of the following recommended practices for working with ELLs?

   (A) Guided practice
   (B) Think-alouds
   (C) Cues
   (D) Scaffolding

68. The weekly quiz average in a grade 11 science class is just above passing. The teacher has tried several strategies to help students better understand new content: minilessons to focus on discrete topics, examples and demonstrations, hands-on work. He wants to motivate the students to try harder, so he offers a five-point bonus if a student's score on each new quiz is higher than on the previous quiz. This strategy primarily addresses which of the following means of engaging students in the learning process?

   (A) Positive reinforcement to promote motivation
   (B) Internal motivation
   (C) Self-directed learning
   (D) The zone of proximal development

69. Ms. Benitez, a grade 2 teacher, includes a 15-minute play period several times throughout the school day. Children can play cooperatively or they can play alone. This strategy is appropriate for this age level because children at this age

    (A) are easily bored and need breaks from academic work.
    (B) develop social, cognitive, and motor skills through play.
    (C) learn content-area material more effectively through play.
    (D) need to feel that school offers the same activities as home.

70. A grade 5 math teacher has two students who are overly talkative. These two students raise their hands to answer every question and frequently blurt out answers without being called on. Which of the following strategies is the best way for the teacher to help these students become more cohesive members of the class community?

    (A) The teacher should call on students randomly rather than inviting students to volunteer to answer
    (B) The teacher should pair these students and have them work together
    (C) During group work, the teacher should ask these students to be observers and recorders for their group's work
    (D) The teacher should tell these students to stop volunteering to answer every question and allow other students to participate

71. Mr. Grissom has guided his fourth-grade students in learning peer assessment techniques, but he also uses informal observations and conferencing to assess students' work on performance tasks. What other approach would be effective in ensuring he is taking student diversity into account during assessment?

    (A) He administers at least five quizzes and four constructed-response exams per subject every grading period
    (B) He uses a variety of objective exams in each subject: matching, multiple-choice, and true/false
    (C) He sends a grade report home each time a student does not perform satisfactorily on a major class project
    (D) He uses a variety of grouping styles—random selection, ability grouping, and student choice—when students have performance tasks to complete

72. A class of first-graders is writing stories based on the format of mentor texts that the teacher has been reading orally and discussing during whole class and small group sessions. The students are completing their story projects in a computer lab using a special software package that allows integration of graphics and animation. Which of the following considerations should be the teacher's primary criterion in designing an evaluation rubric for this project?

    (A) The Technology Application TEKS for this grade level
    (B) Students' prior experience with technology
    (C) Students' home access to technology
    (D) Students' writing proficiency

Use the information below to answer questions 73 to 75.

Ms. Parks's fifth-grade science students are studying sound using interactive videodisc technology. Using computers, appropriate software, and the videodisc resources, each group is to create a lesson on a particular aspect of sound, such as volume or pitch. Each group will then teach the lesson to the rest of the class.

73. Having students teach a lesson to the rest of the class primarily addresses which of the following strategies for promoting student learning?

   (A) When students prepare a lesson to teach peers, students learn about learning theories and consequently become better students
   (B) When students prepare a lesson to teach peers, students learn to better appreciate the efforts of the classroom teacher
   (C) When students prepare a lesson to teach peers, students are highly motivated to learn the subject matter involved
   (D) When students prepare a lesson to teach peers, students learn organizational skills that transfer to academic performance in other areas

74. The videodisc technology enables students to actually observe demonstrations of how sound waves work. Teaching students by allowing them to experience the natural phenomenon of sound waves is developmentally appropriate for Ms. Parks's fifth-graders because these students are likely to be in which of the following stages of cognitive development?

   (A) Piaget's sensorimotor stage
   (B) Piaget's concrete operational stage
   (C) Piaget's formal operational stage
   (D) Piaget's zone of proximal development

75. Following the successful completion of the sound unit, Ms. Parks wants to learn other ways to use technology in her school to enhance her students' learning and technological literacy. Which of the following professional activities would most effectively address this goal?

   (A) Asking colleagues how they use technology in their classes
   (B) Enrolling in a computer-technology course at the local university or community college
   (C) Attending a professional conference on technology in education
   (D) Asking the media-center specialist to teach her how to use the technology available on campus

76. One week at school, Mr. Finch gives his grade 6 math students a variety of class activities including independent work, collaborative projects, and problem-solving scenarios. Mr. Finch takes note of each student's strong points. Throughout the week, he calls a few parents each day until he has called all the parents to tell them about their children's progress. By calling the parents to comment on their children's first-week progress, Mr. Finch is primarily addressing which of the following means of supporting student learning?

    (A) Making sure students know that he will call parents if the students do not perform well in class
    (B) Initiating positive communication with parents early in the year
    (C) Creating internal motivation in students to make sure they work hard to meet learning objectives
    (D) Establishing a social connection with parents so that he'll be able to contact them later in the year in case students do not perform well

77. It is the beginning of the school year. A grade 4 teacher has a class that includes several ethnic groups, several students who require special education services, and several students categorized as ELL. Additionally, the students' records show that they have a wide socioeconomic range. The teacher wants to promote the students' appreciation and celebration of diversity. Which of the following instructional strategies would primarily address this goal?

    (A) Decorating the class with motivational posters that say things such as "Difference rocks," "Let's be friends," and "If we were all the same, things would be boring"
    (B) Providing a generous amount of play time each day to allow students to socialize and get to know each other better
    (C) Creating heterogeneous groups and using cooperative activities for part of every class period
    (D) Talking to the students on the first day of class about the importance of getting along with each other

78. A grade 6 teacher plans a career awareness unit. She sends invitations to all the parents to volunteer to come and talk to the class about their careers and/or work and to answer student questions. Ten parents volunteer, and the teacher schedules two to four parents over several days of the unit. Which of the following explanations primarily addresses the way this activity reflects the teacher's professional responsibilities?

    (A) The teacher is actively engaging families in the children's educational experiences
    (B) The teacher is establishing a foundation for recruiting parent volunteers for field trips, class projects, and other class events
    (C) The teacher will be able to use the level of parent response as a baseline measure of parents' general interest in their children's education
    (D) The teacher is creating an opportunity to meet the students' families

Use the information below to answer questions 79 to 82.

> Ms. Kresmer is preparing her ninth-grade students for the state-mandated writing exam. She has created a unit that will address both the writing process and editing skills.

79. Instead of using traditional spelling lists, Ms. Kresmer introduces memory tricks such as "The moose can't get loose from the noose" to remind students to pay special attention to potential problems such as *loose/lose, knew/new, clothes/cloths, accept/except*. She has students work in groups to devise mnemonic devices for problem pairs, and the groups create illustrated posters displaying the memory trick. Ms. Kresmer's approach to spelling improvement primarily addresses which of the following strategies for implementing effective instruction?

    (A) Impressing on students the importance of earning a satisfactory score on the exam
    (B) Using a fun classroom activity to reduce students' anxieties about the state-mandated exam
    (C) Explaining a concept or skill by providing examples and using age-appropriate learning activities
    (D) Encouraging students to take ownership of their performance on the state writing exam

80. Ms. Kresmer creates several sample prompts modeled on the state writing exam and she explains the rubric in detail. She assigns the first prompt and has short writing conferences with each student to talk about how their drafts address the descriptors in the rubric and to suggest improvements as they proceed to the final version of the essay. Ms. Kresmer is using which of the following approaches to feedback?

    (A) Formative feedback
    (B) Summative feedback
    (C) Guided practice
    (D) Writing-on-demand

81. Ms. Kresmer's conferencing and feedback approach to teaching the writing process reflects which of the following principles for effective, responsive instruction and assessment?

    (A) Creating a climate of trust and encouraging a positive attitude toward writing
    (B) Using an efficient process for scoring student writing assignments
    (C) Showing students how to edit carefully in order to earn a high score on the writing exam
    (D) Reminding students of the importance of planning in producing an effective writing response

82. Philip, a student in Ms. Kresmer's class, receives services from a resource teacher for a learning disability that affects his reading and writing. Which of the following is the most appropriate action that Ms. Kresmer could take to prepare Philip for the state writing exam?

    (A) She should ask the resource teacher to provide writing instruction for Philip
    (B) She should excuse Philip from the writing activities the other students are doing in class and should assign him simpler tasks he can complete independently
    (C) She should work with the resource teacher to determine if Philip qualifies for taking a modified version of the exam
    (D) She should ask the resource teacher to schedule extra tutoring sessions for Philip so that he can complete additional practice essays to ensure he can reach grade 9 writing proficiency

83. A grade 7 science teacher starts each class by having students complete a short independent assignment that involves responding to an open-ended question based on the previous day's lesson. While the students write their responses, the teacher takes attendance by checking off students' names on a seating chart. This approach to taking attendance primarily addresses which of the following principles of effective classroom organization?

   (A) Coordinating noninstructional duties with instructional activities
   (B) Using a short introductory activity to pull students into the day's lesson
   (C) Giving students time to settle down before starting the serious components of the lesson
   (D) Using a short assessment strategy to check on the student's comprehension of the previous lesson

84. Ms. Vidal is starting a geography lesson in her fifth-grade class. She will be teaching several lessons on countries with radically different topographies. To help students remember the landscape features of each of the key countries, she models a graphic organizer that involves drawing a sketch of the country in the center of a blank page and having students create a web of features around the sketch as she presents the lesson. She makes sure each student has several colored pencils or crayons to use in creating his or her geography web. The webbing strategy primarily supports students learning processes in which of the following ways?

   (A) It teaches students a study skill that they can use in this class and transfer to other classes as well
   (B) It facilitates students' acquisition of new knowledge by applying nonacademic art skills in a content-area lesson
   (C) It reduces the amount of direct instruction that the teacher provides each class period
   (D) It creates scaffolding for students to remember information about each country

85. A grade 5 teacher arranges his class sessions to include a cooperative work time when students can share each other's home results and make changes prior to submitting homework for a grade. The teacher notices that some students work alone even while they are in the group, others are easily distracted by environmental factors such as noises and other groups' conversations, and others work together only for a few minutes and then resort to individual work. Which of the following explanations best accounts for the students' behavior during cooperative work times?

   (A) Grade 5 students are not socially or cognitively mature enough to work productively in groups
   (B) Grade 5 students are temperamentally more suited for structured learning environments, such as traditional lecture and demonstration approaches
   (C) Grade 5 students vary greatly in physical, social, and cognitive development and need guidance in working effectively in cooperative settings
   (D) Grade 5 students need to have all classroom behavioral expectations and consequences articulated specifically

86. A grade 7 math teacher plans his lessons to reflect TEKS readiness and supporting standards from the state assessment system in every lesson. This strategy primarily reflects which of the following components of effective instructional design?

    (A) Streamlining the curriculum to eliminate topics not addressed by TEKS
    (B) Constructing meaningful connections between state assessment requirements and daily instruction
    (C) Using TEKS as the basis of instructional design to ensure compliance with TEA curriculum requirements
    (D) Maximizing instructional efforts by focusing on what students need to know for the mandated exam to ensure high campus pass rates

87. Teachers can use a variety of grouping strategies. They can place students in groups based on ability, or they can create heterogeneous groups that reflect a range of abilities. Students can be allowed to self-select groups. Teachers can pair students or they can create groups of four and five members. Flexibility in grouping strategies primarily reflects which of the following aspects of a positive, productive class environment?

    (A) Students thrive in a climate that routinely integrates surprise and limits predictability
    (B) Using a variety of grouping systems allows students to develop cooperative work strategies that reflect their individual abilities
    (C) Using a variety of grouping strategies allows the teacher to test the developmental appropriateness of instructional materials
    (D) Using a variety of grouping strategies ensures fairness by moving low-achieving students from group to group

88. A high-school history teacher introduces a lesson on slavery in America by having students read several Civil War-era documents presenting slave owners' defense of slavery and abolitionist arguments against slavery. The teacher guides students in exploring the arguments posed by both sides. This strategy primarily reflects which of the following principles of effective instructional design?

    (A) Lessons should be devised so as to prompt students to explore ideas from multiple perspectives
    (B) Lessons should include material beyond the textbook to ensure that topics are covered thoroughly
    (C) Lessons should focus on controversial topics in order to fully engage students in content-area subject matter
    (D) Lessons should streamline new knowledge by focusing students' attention on limited views of controversial topics

89. A grade 7 social studies teacher uses cooperative groups for major class projects. He works with each group to help students distribute tasks to every member of the group. As students work in their groups, the teacher moves from group to group to monitor each group's activities and makes sure students are keeping track of their work time. Monitoring students' cooperative work primarily illustrates which of the following principles of effective class organization?

    (A) Ensuring that students do not violate classroom behavior rules during group work
    (B) Facilitating students' cooperative efforts through teacher support and time management
    (C) Monitoring individual students' group participation to keep overachievers from doing all the group work
    (D) Reminding students that group work is as important as lecture and presentation time

90. Which of the following explanations most effectively addresses the benefits of using a computer program to keep up with grading?

    (A) Using a computer program for keeping grade records fulfills components of Technology TEKS
    (B) Computer grade records are more accurate than traditional methods
    (C) Computer grade records allow teachers to send grade reports home more frequently
    (D) Using a computer grading record program reduces time spent on noninstructional duties and maximizes time spent directly with students

PRACTICE TEST 1
ANSWER KEY

1. (C)	24. (B)	47. (A)	70. (C)
2. (B)	25. (B)	48. (B)	71. (D)
3. (D)	26. (C)	49. (D)	72. (A)
4. (A)	27. (D)	50. (C)	73. (C)
5. (C)	28. (A)	51. (A)	74. (B)
6. (B)	29. (B)	52. (D)	75. (D)
7. (C)	30. (C)	53. (B)	76. (B)
8. (B)	31. (A)	54. (C)	77. (C)
9. (C)	32. (D)	55. (A)	78. (A)
10. (D)	33. (B)	56. (B)	79. (C)
11. (D)	34. (A)	57. (C)	80. (A)
12. (A)	35. (C)	58. (C)	81. (A)
13. (C)	36. (B)	59. (B)	82. (C)
14. (B)	37. (A)	60. (A)	83. (A)
15. (A)	38. (B)	61. (A)	84. (D)
16. (C)	39. (B)	62. (D)	85. (C)
17. (A)	40. (D)	63. (C)	86. (B)
18. (D)	41. (A)	64. (C)	87. (B)
19. (B)	42. (B)	65. (B)	88. (A)
20. (A)	43. (C)	66. (B)	89. (B)
21. (C)	44. (D)	67. (D)	90. (D)
22. (D)	45. (A)	68. (A)	
23. (A)	46. (C)	69. (B)	

1.   **(C)**   The correct response is (C). Leading students in an inquiry activity activates prior knowledge and creates student engagement by connecting the instructional task to what students know and what they want to learn. (A) is not the instructional intent of the inquiry activity since the students' questions will cover an array of factual to affective questions. (B) is not the primary focus of this initial activity. (D) misrepresents the instructional intent in this activity.

Competency 008

2.   **(B)**   The correct response is (B). Choice (B) is an important element of creating and sustaining students' motivation to learn. (A), (C), and (D) contradict the original purpose of the inquiry which was to generate student involvement by identifying what each group wants to explore.

Competency 008

3.   **(D)**   The correct response is (D). By focusing on student-generated questions to guide their research, the teacher is supporting an inquiry and problem-solving approach that is likely to sustain a high level of student engagement. (A) does not reflect the intent of the unit activities; direct instruction is highly teacher-centered, with the teacher presenting content and asking questions to monitor comprehension. (B) may be activities that the students integrate into their final presentations but the unit is not concentrated on this instructional approach. (C) misrepresents the unit activities; whole-class discussion and group discussion *is* involved, but the research is learner-driven.

Competency 008

4.   **(A)**   The correct response is (A). The teacher's instructions for the project clearly address the use of technology to support synthesis, production, and presentation of knowledge. (B), (C), and (D) are supporting aspects of the project instructions, but the primary intent of the multimedia project is promoting students' ability to use technology in learning.

Competency 009

5.   **(C)**   The correct response is (C). A reflective essay continues the overall unit objectives, which focused on inquiry, problem solving, and a high-level of student engagement. A reflective essay allows each learner to self-assess his or her own learning experience. (A), (B), and (D) are not congruent with the instructional objectives for the unit.

Competency 010

6.   **(B)**   The correct response is (B). This is what many teachers refer to as an "ice breaker" designed to get students to feel comfortable with each other and to start creating a class climate that values every learner and celebrates individuality. (A) and (D) are integrated into this activity but the primary intent is to start creating the culture of community. (C) is a possible result of the fill-in-the-blank sentence, but students can opt to fill in the blank with personal information rather than career or college intentions.

Competency 005

7.   **(C)**   The correct response is (C). Because they are beginning-level ELLs, the students need to develop both basic communicative skills as well as content-area knowledge. The read-alouds and oral language activities are most likely to integrate the ELL students into meaningful language activities that promote comprehensible input. (A) and (D) address only vocabulary. (B) is not a developmentally appropriate activity at this grade level.

Competency 002

8. **(B)**   The correct response is (B). Under IDEA legislation, an IEP stipulates the instructional plan that the teacher should follow. (A), (C), and (D) incorrectly give the teacher initial responsibility for assessing a special education student's instructional needs.
Competency 013

9. **(C)**   The correct response is (C). Because two students are involved, the teacher needs to rely on school supervisors to address this issue and to ensure that the Code of Ethics and Standard Practices for Texas Educators is not violated. Additionally, the teacher should limit his conversation with the parent to avoid misrepresenting the incident. (A) does not address the parent's concern since it does not involve a classroom activity and since the teacher already said he was not present on the playground. (B) is inappropriate because bringing the parents together will violate the families' right to privacy regarding their children's school records. (D) does not address the parent's concern.
Competency 013

10. **(D)**   The correct response is (D). This response is the most likely in this scenario to promote an effective col- laborative learning experience. Collaborative projects require organization on the part of the learners and efficient use of time. Sequencing the big project promotes individual responsibility and supports team efforts. (A) does not promote the spirit of genuine cooperative learning. (B) would help students appreciate fictionalized accounts of cooperative effort, but it would not help them complete the biology project. (C) promotes a common approach to group projects when students are not guided in principles of cooperative learning. Assigning each member a specific completion task segments responsibility instead of promoting teamwork.
Competency 006

11. **(D)**   The correct response is (D). Providing checklists that students can use to check and evaluate their own efforts is a frequently implemented formative feedback strategy. It fosters students' independence as learners and promotes higher levels of achievement. (A), (B), and (C) are typical in-class activities but they lack the formative assessment component offered by the checklist.
Competency 010

12. **(A)**   The correct response is (A). Teachers are obligated to do everything the state, district, and campus re- quires to prepare students for mandated exams. Benchmarking and practice materials provide formative feedback and familiarize students with the format of the exam. The testing environment must also be rigidly controlled in order to create equitable testing circumstances for learners throughout the state. (B) ignores the importance of test practice in providing exam-readiness. (C) is irrelevant because the Common Core State Standards are not used in Texas. (D) incorrectly represents the purpose of state-mandated assessment exams in Texas.
Competency 010

13. **(C)**   The correct response is (C). The Texas Education Code stipulates these procedures for designating a student LEP/ELL. Additionally, the school seeks written parental consent to place the child in a special language program. (A) and (D) misrepresent the teacher's role in determining a student's LEP status. (B) Parents can request that students be placed in special language programs, but LEP/ELL designation applies only if students meet the criteria set by the TEC and TEA.
Competency 013

14. **(B)**   The correct response is (B). Once a student has been identified as ELL, the teacher needs to offer dif- ferentiated, adjusted, or adapted instruction to meet the learner's needs. Observing the learner's capabilities through formal and informal assessments offers an excellent starting point for helping ELLs meet ELPS expectations. (A) assumes that the ELLs needs are grammar-based. The teacher needs to take into account content-area knowledge

and strategies that promote comprehensible input in basic communication and academic areas. (C) shows lack of appreciation for the family's home language and culture and promotes a deficit view of diversity. (D) also promotes a deficit view by essentially penalizing ELLs by asking them to give up opportunities for socializing meaningfully with classmates in order to complete academic tasks.
Competency 002

15.　**(A)**　The correct response is (A). The teacher's concern reflects awareness of the ELL students' affective needs: they need to know that success is as attainable for them as it is for all other learners. The teacher's concern focuses on the importance of creating a culture of high expectations for all learners. (B) represents a language concern rather than the affective concern expressed in the scenario. (C) inaccurately suggests a disconnect between the ELPS expectations and the possibilities for operationalizing those expectations in authentic language learning experiences in the classroom. (D) misrepresents the intent of special language programs: all programs strive to help ELLs achieve reasonable levels of independence and to transition into mainstream programs as soon as possible on the basis of assessed English language proficiency.
Competency 001

16.　**(C)**　The correct response is (C). This activity is most likely to cause students to reflect and then move on to the other higher-order thinking skills that the teacher has targeted for this unit. (A) would certainly engage the students but it does not promote the higher-order thinking skills the teacher has targeted. (B) would give students the opportunity to generate a list but does not encourage reflection. (D) is not an appropriate initial activity given the teacher's instructional goals.
Competency 004

17.　**(A)**　The correct response is (A). Having a variety of reading levels gives students a choice to attempt a more challenging text on their own rather than as a mandated class assignment. Choice encourages self-directed learning and supports high levels of motivation. These factors impact all levels of learners, including the ELLs targeted in this scenario. (B) creates the possibility of frustration if students are unable to self-select materials at their current reading levels. (C) misrepresents the intent of SSR and other free reading times; students could choose materials related to content-area topics, but they should have a choice of a wide variety of topics. (D) Since the students are in grade 3 and are mainstreamed, the students should be past the need for L1 materials for scaffolding.
Competency 004

18.　**(D)**　The correct response is (D). According to Erikson's theory of psychosocial development, adolescents define their identity in part through career and life work interests. (A), (B), and (C) do not accurately reflect the grade 7 students' developmental stage according to Erikson's theory.
Competency 001

19.　**(B)**　The correct response is (B). The teacher is trying to get parents to encourage self-selected reading at home as a means of promoting the child's literacy development. (A) exceeds the parameters of the teacher's efforts. (C) is beyond the scope of the advice the teacher gives the parents. (D) misrepresents the teacher's at-home reading initiative; at-home reading is not homework but is instead student-driven, student-selected reading.
Competency 011

20.　**(A)**　The correct response is (A). This class activity shows that the teacher knows how to use diversity to enrich students' learning experiences. (B) is not addressed by the scenario. (C) is not the primary goal of the activity, although students' geography and history knowledge is likely to be enhanced through this culture-based activity. (D) could be a result of the activity but the lessons are focused on cultures from throughout the world rather than on the student's own culture.
Competency 002

21. **(C)** The correct response is (C). Enlisting the help of parents is appropriate at this time since the student seems able to work in the teacher-supported class environment but not at home. (A) is punitive and does not address the focal issue which is the student's apparent inability to work effectively on his own. (B) is inappropriate because the teacher has no evidence for this conclusion. (D) does not address the focal problem which is supporting the student's independent work habits.
Competency 011

22. **(D)** The correct response is (D). The teacher's nonverbal gestures are intended to communicate informally with the students about meeting a class goal—homework success. (A) and (C) misconstrue the intention of the teacher's communication; the teacher is targeting a specific student even though the "interruption" is likely to attract all the students' attention. (B) incorrectly suggests that classroom interactions and activities should focus on pleasing the instructor.
Competency 007

23. **(A)** The correct response is (A). The teacher is using effective questioning strategies to move students into productive discussion that will promote higher-order thinking. (B) does not correctly represent the intent of the activity; the teacher is not directly targeting real-world applications of math content. (C) suggests that the teacher has a preconceived outcome in mind. (D) suggests that the discussion is perfunctory and intended to give students a chance to vent.
Competency 007

24. **(B)** The correct response is (B). Working across grades with teachers whose instructional goals mesh shows cooperative teaching intended to promote student learning. (A) is not addressed by the scenario. (C) misconstrues the intent of the teachers' cooperative efforts. (D) is not a requirement of the state teacher appraisal system.
Competency 012

25. **(B)** The correct response is (B). This collaborative targets a very specific learning situation and purpose that coordinates out-of-classroom resources. The middle-school-kindergarten collaborative will put both sets of learners in a highly social reading situation involving questions from the emergent readers and confidence-boosting expertise from the struggling middle-school readers. (A) misrepresents the student mentoring aspect of the collaborative. (C) is not the primary goal of the activity, although it is likely that both sets of students will learn quite a bit about their reading strategies during this collaborative. (D) incorrectly suggests that students' reading skills improve by reading below grade-level texts.
Competency 003

26. **(C)** The correct response is (C). Compiling research- and practice-based information from a professional journal is an effective use of professional development resources to enhance teacher's knowledge and instructional skills. (A) reduces the student mentoring activity to vocabulary development and does not address professional development. (B) misrepresents the intent of the collaborative initiative. (D) is likely to be relevant eventually but this does not address professional development.
Competency 012

27. **(D)** The correct response is (D). A well-constructed lesson includes time for students to reflect on what they learned and to bring meaningful closure to the lesson. (A) and (B) remove the intellectual component from the task described in the scenario. (C) should occur before the activity described in the scenario.
Competency 003

28. **(A)** The correct response is (A). This class activity shows the teacher implementing effective communication to foster student engagement and promote learning. (B) could be a result of the daily logs, but it is not the

motivating factor. (C) and (D) are not supported by the scenario, where the teacher is shown simply responding communicatively rather than critically.
Competency 007

29.   **(B)**   The correct response is (B). The Daily Learning Log offers the teacher immediate feedback on the effectiveness of the lesson, thus creating an opportunity for flexible adjustment to meet learner needs revealed by the logs. (A) and (C) turn the highly student-centered learning logs into traditional testing which is likely to compromise the teacher's original intent in creating this activity. (D) is a pointless activity unless the class develops criteria for each level of response.
Competency 010

30.   **(C)**   The correct response is (C). A research project is a daunting task; students need scaffolding, such as sequenced activities and deadlines, to complete the task in a way that genuinely promotes learning. (A) will enhance student motivation but will not provide guidance in helping the students complete the task. (B) is an important component of research, but it lacks the support provided by (C). (D) misrepresents the purpose of using a mentor text: a sample assignment should show students what an effectively completed assignment might look like.
Competency 004

31.   **(A)**   The correct response is (A). Thematic units are highly praised as ways of bringing cross-disciplinary and multiple viewpoints into unit of study. (B), (C), and (D) are likely to result from the unit described in the scenario but individually do not adequately explain the instructional value of thematic units.
Competency 003

32.   **(D)**   The correct response is (D). A rubric, especially when the teacher uses it in the formative way described in the scenario, is an excellent means of promoting students' self-advocacy through self-assessment. (A) is incorrect because rubrics generally do not include specific instructions for a task. (B) is incorrect because in the scenario, the rubric has already been created. (C) does not represent the teacher's intent in explaining the rubric.
Competency 010

33.   **(B)**   The correct response is (B). Using a timer to keep students on-task during group activities is considered a practical way to guide students in managing group activities and developing individual and collective responsibility for completing the collaborative task. (A) misrepresents the teacher's concerns: the students know how to work together; the focal problem is managing time. (C) also fails to address the time management issue. (D) will not address the teacher's goal; the students obviously need some guidance and the threat of a bad grade will not help them understand how to manage group work time.
Competency 006

34.   **(A)**   The correct response is (A). A spreadsheet, which allows data to be entered, sorted, rearranged, and displayed in multiple ways is a task-appropriate tool for this instructional unit. (B), (C), and (D) offer only partial ways of dealing with the interview data; none of these provides the platform for the necessary synthesis and analysis of data.
Competency 009

35.   **(C)**   The correct response is (C). The posters promote a positive, productive classroom environment that supports students' affective needs as a route to promoting their cognitive growth. (A) and (B) do not reflect the intent of the posters. (D) is not addressed by the scenario. (D) incorrectly reduces asking questions to an oral language development activity.
Competency 005

36. **(B)** The correct response is (B). According to TEA, TEKS are state standards for what students should know and be able to do. (A), (C), and (D) misrepresent how TEKS impacts instructional goals and objectives.
   Competency 003

37. **(A)** The correct response is (A). The Texas Education Code locates teacher appraisal within the system recommended by the Texas commissioner of education or adopted by the local school district. (B), (C), and (D) do not establish procedures for teacher appraisal in Texas.
   Competency 012

38. **(B)** The correct response is (B). Children at this age level are egocentric and generally see others' needs and desires as a direct threat to fulfilling their own desires. By giving each child a designated task, the teacher is focusing the individual child on a specific task and promoting responsibility for helping the group meet its goals. (A) and (C) are not developmentally appropriate because they require a level of cooperative ability which second graders may not yet have attained. (D) requires evaluative skills that second graders generally do not yet possess.
   Competency 006

39. **(B)** The correct response is (B). Checking the sponsoring organization, author, and date are basic guidelines for evaluating electronic sources. Students need to know that websites are not vetted by an overarching Internet clearing system; thus, it is crucial to investigate the credentials of the individual or organization responsible for a site. (A) and (D) represent a widely held misconception about the general reliability of Internet sources. (C) underscores the need to be vigilant about investigating the creators of a site; when users can change information, there is no way to ensure the legitimacy and accuracy of that information.
   Competency 009

40. **(D)** The correct response is (D). The state assessment system reflects the federal No Child Left Behind call for accountability in helping students meet challenging standards and the state's College and Career Readiness initiatives. (A), (B), and (C) reflect ways that data from the state assessment systems could be used but these are not the primary goals of state assessment.
   Competency 013

41. **(A)** The correct response is (A). Replacing the row arrangement with desk clusters is generally recognized as a means of establishing a classroom environment that emphasizes collaboration and encourages a high level of interaction among learners. (B) incorrectly suggests that grouping desks into clusters is primarily intended to police student behavior. (C) is incorrect because arranging desks into clusters does not mean abdication of teacher authority. (D) could be a result of this classroom arrangement, but grouping on the basis of ability is only one approach to grouping.
   Competency 005

42. **(B)** The correct response is (B). By providing two start-up questions, the teacher is promoting the students' understanding of inquiry as the initial step in research. (A) is incorrect because the teacher has created questions to which the students are not likely to know the answers to. (C) is not relevant to the scenario. (D) is a side effect not the primary intent of the assignment.
   Competency 004

43. **(C)** The correct response is (C). The teacher is responsible for guiding students in using productivity tools to communicate and publish information in various ways. Additionally, the teacher would be able to connect the project to available campus technology. (A) would not provide sufficient guidance since students would have to infer

what is effective or ineffective in the videos. (B) would not show students *how* to create an effective presentation. (D) would not focus on technology resources available on campus.

Competency 009

44.　**(D)**　The correct response is (D). Under copyright laws, using the photographs and documenting the source is considered fair use because the materials are being used for educational purposes. (A) is not necessary under fair-use principles. (B) and (C) are incorrect representations of fair use guidelines.

Competency 002

45.　**(A)**　The correct response is (A). The panel of family members was not originally part of the teacher's project, but she recognizes an unanticipated learning opportunity when students start reporting the results of their research. (B) and (D) might result from the creation of the panel but are not the triggers for creating the panel. (C) is not initiated by the panel in the context of the decision set. The teacher is already relying on students' funds of knowledge by having them interview members of the community.

Competency 010

46.　**(C)**　The correct response is (C). Teachers' professional responsibilities include engaging family members in various aspects of the educational program. The panel is a perfect opportunity for such engagement. (A), (B), and (D) are likely outcomes of the teachers' decision to invite family members to serve on a panel but item (C) most clearly connects that decision to a specific professional responsibility.

Competency 011

47.　**(A)**　The correct response is (A). This activity would give students' first-hand understanding of the role they'll play as audience members in the panel; it would promote students' active engagement in this class activity. (B) misrepresents the role of the audience in a panel discussion. Creating questions beforehand overlooks the immediacy of the information to be presented by the panelists. The questions should reflect the students' active listening on the day of the panel. (C) might be a good companion strategy after doing the mock panel described in (A). (D) would clearly provide interesting information but it does not address the teacher's goal as presented in the scenario.

Competency 002

48.　**(B)**　The correct response is (B). Since the students have been informed of the curator's expertise, creating questions is a good strategy for promoting students' ownership of their own learning. (A) is unnecessary since the teacher has already explained the basic role of a curator. (C) is also unnecessary since the students have already compiled a significant amount of information in the course of the project. (D) will not promote students' abilities to be active participants during the curator's talk.

Competency 004

49.　**(D)**　The correct response is (D). Successful completion and presentation of the culminating multimedia presentation brings together a variety of technology applications in a cooperative effort. (A) is incorrect because the decision set suggests that students are already adept at using technology and are applying and expanding their existing knowledge through this project. (B) and (C) misrepresent the scenario established by the decision set.

Competency 009

50.　**(C)**　The correct response is (C). This class activity shows that the teacher knows how to create a positive, productive learning environment by creating a culture of high expectations for all learners. (A) and (D) are irrelevant in the structure of this activity. (B) also misrepresents the intent of the activity; the stars system is intended to push students to attempt new things.

Competency 001

51. **(A)** The correct response is (A). The teacher is using the rubric to provide formative feedback by directing students to the areas they need to address. This also develops the students' independence as learners. (B) provides formative feedback but does not use the rubric as a tool for helping students promote their learning success. (C) and (D) are not formative assessment strategies.
    Competency 010

52. **(D)** The correct response is (D). The computer-based reading program is an example of collaboration between the classroom teachers and the media specialist to enhance student learning. (A) will result as part of the collaborative effort but it is not the primary learning principle demonstrated by the media specialist-classroom teacher collaboration. (B) is incorrect because the reading program is not an assessment initiative. (C) is incorrect because taking a quiz until a passing score is attained shows low expectations.
    Competency 009

53. **(B)** The correct response is (B). To ensure students understand how to carry out desired behaviors, teachers should model the behavior and allow students opportunities to practice the behavior. (A) makes the principal an external reason for the behavior when in fact, hallway procedures are motivated by safety concerns. (C) does not give students the opportunity to practice the desired behavior. (D) also provides no practicing opportunities and is focused on negative rather than positive behavior.
    Competency 007

54. **(C)** The correct response is (C). In Erikson's stages theory, Joel's behavior is explained by the intimacy versus isolation crisis. (A), (B), and (D) do not correctly match Erikson's stages to the student's behavior.
    Competency 001

55. **(A)** The correct response is (A). According to ELPS, teachers should make linguistic accommodations to help students achieve higher levels of English language proficiency. (B) and (C) are special language program delivery methods not strategies that teachers can implement on their own. (D) suggests that ESL teachers hold the primary responsibility for helping ELLs attain higher levels of language proficiency. While ESL teachers are advocates for ELL students, team teaching is a limited approach that would stretch ESL teachers' abilities beyond reasonable expectations.
    Competency 002

56. **(B)** The correct response is (B). Recognizing each student's birthday is a strategy for creating a nurturing environment in which all students feel included and valued. (A) is not addressed by the scenario. (C) is not the primary goal of the birthday recognition. (D) is not suggested by the scenario.
    Competency 005

57. **(C)** The correct response is (C). The teacher's use of whole-class and small-group activities shows the use of a variety of instructional techniques designed to boost student engagement. (A) is incorrect because that scenario describes teaching techniques rather than a ZPD opportunity. (B) is not the primary goal of the whole class and small group teaching strategies in the scenario. (D) is not reflected by the scenario.
    Competency 008

58. **(C)** The correct response is (C). By briefly joining in each group's deliberations, the teacher is modeling effective small group communication strategies. (A) and (B) misrepresent the rigor of collaborative work. (D) incorrectly represents the teacher's intent in joining the small-group discussion; prior knowledge would have been activated much earlier in the lesson.
    Competency 007

59.   **(B)**   The correct response is (B). Creating a competition should provide motivation for students to work independently to achieve a class goal, in this case, a goal to reach for higher levels of reading achievement. (A) is not developmentally appropriate for the students in the scenario. (C) might be a motivating factor for some students, but it is not likely to result in all-around greater interest in reading since low-achieving students might not be sufficiently motivated to read more. (D) would be a motivating factor for high-achieving students to carry the responsibility for reaching the class goal and the low achieving students would reap the benefits of the reward without meaningfully contributing.
Competency 008

60.   **(A)**   The correct response is (A). This is a typical definition of scaffolding. (B) misrepresents the intent of scaffolding. (C) and (D) are examples of scaffolding that might be used in early in dual language immersion programs.
Competency 004

61.   **(A)**   The correct response is (A). This is the recommended approach to initiating contact with parents early in the year and establishing a friendly context for future communication. (B) is not a teacher-initiated contact. (C) lacks the positive, friendly tone that is recommended for the initial contact from the teacher. (D) is ideal but it would be unrealistically time-consuming. In the context of parental contact, phone calls are generally reserved for immediate, specific concerns.
Competency 011

62.   **(D)**   The correct response is (D). The workshop is a professional development activity designed to help teachers improve classroom instruction. (A) is an obvious result of a professional development workshop but not the primary motivation for conducting and attending such workshops. (B) is incorrect because the scenario suggests that the workshop is being led by a specialist rather than colleagues. (C) misrepresents the primary intent of professional development opportunities.
Competency 012

63.   **(C)**   The correct response is (C). Listing the presidents is a memorization activity in the Bloom's Taxonomy framework. (A), (B), and (D) do not correctly match listing the presidents to a Bloom's Taxonomy level.
Competency 003

64.   **(C)**   The correct response is (C). The poster project pulls together several of the higher skills in Bloom's Taxonomy but is collectively a creating activity. (A), (B), and (D) do not adequately describe the competencies required in the poster project.
Competency 003

65.   **(B)**   The correct response is (B). A reflective essay is the most appropriate instrument for assessing the students' achievement of the unit goal set up in the scenario. (A) and (C) are not the best means of assessing the overall unit goal. (D) does not permit assessment of individual students.
Competency 010

66.   **(B)**   The correct response is (B). The passage is comprehensible although it shows features of L1 transfer and interference; the student manages to convey simple information about the concrete, familiar topic but shows potential for moving to higher levels of cognitive and linguistic ability by offering cause-and-effect observations. (A), (C), and (D) do not accurately match the student's writing to ELPS proficiency-level descriptors.
Competency 002

67.   **(D)**   The correct response is (D). Using visuals, props, and realia to support ELL students' understanding of new content is an example of scaffolding. (A) does not apply in this scenario because the students are not applying their knowledge in a learning task. (B) generally describes oral modeling of a thinking process; the scenario suggests that the teacher is simply defining and illustrating the various geographic terms. (C) refers to prompting students to recall previous information.
   Competency 004

68.   **(A)**   The correct response is (A). Rewarding students for desired behavior is an example of positive reinforcement to promote student motivation. For grade 11 students, the five-point bonus is a developmentally appropriate strategy. (B) describes attitudes that students already have about achievement, goal setting, and personal desires. (C) and (D) are concepts that do not apply to the scenario.
   Competency 008

69.   **(B)**   The correct response is (B). For young children, integrating play into the school day is considered an important means of developing social, cognitive, and motor skills. (A) touches on an important developmental factor at this age—relatively short attention spans—but is not the primarily reason for integrating play. (C) and (D) incorrectly represent the reasons for integrating play into early elementary curriculum activities.
   Competency 001

70.   **(C)**   The correct response is (C). This option addresses the talkative students' apparent need to be the center of attention and gives them a valuable, productive role within the classroom community. (A) and (B) do promote the talkative students' ability to become productive members of the class community. (D) is not a student-centered approach to the situation described in the scenario.
   Competency 005

71.   **(D)**   The correct response is (D). This option gives the teacher the best means of assessing individual students' abilities by observing them as they interact with classmates to complete assigned tasks. (A) and (B) do not take student diversity into account. (C) does not address the instructional goal presented in the scenario.
   Competency 002

72.   **(A)**   The correct response is (A). The Technology Applications TEKS offers general guidelines on what students should know and be able to do with technology and would thus provide a good framework for creating a rubric for this project. (B) should be addressed while the project is ongoing rather than during assessment. The project should move students toward higher levels of facility with technology. (C) is irrelevant because the project is being completed at school. (D) is not the primary goal of the project as presented in the scenario.
   Competency 009

73.   **(C)**   The correct response is (C). The need to teach a skill or concept to someone else is widely considered a major motivation for learning the topic involved. (A) and (B) are not relevant to the scenario. (D) might result upon completion of the teaching project, but it is not the teacher's primary motivation in making this assignment.
   Competency 008

74.   **(B)**   The correct response is (B). Grade 5 students are in the concrete operational stage; they understand complex ideas by seeing specific examples, such as what would be provided by the videodisc. (A) and (C) do not apply to this age level. (D) is not one of Piaget's stages of cognitive development.
   Competency 001

75.   **(D)**   The correct response is (D). The media specialist is the best professional resource for integrating available campus technology into teaching. (A) would be limited to what the colleagues know about technology and

would not address all the possibilities based on available campus resources. (B) and (C) would be long-term possibilities for addressing the teacher's goal, but neither of these options would effectively address the goal of using available campus technology.

Competency 012

76. **(B)** The correct response is (B). The teacher is initiating positive communication with parents by sharing specific information about their children's success in class. (A) is punitive and threatening. (C) incorrectly describes the development of internal motivation. (D) misrepresents the intent of the teacher's initial contact with parents.

Competency 011

77. **(C)** The correct response is (C). Heterogeneous grouping is the best strategy for addressing the teacher's goals. Implied in this response is the expectation that the teacher would guide the students in learning effective cooperative strategies. (A) and (D) are superficial attempts to promote respect for diversity but do not operationalize the teacher's goal. (B) is incorrect because playtime does not automatically address the teacher's goal.

Competency 002

78. **(A)** The correct response is (A). By inviting parents to talk about their work or careers, the teacher is integrally involving parents in their children's educational experiences. (B) turns the parent guest day into an opportunistic venture for recruiting parent volunteers. (C) misrepresents the intent of the parent guest project. (D) should have occurred at the beginning of the school year; furthermore, the parent guest project would be based on previously established positive communication with the parents.

Competency 011

79. **(C)** The correct response is (C). Encouraging students to create their own mnemonic devices for confusing spelling words illustrates how teachers can use examples and devise grade-appropriate learning strategies. (A), (B), and (D) focus on performance on the state-mandated exam instead of the instructional goals presented in the scenario.

Competency 007

80. **(A)** The correct response is (A). Providing feedback during conferencing is an example of formative feedback designed to improve student performance. (B) is incorrect because the teacher is offering suggestions for improvement; summative feedback does not include possibilities for improvement. (C) is incorrect because conferencing and rubric-based feedback is not guided practice. (D) is not a feedback strategy. Writing on demand describes the high-stakes essay writing used in many state assessment systems.

Competency 010

81. **(A)** The correct response is (A). Conferencing is considered the best delivery method for helping students improve their writing. The one-to-one conferencing allows two-way communication between writer and teacher, thereby fostering a climate of trust and promoting high expectations. (B) is incorrect because feedback occurs prior to scoring. (C) and (D) address limited components of writing assessment.

Competency 007

82. **(C)** The correct response is (C). Students who are designated as special education students could qualify for modified versions of the state exam; the classroom teacher should explore all options for ensuring special education students have the best chances to perform effectively on state-mandated exams. (A) and (D) incorrectly suggest that the resource teacher is responsible for the academic achievement of special education students. (B) does not address the teacher's goal.

Competency 012

83. **(A)** The correct response is (A). The teacher integrates necessary record keeping with an instructional activity, thereby maximizing learning and teaching time. (B), (C), and (D) are side effects of the activity described in the scenario, but the scenario focuses on the integration of record keeping into instructional time.
Competency 006

84. **(D)** The correct response is (D). Graphic organizers provide scaffolding for students to acquire new knowledge. (A) is incorrect because the immediate concern is helping students remember basic information relevant to a specific content area. (B) incorrectly assesses the teacher's use of colored pencils in creating the graphic organizer. (C) does not reflect the teacher's goal.
Competency 004

85. **(C)** The correct response is (C). Developmentally, fifth-graders are working through Erikson's Stage 4 and moving into Stage 5. Cognitively, they are moving toward Piaget's formal operational stage. Thus, they need guidance in adjusting to classroom tasks that call for assimilating individual and group responsibilities. (A) incorrectly pairs group work with a standard of maturity. Even very young children can be taught to work cooperatively in classroom settings. (B) is reductive; fifth-graders cannot be classified collectively as being more suited to one delivery method over another. (D) interprets the scenario as a behavior management issue when it is more appropriately a delivery system issue.
Competency 001

86. **(B)** The correct response is (B). Instructional planning and design should integrate required standards for state assessment. (A) misrepresents the scenario. (C) incorrectly suggests that TEKS restricts options for instructional design. (D) promotes teaching to the test as a guiding principle of instructional design.
Competency 003

87. **(B)** The correct response is (B). Using a variety of strategies for grouping students for cooperative work allows students to discover their strengths and weaknesses as group members. (A) incorrectly promotes a class atmosphere that lacks consistency. (C) is incorrect because assessing the effectiveness of grouping strategies is separate from assessing the appropriateness of instructional materials. (D) inappropriately suggests that low-achieving students are undesirable members of class groups.
Competency 005

88. **(A)** The correct response is (A). The approach described in the scenario allows students to explore a controversial issue from multiple perspectives. (B) inappropriately suggests that textbooks present limited versions of curricular topics. (C) suggests that student interest should be cultivated by focusing on controversial topics. (D) contradicts the teacher's intention as described in the scenario.
Competency 003

89. **(B)** The correct response is (B). In helping students learn to work effectively in groups, teachers need to provide guidance in delegating group tasks and monitoring time on task. (A) ineffectively integrates behavior management into productive group work. (C) inappropriately targets high achievers as foils to effective collaborative efforts. (D) misrepresents the teacher's intent as described in the scenario.
Competency 006

90. **(D)** The correct response is (D). Computer grading programs streamline the teacher's record keeping time thereby creating more opportunities to work with students directly on instructional tasks. (A) is incorrect because the Technology TEKS apply to student learning. (B) is incorrect because errors are possible in any grading approach including computer grading programs. (C) incorrectly suggests that a primary reason for efficient record keeping is reporting grades to parents.
Competency 006

ANSWERS SORTED BY DOMAIN AND COMPETENCY

Domain	Competency	Question	Answer	Did You Answer Correctly?	Domain	Competency	Question	Answer	Did You Answer Correctly?
I	001	15	A		II	005	6	B	
I	001	18	D		II	005	35	C	
I	001	50	C		II	005	41	A	
I	001	54	C		II	005	56	B	
I	001	69	B		II	005	70	C	
I	001	74	B		II	005	87	B	
I	001	85	C		II	006	10	D	
I	002	7	C		II	006	33	B	
I	002	14	B		II	006	38	B	
I	002	20	A		II	006	83	A	
I	002	44	D		II	006	89	B	
I	002	47	A		II	006	90	D	
I	002	55	A		III	007	22	D	
I	002	66	B		III	007	23	A	
I	002	71	D		III	007	28	A	
I	002	77	C		III	007	53	B	
I	003	25	B		III	007	58	C	
I	003	27	D		III	007	79	C	
I	003	31	A		III	007	81	A	
I	003	36	B		III	008	1	C	
I	003	63	C		III	008	2	B	
I	003	64	C		III	008	3	D	
I	003	86	B		III	008	57	C	
I	003	88	A		III	008	59	B	
I	004	16	C		III	008	68	A	
I	004	17	A		III	008	73	C	
I	004	30	C		III	009	4	A	
I	004	42	B		III	009	34	A	
I	004	48	B		III	009	39	B	
I	004	60	A		III	009	43	C	
I	004	67	D		III	009	49	D	
I	004	84	D		III	009	52	D	

(continued)

Domain	Competency	Question	Answer	Did You Answer Correctly?
III	009	72	A	
III	010	5	C	
III	010	11	D	
III	010	12	A	
III	010	29	B	
III	010	32	D	
III	010	45	A	
III	010	51	A	
III	010	65	B	
III	010	80	A	
IV	011	19	B	
IV	011	21	C	
IV	011	46	C	
IV	011	61	A	
IV	011	76	B	
IV	011	78	A	
IV	012	24	B	
IV	012	26	C	
IV	012	37	A	
IV	012	62	D	
IV	012	75	D	
IV	012	82	C	
IV	013	8	B	
IV	013	9	C	
IV	013	13	C	
IV	013	40	D	

PRACTICE TEST 2

TExES Pedagogy and Professional Responsibilities EC–12 (160)

Also available at the REA Study Center (*www.rea.com/studycenter*)

This practice test is also offered online at the REA Study Center. We recommend that you take the online version of the test to simulate test-day conditions and to receive these added benefits:

- **Timed testing conditions**—helps you gauge how much time you can spend on each question

- **Automatic scoring**—find out how you did on the test, instantly

- **On-screen detailed explanations of answers**—gives you the correct answer and explains why the other answer choices are wrong

- **Diagnostic score reports**—pinpoint where you're strongest and where you need to focus your study

TIME: 5 Hours
              90 Multiple-choice questions

In this section, you will find examples of test questions similar to those you are likely to encounter on the TExES Pedagogy and Professional Responsibilities (160) Exam. Read each question carefully and chose the best answer from the four possible choices. Mark your responses on the answer sheet provided on page 240.

1. A seventh-grade history teacher dresses up as a relevant historical figure each time he introduces a new unit and offers an account of historical events from the perspective of the persona of the historical character. This strategy primarily reflects which of the following aspects of creating a positive, productive classroom environment?

    (A) The teacher wants to present historical information from multiple perspectives
    (B) The teacher is presenting instruction is a way that communicates the teacher's enthusiasm for learning
    (C) The teacher wants to make history more fun for the students
    (D) The teacher wants to promote students' ability to remember historical facts

Use the following information to answer questions 2 to 4.

Mr. Banks, an eighth-grade math teacher, uses several techniques to optimize students' abilities to learn important math concepts. For example, he has taught students to adapt lyrics from their favorite songs to remember math formulas. And he schedules monthly field trips to local businesses where the owners talk about how they use math in their day-to-day business affairs.

2. Using lyrics of songs familiar to students for remembering academic concepts best represents which of the following instructional strategies?

    (A) The teacher is drawing on students' prior knowledge to make learning meaningful
    (B) The teacher wants students to recognize the importance of math concepts
    (C) The teacher wants to reduce students' anxieties about understanding math
    (D) The teacher wants to show students that he understands how important music is to them

3. Taking students on field trips and having businesspeople talk to the students about math applications primarily reflects which of the following strategies for enhancing student learning and engagement?

    (A) Changing the physical learning space to promote student interest in the subject
    (B) Showing students that textbook materials are not enough for fully understanding a subject
    (C) Addressing TEKS standards related to field research in math and science areas
    (D) Using resources outside the school to help students relate course content to real-world situations

4. The day after the field trip, Mr. Banks creates a sample math problem based on the business the students visited. Then, he breaks students into groups and has each group create their own math problem based on what they learned about math by listening to the business people. This strategy reflects which of the following approaches to assessment?

   (A) Formative feedback to encourage higher levels of student learning
   (B) Summative assessment at the conclusion of a major unit
   (C) Assessment that reflects real-world applications
   (D) Instructional flexibility triggered by an unanticipated learning situation

5. A grade 4 teacher uses whole-class discussions to ask questions about the lesson he has just presented. Several students never raise their hands and when he calls on them, they shrug their shoulders or they say "I don't know." The teacher knows that the students understand the material because their homework, seatwork, and quiz averages are strong. Which of the following strategies would best address the teacher's goal to get the nonresponsive students to participate in whole-class discussions?

   (A) Having more group discussions so that these students will not be overwhelmed by speaking in front of the whole class
   (B) Assigning participation grades each week based on the number of times students respond to questions throughout the week's discussions
   (C) Allowing the unresponsive students to independently develop their abilities to speak confidently before the whole class
   (D) Asking the students to stay after class to discuss their reasons for not participating

6. A grade 5 math teacher and a science teacher at an elementary school are planning a celebration of Galileo's birthday. The students will research Galileo's discoveries, create posters and other artifacts showcasing the discoveries, and prepare short plays depicting important events in his life. The posters will be displayed throughout the school and the students will present the plays to students in grades 1 to 4. This projects primarily illustrates which of the following types of professional activities?

   (A) Team teaching
   (B) Horizontal teaming
   (C) Improving teaching performance
   (D) Taking leadership roles within the school community

7. Which of the following explanations correctly describes what an IEP is?

   (A) A written statement for each child with a disability that identifies measurable, annual goals that allow the child to make progress in the general education curriculum
   (B) A TEKS-based curriculum modified to enable a child with a disability to participate fully in a mainstream class
   (C) An educational plan for children with disabilities based on TEA regulations for special education
   (D) An educational plan developed for children with disabilities based on the teacher's recommendations regarding the child's ability to complete instructional tasks

8. A grade 9 history teacher has completed a lecture on the key points of a chapter on the events leading up to World War I. For the whole-class discussion, the teacher prepared a list of questions designed to focus on higher-order thinking skills. Which of the following procedures should the teacher observe in using the questions to guide class discussion?

    (A) If no one answers the question right away, the teacher should move on to the next question
    (B) The teacher should write all the questions on the board, ask students which ones they know the answers to, and start with the ones they do not know
    (C) Because the questions have been designed to focus on higher-order thinking skills, the teacher needs to allow sufficient wait time for students to construct their answers
    (D) The teacher should assign each question to a group and then have the groups report on their findings

9. Teachers at a middle school have received the results of the previous year's mandated exam. The teachers discuss the results and set a goal to reach 75 percent satisfactory ratings on this year's exams. Which of the following initial strategies will most effectively enable teachers to use the results of mandated exams to improve instruction?

    (A) The teachers distribute the sample exams available from TEA, go over each question, explain the correct response, and explain why the incorrect responses are wrong
    (B) The teachers create pretests based on sample exams and released exams to identify the students' strengths and weaknesses in understanding the TEKS readiness and supporting standards addressed by the state exams
    (C) The teachers review their semester curriculum and connect each unit and each lesson to TEKS readiness standards
    (D) The teachers administer the released tests continually until all the students score satisfactory or higher

10. A grade 6 language arts teacher distributes a list of class rules and procedures on the first day of class. He gives students time to read the rules independently and then to talk in groups about the fairness and/or scope of each rule. He makes changes to some of the rules based on the students' comments but he leaves most of the rules in their original form. This teacher's approach to managing student behavior reflects which of the following classroom discipline models?

    (A) The contract approach
    (B) Low teacher control
    (C) Medium teacher control
    (D) High teacher control

11. Which of the following explanations best expresses the motivation for informing parents of class rules, procedures, and key educational goals early in the school year?

   (A) To avoid potential legal problems, teachers need to inform parents about all aspects of curriculum, instruction, and procedures
   (B) Students need to know that parents are working cooperatively with the teacher to ensure that all class policies are observed
   (C) Teachers need to be able to rely on parents to help their children participate in challenging class projects, bring required materials to class, and complete homework each night
   (D) When parents are actively involved in their children's education, students have positive attitudes toward school and generally have higher levels of achievement

12. When students do not respond to a question during whole-class discussions, which of the following actions would enable the teacher to sustain an effective, responsive instructional environment?

   (A) The teacher rephrases the question
   (B) The teacher calls on specific students to answer the question
   (C) The teacher asks the question again
   (D) The teacher moves on to the next question

13. A grade 5 elementary school teacher arranges to have her students take a field trip to the middle school that they will be channeled into the following year. Her students will be divided into groups of five and will visit language arts, social studies, math, science, and computer classes throughout the day. Each teacher will include a short talk about middle-school expectations. This initiative is an example of which of the following professional interactions?

   (A) College and career readiness
   (B) Vertical teaming
   (C) Mentoring
   (D) Supporting district goals

14. A grade 9 teacher has several special education students in her English class. The students participate fully in all activities, but they have trouble keeping up with the pace of class activities. Which of the following adjustments would most appropriately address the special educational students' instructional needs?

   (A) Pairing each special education student with a class buddy who helps him or her complete class work
   (B) Giving the special education students simpler assignments
   (C) Sequencing the class assignments so that all students can work at their own pace
   (D) Grouping the special education students and providing targeted attention while the other students complete the regular assignment

15. A grade 2 teacher hangs a large analog clock at the back of the room. Early in the semester, the teacher sets a timer for one minute and has students watch the clock as the minute ticks away. She wants students to "feel" how long one minute lasts. Now, when she gives students short class work, she tacks a large cardboard number next to the class to display the number of minutes they have to complete the task, sets the timer, and reminds students to look at the clock every once in a while as they work. Which of the following statements best explains the teacher's rationale for these actions?

   (A) The teacher wants to make sure students do not waste their time when they are supposed to be working
   (B) The teacher is modeling and monitoring the students' time-management skills
   (C) The teacher is integrating lessons on telling time
   (D) The teacher wants to gently pressure students into working faster

16. A fourth-grade teacher has set up the classroom with several centers that allow students to play simulation games and other video games that are designed to reinforce academic skills. The teacher's use of video games reflects which of the following principles of effective instructional design?

   (A) The teacher understands that students need down time from challenging academic tasks
   (B) In creating short free periods for the students, the teacher is making time for noninstructional duties
   (C) The video games create an opportunity for real-world assessment of academic skills
   (D) For grade 5 students, video games are considered age-appropriate play that promotes cognitive, social, and motor skills

17. A grade 6 teacher is conducting a parent conference about Danny's math performance. The teacher comments that Danny could be doing much better than he is. The parents want to know how he stands in comparison to the other students in class and want to see his grades in the context of the other students' grades. Which of the following actions is the most appropriate response to the parents' request?

   (A) The teacher tells the parents that they should concentrate on Danny's strengths in other classes and give him time to develop more interest in math
   (B) The teacher shows the parents her grade book, pointing to students' records that show lower achievement than Danny's
   (C) The teacher shows the parents three exams—Danny's and two other students—to show the quality of Danny's work in comparison to the two other students
   (D) The teacher shows the parents several of Danny's exams, pointing to areas where he made careless mistakes that resulted in incorrect responses

Use the information below to answer questions 18 to 21.

Mr. Drake, a first-grade teacher, is starting a reading unit on animals. Students read at different level; additionally, the class includes several beginning level ELLs.

18. Before reading a story to the students, Mr. Drake tells the students their purpose for reading the story and what they are expected to learn. This strategy primarily supports which of the learning processes?

   (A) The students should know why the instructor chose the story over others
   (B) It is important for teachers to share personal ideas with their students in order to foster an environment of confidence and understanding
   (C) Mr. Drake is modeling a prereading skill in order to teach it to the young readers
   (D) Mr. Drake wants to activate students' prior knowledge about the topic of the story

19. Mr. Drake leads the class in a whole-class discussion about pets. Some of the students have pets; others talk about how they would like to have pets but their parents keep saying pets are too much trouble. Mr. Drake asks, "What kinds of things might make pets seem like too much trouble?" This exercise presents what level of questioning?

   (A) Evaluation
   (B) Analysis
   (C) Comprehension
   (D) Synthesis

20. For reading practice, Mr. Drake pairs students at different reading levels: a skilled reader with a lower-level reader. The students read the stories aloud to each other and ask each other questions. This approach reflects which of the following understandings about students' developmental levels?

   (A) Guiding students in setting their own learning goals
   (B) Maximizing class time by having students teach each other
   (C) Promoting a culture of high expectations by having students of different abilities collaborate on learning tasks
   (D) Reducing students' anxieties about reading aloud in front of the whole class

21. Following the paired reading, Mr. Drake hands out an index card to each student and gives them these directions: "On one side of the card, I want you to write a sentence about the story. On the other side, I want you to draw a picture of your favorite part of the story." This activity primarily represents which of the following strategies for promoting student learning?

   (A) Summative assessment
   (B) Authentic assessment
   (C) Formative assessment
   (D) Real-world applications

Use the following information to answer questions 22 and 23.

> Mr. Drake has 10 computer stations in the classroom, each set up with several phonics software programs that allow students to create flash cards, practice initial sound recognition, and spell simple words through interactive prompting. Mr. Drake groups the children, making sure the ELL students are with native speakers.

22. Mr. Drake has the students work together on phonics using a program that focuses on the animal kingdom. This assignment primarily addresses which of the following means of implementing effective instruction?

    (A) Using developmentally appropriate technology applications to support instructional goals
    (B) Integrating time for play into school activities
    (C) Integrating rest time to balance active movement time
    (D) Using heterogeneous grouping to help students appreciate each other's differences

23. As a culminating activity, Mr. Drake assigns a poster project to be done on a sheet of construction paper. Students pick a favorite animal from the phonics program, draw a picture of it, and write 10 words that describe the animal. Students will present their posters to the whole class. Most of the ELL students tell Mr. Drake that they do not know how to say their descriptive words in English. Which of the following adjustments would best represent a linguistic accommodation for the ELL students?

    (A) The teacher shows the ELL students how to translate the words using a program on the computer
    (B) The teacher asks for volunteers to tell the students the translation
    (C) The teacher tells the students to pick words that they know in English
    (D) The teacher tells the students to go back to the phonics program to find the words or to pick new words

24. A high-school biology teacher has completed an introductory lesson addressing how environmental change can impact ecosystem stability. He has students read the chapter in the textbook and presents a PowerPoint lesson connecting real-world examples to the information in the textbook. He wants to conclude this lesson with a class activity that allows students to demonstrate their ability to apply the terms and concepts he introduced. Which of the following activities primarily focuses on application of new knowledge?

    (A) Students are given scenarios from real-world ecological environments. Working in groups, students connect terms and concepts from the lesson to details in the scenario.
    (B) Working in groups, students devise a short list of questions about things they want to learn about environments and ecology.
    (C) Working independently, students create a hypothetical example of how ecological change impacts environment.
    (D) Students take a multiple-choice objective exam based on their reading and the presentation. The teacher uses the results of the exam to identify areas that he needs to reteach.

25. A high-school teacher has a language arts class that includes 25 percent ELL students and 75 percent native speakers. Although the ELL students are at the intermediate and advanced levels, they do not readily participate in class discussions. Which of the following adaptations could the teacher make to most effectively help the ELLs meet ELPS expectations for listening and speaking?

   (A) The teacher does several round-robin activities in a fishbowl format, making sure every student in class is in the fishbowl at least once.
   (B) The teacher has a minilesson on how to ask questions and volunteer responses during class discussions.
   (C) The teacher assigns each student a number. During whole-class discussion, instead of asking for volunteers to respond or comment, the teacher randomly calls out numbers.
   (D) The teacher stops having whole-class discussions for a few weeks; instead, she has students work independently and creates open-ended seat-work activities to assess students' understanding of new material.

Use the following information to answer questions 26 to 29.

   Ms. Vidal is starting a lesson on South America in her middle-school social studies class. As an introductory activity, she posts a large map of South America on the wall. Each country is identified by its name and an illustration representing an important geographical, historical, or cultural feature associated with the country. In a whole-class discussion, she answers questions about the countries. She tells students that for the next two weeks, they will be working on group projects researching the main countries because there are not enough class members to form a group for each country. She also explains that at the end of the research period, each group will teach basic information about their country to the whole class. Then she puts four labels on the selected countries and has students write their names on the country they want to research.

26. The grouping strategy used by Ms. Vidal is known as

   (A) ability-based grouping.
   (B) heterogeneous grouping.
   (C) self-selected grouping.
   (D) homogenous grouping.

27. Ms. Vidal's decision to have students research a country and then teach the information to the whole class primarily reflects which of the following understandings about how student learn?

   (A) Constructivism
   (B) Cooperative learning
   (C) Student-driven curriculum
   (D) Behaviorism

28. Through her membership in the National Council for the Social Studies, Ms. Vidal is able to connect with several teachers throughout the country who are doing similar projects. She arranges a video conference with one of these teachers. The teachers will give students a chance to exchange ideas and set up online communication opportunities. This activity primarily enhances student learning in which of the following ways?

   (A)   Ensuring that students incorporate opinions and personal observations from a wide variety of learners into the class project
   (B)   Reducing the amount of time that students need to spend in traditional, library research
   (C)   Using technology to synthesize knowledge, share information, and participate electronically in a learning community
   (D)   Expanding the class community by using resources outside the school environment

29. The students decide they want their parents to attend the presentations. Several students say that they do not think their parents will want to attend. The teacher suggests that students write individual invitations for their families, illustrating the card or letter with images of their country. The students do not think that will be enough to bring in all the parents. Which of the following strategies would be most appropriate for more fully engaging families in the students' projects?

   (A)   The teacher sends notes to the parents explaining that students will receive extra credit on the assignment if one or more family members shows up
   (B)   The teacher suggests that the students expand the presentation to include a sample food from their country and ask their parents to help prepare it
   (C)   The teacher sends notes to the parents asking for volunteers to bring refreshments and inviting the parents to attend
   (D)   The teacher calls all the parents and informs them of how hard their children have worked on this project

Use the following information to answer questions 30 and 31.

   The day following all the group presentations, Ms. Vidal delivers a direct instruction lesson to fill in gaps which she thinks are important in the students' holistic understanding of South American countries. The students work in groups to discuss this new information and to review for the upcoming multiple-choice test. These are the first five questions from the exam:

---

1. Which country has Bogota as its capital?
   a. Colombia   b. Argentina   c. Chile
2. Which country is most likely to directly affect U.S. climate?
   a. Brazil   b. Chile   c. Paraguay
3. Where would the people be most likely to wear little clothing?
   a. Central Chile   b. Southern Colombia   c. Southern Argentina
4. Which country is the largest?
   a. Colombia   b. Argentina   c. Brazil
5. Which of these factors most closely ties together Brazil and Argentina?
   a. Religion   b. Language   c. Vegetation

---

30. Based on these samples, what type of knowledge does the test assess?

    (A) Higher-level and lower-level thinking
    (B) Lower-level thinking only
    (C) Higher-level thinking only
    (D) Informational knowledge only

31. Ms. Vidal's strategy to have students research a country and teach the information to the whole class primarily reflects which of the following techniques for actively engaging students in the learning process?

    (A) A variation in teacher and student roles promotes students' intellectual involvement in the learning task
    (B) Providing a traditional test at the end keeps students alert and engaged throughout the duration of the unit
    (C) Having parents attend the presentations creates a greater responsibility and higher involvement in the learning task
    (D) The wide variety of activities incorporated in this unit allows the teacher to constantly revise activities that are not working

32. Ms. Davis is about to start a research project in her tenth-grade language arts class. She has decided to work closely with students to identify topics that they are interested in exploring instead of assigning a teacher-selected topic. Ms. Davis's approach to the research project primarily reflects which of the following strategies for implementing effective, responsive instruction?

    (A) Allowing students to do a personal-experience research paper
    (B) Relying on students' prior knowledge and experience to devise a relevant, meaningful research project
    (C) Devising a research project that requires innovative research strategies instead of completely relying on traditional library research
    (D) Devising a research project that will help students distinguish between material that needs to be documented and information that falls under fair-use guidelines

Use the following information to answer questions 33 to 35.

A grade 2 teacher is starting a unit on three-dimensional figures (cylinder, cube, sphere, cone, pyramid, etc.).

33. Which of the following instructional strategies is most developmentally appropriate for helping students learn the features of each figure?

    (A) The teacher has students make construction-paper models of the figures.
    (B) The teacher devises a quiz in which students have to correctly match the figure to its name. The quiz is administered every day until all the students get 100 percent correct.
    (C) The teacher draws each figure on the board and has students copy the figures into their notebooks.
    (D) The teacher posts large, labeled illustrations of the figures throughout the room.

34. After the students learn the names and features of each figure, the teacher organizes the class into small groups, and each group picks a different figure. As a group project, each group has to find examples of how their figure is used in the real world. As an example, the teacher shows slides of architectural structures based on the figures. Then the teacher suggests that the students look around their homes for examples of their figure. This group activity primarily addresses which of the following strategies for promoting learning?

    (A) Using play to present academic content
    (B) Presenting content in a meaningful, relevant way
    (C) Assessing understanding through real-world applications
    (D) Creating homework assignments that encourage family participation

35. This group activity is an example of which level of Bloom's Taxonomy?

    (A) Remembering
    (B) Understanding
    (C) Applying
    (D) Creating

36. A grade 10 science teacher lectures almost every day and wraps up the class with a few questions on the key points of the lesson. The students rarely are able to answer the questions. Which of the following adjustments to his delivery method would most effectively engage his students in exploring the content of each class lesson?

    (A) The teacher starts making audiotapes of each lesson. He invites students to come in before school, during lunch, or after school to listen to the tapes as many times as they want to.
    (B) The teacher ends each class period with a quiz to encourage students to listen actively throughout the lecture.
    (C) The teacher starts using a jigsaw approach with each new chapter. Instead of lecturing, he divides the chapter into sections and makes each group responsible for teaching its assigned section to the class.
    (D) The teacher divides the lecture into minilessons of no more than 10 minutes each and does a think-pair-share at the end of each minilesson.

37. A middle-school social studies teacher has the classroom arranged with his desk at the back of room. When he presents class material, he walks around the room as he lectures, sometimes stopping at a student's desk to ask a question. The teacher's delivery method primarily illustrates which of the following features of a productive classroom climate?

    (A) The teacher is ensuring that students are paying attention
    (B) The teacher is using the physical space of the classroom to facilitate learning
    (C) The teacher realizes that if he constantly moves around, students will not get bored
    (D) The teacher is promoting effective class discussion

38. A grade 6 physical education teacher has attended several training sessions designed to help teachers spot signs of child abuse. The teacher suspects that one of her students may be a victim of child abuse. Which of the following options explains the action that the teacher is required to take?

    (A) The teacher must contact the child's parents before taking any action
    (B) The teacher must contact the principal before taking any action
    (C) The teacher should contact the Texas Child Abuse Hotline
    (D) The teacher should set up a meeting with the school counselor to discuss the proper course of action

39. A middle-school social studies teacher is presenting a unit on civil rights issues in the 1960s. After she presents several lectures and demonstrations on key civil rights events in that period, she wants to integrate technology to encourage students to explore their understanding and perceptions of the issues in a collaborate format. Which of the following applications would most effectively address the teacher's goal?

    (A) Setting up a class discussion board where students are allowed to create threads
    (B) Having students do online research to find 1960s-era responses to the civil rights events of the period
    (C) Posting electronic copies of newspaper and magazine articles on civil rights issues
    (D) Using a spreadsheet to create a timeline of key civil right events over the past 50 years

40. A grade 3 teacher has an "our stories" period once a week. Students bring a special object or toy and tell the whole class about it explaining why it is so special to them. There are several ELL students in the class. This activity primarily addresses which of the following ELPS for listening and speaking?

    (A) Integrating home language into academic activities
    (B) Making an informal oral presentation
    (C) Narrating, describing, and explaining
    (D) Using grade-level content-area vocabulary

41. A grade 2 teacher likes to work one-on-one with students as they do independent reading and other seat work. She purchases a small plastic child's chair, and each time she works with a student, she places her chair next to the student's desk so that she can sit at the child's level. This strategy primarily addresses which of the following principles for creating a positive classroom environment?

    (A) The teacher is creating a nurturing environment
    (B) The teacher wants to make sure that the students pay attention while she is working with them one-on-one
    (C) The teacher wants to eliminate students' discomfort over working one-on-one at the teacher's desk
    (D) The teacher wants to motivate students to try their best on challenging tasks

42. Which of the following terms is used to describe a collaborative tool that allows students to contribute and modify content on a web-based class document?

    (A) Blog
    (B) Chat room
    (C) Wiki
    (D) Web page

43. A grade 2 teacher has several class helper opportunities, such as pencil sharpener, paper collector, board eraser, and workbook distributor. Students take turns volunteering for these positions each week. She also has several free-time centers set up. Students can choose to do extra reading, play with building sets, do art projects, or play video games during the 30-minute play period the teacher schedules each day. The variety of activities and helper choices reflects the teacher's understanding that the children are in which of the following stages of psychosocial development?

    (A) Identity versus identity confusion
    (B) Trust versus mistrust
    (C) Industry versus inferiority
    (D) Initiative versus guilt

44. A grade 9 language arts teacher changes her essay-grading strategy. She tells students that if they score below a B on the final version of any writing assignment, they can arrange a one-on-one conference with her to come up with an improvement plan and resubmit the improved essay within one week. This strategy primarily illustrates the teacher's understanding of which of the following principles for engaging students in the learning process?

    (A) Using formative assessment
    (B) Encouraging self-motivation
    (C) Guiding students through the writing process
    (D) Adapting grading criteria according to each student's needs

45. A middle-school science class of 25 includes 10 beginning- to intermediate-level ELL students. Which of the following instructional strategies best supports the ELL students' language needs as they acquire new content knowledge?

    (A) Pairing each ELL student with students of similar language backgrounds to support each other in learning new content
    (B) Adapting a total immersion approach to motivate the ELLs to set higher learning goals for themselves
    (C) Assigning supplemental homework to the ELL students
    (D) Providing a class library of illustrated books at various reading levels to present science concepts at language and cognitive levels accessible to the ELL students

46. Ms. Berry is a first-year ninth-grade science teacher. Each day, she lectures for almost the entire class to make sure she is covering all the material assigned for the day. She is usually still lecturing when the bell rings, and students linger to ask questions about the assigned homework and about terms and topics she covered in the lecture. A lot of Ms. Berry's students are in Mr. Gordon's English class the next period. One day during lunch, Mr. Gordon complains to Ms. Berry about the number of tardy students coming from her class. Which of the following adjustments will effectively address Ms. Berry's time allocation problem?

    (A) Allowing Mr. Gordon's students to leave a few minutes early each day to avoid conflict with a colleague
    (B) Ending the lecture a few minutes before the end of class to give students time to gather their materials and be on time to the next class
    (C) Using a slide-presentation program to allow presentation of more material in a short period of time
    (D) Planning daily lessons to include presentation time, application opportunities, questioning and reflection, and closure within the boundaries of the period

47. Mr. Juarez is a first-year grade 4 teacher. When the bell rings for lunch on the first few days of class, the students rush to the door and run out into the hallway. Mr. Juarez has posters all over the classroom stating class procedures, including "No running, pushing, or shoving." Which of the following actions is likely to promote appropriate behavior for exiting the room?

    (A) The teacher talks with the students about the importance of exiting the room calmly, emphasizing the hazards of tripping or knocking someone over.
    (B) The teacher stops his prelunch lesson a couple of minutes early, locks the classroom door, and has students stand up one row at a time, calmly exit the row, and quietly line up against the wall to wait for the lunch bell.
    (C) The teacher tells the students that from now on, everyone will get a 10-point deduction in their daily grade if they run, push, and shove on the way to lunch.
    (D) The teacher starts having lunchtime exit practice lessons first thing in the morning and in the middle of the afternoon. He tells the students the practice lessons will continue until they remember to follow the lunchtime exit rules at an actual lunch period.

48. Ms. Garza, a new middle-school science teacher, is concerned about her upcoming teacher appraisal observation. Which of the following actions is most likely to strengthen her chances of getting a good rating from the observer?

    (A) Reading professional articles on learner-centered science class activities and applying the strategies in her classes
    (B) Video-recording several of her classes and then watching the recordings to identify teaching practices she should change
    (C) Asking an experienced teacher to observe her and offer constructive feedback on her strengths and weaknesses as a teacher
    (D) Integrating technology into every class lesson to ensure that her observer sees that she uses a variety of delivery methods to promote student learning

49. Which of the following features of word-processing software primarily supports effective application of the writing process?

    (A)   The spelling and grammar check function
    (B)   The cut-and-paste function
    (C)   The thesaurus function
    (D)   The style set options

50. A middle-school social studies teacher has several ELL students in his class. He wants to promote the ELL students' understanding of social studies content-area vocabulary. Which of the following instructional strategies provides focused instruction to promote ELLs' acquisition of content-area vocabulary?

    (A)   The teacher distributes a list of new content-area words each Monday and provides in-class time for students to look up the words.
    (B)   The teacher identifies a focal concept in the next reading assignment and models how to create a semantic map.
    (C)   The teacher makes sure all the ELL students know how to use computer translation programs to find L1 definitions of social studies terms.
    (D)   He has a student volunteer read aloud the chapter title and all the subheadings. Then he asks for another volunteer to predict what topics the chapter might cover.

Use the information below to answer questions 51 to 54.

    A fourth-grade science teacher has set up learning centers that allow students to study science in a variety of ways: hands-on projects and experiments, reading, computer simulations, interactive videodiscs, targeted research, and videos that discuss important scientific discoveries.

51. The centers created by this teacher demonstrate which of the following understandings about factors and processes that impact student learning?

    (A)   To stay actively involved in learning, students need to have classroom experiences that incorporate activities other than sitting at their desks
    (B)   Students have different approaches to learning (tactile, visual, auditory, kinesthetic)
    (C)   Providing learning centers gives learners autonomy in determining what they learn through the activity
    (D)   Learning centers allow some discretionary classroom time for the teacher to complete noninstructional duties while students are meaningfully involved in independent learning activities

52. In selecting the scientists for the videos of important discoveries, the teacher chooses materials that represent men and women from different countries. This strategy primarily addresses which of the following instructional principles?

    (A)   Instructional materials should be interesting to a wide variety of students
    (B)   Instructional materials should reflect diversity and equity
    (C)   Instructional materials presented through centers should be different from material presented in the textbook
    (D)   Instructional materials presented through centers should target higher cognitive levels than other delivery methods

53. As the students work in the science centers, the teacher moves from group to group asking questions and commenting on each student's progress. This procedure indicates that the teacher most likely views her role during center activities as

    (A) facilitator.
    (B) supervisor.
    (C) partner.
    (D) evaluator.

54. What is the main advantage of using hands-on activities to teach content area in elementary schools?

    (A) Hands-on activities can promote higher-order thinking and increase intelligence
    (B) Hands-on activities can lead to active learning and collegiality among children
    (C) Hands-on activities can promote higher-order thinking skills and can guide students to construct their own knowledge
    (D) Hands-on activities can promote equity among diverse ethnic groups in the classroom

55. A grade 1 teacher at a school where about half of the students are classified as ELL is having the first parent-teacher conferences of the year. Which of the following guidelines should primarily direct the way the teacher conducts this first conference?

    (A) Include positive comments about each child and make suggestions for how families can help the child at home
    (B) Keep the conversation light and objective, saving any negative comments for the next conference
    (C) Discuss the importance of speaking only English at home at all times and insisting that the child communicate with all family members in English
    (D) Discuss the results of diagnostic testing using technical terms so that parents understand how the teacher can help their child

56. Which of the following terms is used to describe an assessment tool that provides performance level categories and descriptors for ranges of performance in each category?

    (A) Student self-assessment grid
    (B) Performance checklist
    (C) Holistic scoring
    (D) Rubric

57. Which of the following descriptions most accurately explains the impact of No Child Left Behind (NCLB) on ESL/ELL education in America?

    (A) NCLB stipulates the kinds of special language programs that must be taught at all schools that enroll ELLs
    (B) NCLB identifies strong special language programs as a vital component of achieving educational equity for all learners
    (C) NCLB sets limits on the number of years that ELLs can be in special language programs
    (D) NCLB establishes minimum percentages of ELLs necessary for schools to offer special language programs

58. A high-school teacher notices that a student who has been enthusiastic and participatory gradually seems to lose interest in class, stops turning in her homework, refuses to do class work, and does not want to do group projects. Which of the following initial actions should the teacher take to maintain a positive, classroom environment for this student?

    (A) Contact the student's family to inquire about family problems that might be affecting the student
    (B) Confer with other teachers to determine if the student is acting the same in other classes
    (C) Ask the student if something is wrong and point out that her schoolwork is suffering and her performance in class has changed
    (D) Give the student extra credit work to help her catch up and improve her grades

Use the information below to answer questions 59 to 62.

Ms. Trussel is developing a tenth-grade world history unit focused on Virgil's attempt to connect the origins of Rome to the events that followed the destruction of Troy by the Greeks. She wants the unit to be challenging, but she realizes that the students must be able to handle the work. She also knows that this semester, the sophomores will be taking their first college entrance exams. Additionally, the curriculum coordinator wants all the teachers to integrate techniques and information from the cooperative learning workshop the school district sponsored for professional development.

59. What should be Ms. Trussel's first step in planning the unit?

    (A) Combining cooperative learning and content
    (B) Deciding on assessments that will be fair to all students
    (C) Developing objectives for the unit
    (D) Finding available materials and resources

60. Ms. Trussel's understanding of students' developmental processes and characteristics is illustrated by which aspect of her planning?

    (A) She realizes that challenges promote higher levels of achievement but also acknowledges that a positive learning environment is sustained through expectations of success
    (B) She wants to focus on higher-order thinking skills that will promote students' success in the real world
    (C) She plans to integrate a substantive amount of cooperative learning into the unit
    (D) She knows students will be distracted by the need to prepare for their college entrance exams

61. Which of the following is an indication that Ms. Trussel is aware of the environmental factors that may affect learning?

    (A) She knows cross-curricular units promote students' ability to see things from multiple perspectives
    (B) She knows that external challenge will make learners work harder
    (C) She is aware that her students will take their first college entrance exams this semester
    (D) She knows cooperative learning will reduce individual students' responsibility for completing unit work

62. How can Ms. Trussel most effectively keep gifted students challenged throughout the unit?

    (A) She assigns an extra report on Greek history
    (B) She pairs gifted students with low-achieving students
    (C) She invites the gifted students to suggest additional aspects of the unit that they want to pursue
    (D) She targets the unit at the gifted students because they are the most challenging learners

63. Which of the following explanations most effectively identifies the prime benefit students derive from cooperative learning activities?

    (A) Students are allowed to socialize and practice communication skills without the intrusion of the teacher
    (B) Students assume responsibility for the learning process and work together under reduced teacher directiveness
    (C) Teachers function as facilitators in constructing knowledge rather than as dispensers of knowledge
    (D) Students are allowed opportunities to be creative and plan daily instructional activities

64. Which of the statements below best explains the basic attributes of the portfolio method of assessment?

    (A) It allows for the gathering of students' work completed throughout the year
    (B) It reduces student anxiety over deadlines
    (C) It offers students an opportunity to show the range, quality, and breadth of their work
    (D) It allows teachers to generate data on students' proficiency in discrete aspects of the content being assessed

Use the information below to answer questions 65 to 67.

   Mr. Smith is a first-year teacher in the process of setting up classroom rules for his grade 8 class.

65. Which of the guidelines below is the first consideration he needs to take into account in developing classroom rules?

    (A) Rules must be stated clearly but succinctly to avoid misinterpretations
    (B) Rules must be long and specific enough to cover all possible behavioral variations
    (C) Rules must be consistent with district and campus rules
    (D) Rules must include a rationale so that they do not seem arbitrary

66. Mr. Smith is considering asking for student input in finalizing class rules. What is the main benefit of allowing students to participate in creating classroom rules?

    (A) It promotes a sense of ownership which increases the likelihood that students will comply with the rules they helped create
    (B) It establishes an external locus of control which creates a culture of compliance
    (C) It teaches students the process for setting up a classroom-management program
    (D) It values students' abilities to do the right thing and conditions them to obey rules without questioning their appropriateness

67. When Mr. Smith assigns the first cooperative project, the issue of rules comes up again. After monitoring students' first cooperative work session, he realizes the students need guidance in learning how to work together productively. Which of the following guidelines for group work should be the foundational principle for developing collaborative skills and individual responsibility in group work?

(A) Allow group members opportunities to communicate, talk in a low voice, and not be hesitant to criticize each other's work

(B) Listen to each others' ideas but develop a system for making sure no one dominates the discussion at any time

(C) Support each other during the project and make sure all contribute meaningfully to the group effort

(D) Remember that the group effort will be scored both individually and jointly, so make sure everybody does something to showcase his or her individual efforts

Use the information below to answer questions 68 to 70.

Ms. Palomo, a grade 9 English teacher, has two years teaching experience but is new to her campus. She has recently attended a cooperative learning workshop and wants to integrate some of the suggestions to create more interaction and participation in her classroom. She plans a cooperative grouping approach for the upcoming unit on a historical novel.

68. During the in-service week before the beginning of classes, Ms. Palomo wants to become better acquainted with the campus grounds, faculty, curriculum, and available resources. Which of the following optimally addresses her goal?

(A) Touring the school, finding the teacher's workroom, materials storage, and the library

(B) Talking to the principal about what is expected of her

(C) Identifying a colleague from her subject area who has spent several years at the school and talking about the campus community, curricular expectations, and good teaching practices

(D) Reviewing the curriculum for her grade level and finding materials to supplement the textbook

69. From the workshop, Ms. Palomo has learned that a cooperative approach promotes student engagement numerous ways. Which of the following statements does *not* reflect the role of cooperative learning in student engagement?

(A) Cooperative projects allow students to demonstrate leadership abilities

(B) Cooperative projects encourage organization and distribution of appropriate work for all members

(C) Cooperative projects allow high-achieving students to work with other high-achieving students and cluster low-achieving students together

(D) Cooperative projects include self-evaluation of each member's contribution

70. Ms. Palomo asks a social studies teacher to demonstrate how students can prepare a timeline of historical facts by analyzing the events in the novel. In addition, she asks the librarian to speak to the class about books and other resources that will help the students connect historical events to the narrative. Ms. Palomo's reliance on these speakers primarily reflects which of the following professional responsibilities?

    (A) Reducing preparation time by bringing in guest speakers
    (B) Introducing students to other teachers and resource persons on campus
    (C) Easing the work involved for students
    (D) Relying on professional colleagues' expertise and experience to support student learning

71. Mr. Chavez, a middle-school teacher, notices that a few students in the class have exchanged heated words as class begins. Once class begins, he notices that the interactions among these students appear strained. Which of the following actions should Mr. Chavez take to secure a positive, productive class environment?

    (A) Address the issue in front of the whole class by asking the students to share what is causing their problems
    (B) Ignore the situation because the students are likely to resolve their differences on their own
    (C) Put the students in groups so that they work out problems by cooperating
    (D) Communicate and illustrate clear guidelines about respecting and valuing each other

72. Ms. Riley, a grade 10 history teacher, has a number of L1 Spanish intermediate ELL students in her class. As she analyzes student assignments, she realizes that the ELL students consistently score the lowest scores on all assignments. Which of the following actions should be Ms. Riley's initial strategy for adapting instructional materials to address the needs of the ELL students?

    (A) Adjust assignments to reflect students' academic abilities and not their limited English proficiency
    (B) Create assignments for the ELLs that are easier than the assignments given to the other students
    (C) Have a bilingual student translate the lessons into Spanish for the ELLs
    (D) Request that the ELLs be transferred to an ESL class

Use the information below to answer questions 73 to 75.

Mr. Nelson wants his grade 9 students to use computer applications to configure chemical equations for a number of substances. The equations require that students enter several elements and conduct mathematical computations on them to derive the results.

73. For this particular assignment, the most task-appropriate technology tool is

    (A) simulations.
    (B) word processing.
    (C) spreadsheets.
    (D) graphics.

74. To help his students learn to acquire information electronically, Mr. Nelson demonstrates how to use several chemistry-specific software programs and how to use science-related websites. Which of the following actions should Mr. Nelson take to ensure students are able to evaluate digitally retrieved information sources?

    (A) Warn students not to use major search engines since they produce too many results for students to choose from
    (B) Show students how to determine the validity of a website by checking the credentials of the sponsor and/or creator
    (C) Remind students that information retrieved from the web is better than material provided by books because web materials are regularly updated
    (D) Have students practice looking for information on the Internet by looking for answers to specific questions

75. Mr. Nelson sets up an experiment in which students examine new substances created by various combinations of the original substances. Mr. Nelson identifies the objectives and procedures and explains the paradigm for completing the required lab report. Mr. Nelson's approach primarily addresses which of the following strategies for promoting student engagement in learning processes?

    (A) It ensures that most of the experiments will yield the desired outcome
    (B) It enables students to work more quickly so that they are able to stay on the curricular schedule
    (C) It enables students to develop a conceptual framework for the work they are about to do
    (D) It ensures that all students have an equal chance of successfully completing the experiment

76. Which of the following assessment methods primarily examines students' efforts, progress, and achievements in the context of a specific instructional content area and/or setting?

    (A) Standardized testing
    (B) Constructed responses
    (C) Observation
    (D) Portfolio

77. Which of the following methods primarily generates objective data about student achievement in meeting specific content-area learning outcomes?

    (A) Self- and peer evaluations
    (B) Multiple choice exams
    (C) Interviews
    (D) Performances

Use the information below to answer questions 78 and 79.

In the first week of school, a middle-school teacher assigns a short writing project aimed at encouraging students to engage in introspective activities. She asks students to make a list of the things they like about themselves. Then, she asks them to write two paragraphs in class: one paragraph describing their personal strengths in the context of classroom behavior and a second paragraph describing their strengths in situations outside the class.

78. Starting the assignment by asking students to list qualities they like about themselves, the teacher is primarily demonstrating an understanding of which of the following features of effective instructional design?

    (A) Creating an assignment that will be easy for students to complete
    (B) Ensuring that each student is able to respond to the writing assignment
    (C) Logically sequencing the assignment by starting with prewriting and moving to short drafting
    (D) Devising an assignment that combines discussion, student work, and possibilities for improvement in one class period

79. By asking the students to think about their own characteristics, the teacher is supporting the students' cognitive development by promoting their ability to

    (A) activate prior knowledge as a basis for understanding new concepts.
    (B) demonstrate their ability to write a personal narrative.
    (C) generate grammatically correct writing.
    (D) develop positive self-esteem by identifying their assets and skills.

80. Ms. Ricci is an eleventh-grade science teacher at a campus located in a city that also houses a large regional university. She knows several of the professors from the university college of science and invites them to her class to lecture about some of the topics that she has covered in class. This activity primarily illustrates which of the following understandings about creating effective educational experiences for students?

    (A) Relying on resources outside the school to address specific educational purposes
    (B) Ensuring that students know content-area expectations for college readiness
    (C) Demonstrating connections between class lessons and real-world experience
    (D) Addressing students' concerns about applying for college

Use the following information to answer questions 81 and 82.

A grade 2 teacher has assigned students a short research project. The students are supposed to pick a favorite animal and write a research card about the animal. The teacher puts these instructions on the board:

> 1. On one side of the card, draw a picture of your animal and write its name clearly.
>
> 2. On the other side, write five interesting facts about your animal.

81. The teacher schedules several days at the library for students to look up information about their selected animal and also arranges for a computer lab session so students can find information online. These instructional strategies primarily address which of the following means of promoting student learning?

    (A) Using cross-disciplinary approaches to promote higher-order thinking skills
    (B) Relying on campus specialists to help students complete their assignments
    (C) Promoting students' research skills through developmentally appropriate learning tasks
    (D) Devising assignments that are easy for all students to complete

82. The teacher makes large research cards of several unusual animals that she knows have not been chosen by any of the students. She posts these on the display area where the students will eventually post their cards. This teaching strategy primarily addresses which of the following principles of effective, responsive instruction?

    (A) Doing the same assignment as the students in order to work out problems in the design of the assignment
    (B) Providing examples so as to effectively communicate expectations to students
    (C) Demonstrating that the teacher is an active member of the classroom community
    (D) Creating a model assignment to ensure students do not make mistakes

83. A high-school science teacher shows students a clip from the film *Apollo 13* showing the cinematic astronauts creating a new carbon monoxide filter out of materials available on their spacecraft. She writes the words *collaboration, creativity, innovation,* and *resourcefulness* on the board. She has students brainstorm in groups about personal experiences they have had in finding solutions to challenging problems. This activity focuses on which of the following elements of effective, responsive instruction?

    (A) Promoting higher-order thinking by guiding students toward exploration and inquiry
    (B) Using film to promote students' understanding of complex topics
    (C) Connecting class content to real-world experience
    (D) Stimulating students' prior knowledge about key concepts in a lesson

Use the information below to answer questions 84 to 86.

> Ms. Blanco, a grade 3 teacher, wants students to start reading self-selected materials for 15 minutes at home every night.

84. Which of the following actions will most effectively enlist parents' help in meeting this goal?

    (A) Sending parents an article about declining reading scores on standardized exams
    (B) Sending parents a flyer on books that students can purchase at the next campus book fair
    (C) Sending parents a questionnaire about the family's reading habits
    (D) Sending home a reading log for students to fill in every night and parents to initial

85. Mindy is one of the children in the class. Mindy's mother drops in during Ms. Blanco's conference period to explain that she is too busy to keep track of Mindy's at-home reading. Which of the following responses most effectively addresses the parent's concern?

    (A) The teacher tells the parent that her child will be excused from this class requirement and will be given class time to complete the assignment
    (B) The teacher suggests that the parent buy an inexpensive timer and show the child how to monitor her own at-home reading time
    (C) The teacher gives the parent several articles on the importance of family support in building young children's literacy
    (D) The teacher asks the parent for suggestions on how they can collaborate in getting Mindy to read at home

86. Ms. Blanco wants to promote her students' literacy experiences beyond the school environment. She contacts the public library to ask one of its staff members to visit the class and read a few books from the public library shelves. She also asks the public library staff member to bring flyers about acquiring a public library card. Ms. Blanco's initiative primarily demonstrates her understanding of which of the following professional responsibilities?

   (A) Supporting students' literacy experiences by facilitating their access to the public library
   (B) Relying on the library to offer instructional support in areas that the school library cannot cover
   (C) Advocating for good professional relationships between public library staff and school personnel
   (D) Initiating a reading program at the public library that coordinates school reading requirements with library services

87. Which of the following explanations best addresses the instructional principle behind wait time?

   (A) Wait time allows students time to construct a response appropriate to the cognitive level of the questions posed by the teacher
   (B) Wait time means that the teacher extends a deadline to accommodate special student circumstances
   (C) Wait time is the maximum time period a teacher can legally allow for a student to submit an assignment
   (D) Wait time supports the application of the zone of proximal development in specific circumstances involving specific students

88. A high-school teacher is hosting an end-of-year celebration at his home to honor the graduating seniors in his class. During the party, the teacher realizes that many of the parents are allowing their children to drink alcoholic beverages. Which of the following statements stipulates the teacher's professional responsibilities in this situation according to the Code of Ethics and Standard Practices for Texas Educators?

   (A) Because the party is being hosted at his home, the teacher can respect the parents' rights to let their children drink alcoholic beverages
   (B) The teacher should contact the school principal to get official permission for the students to consume alcohol throughout the rest of the party
   (C) The students are not his children, so the teacher has no legal responsibility to control their drinking even if they are on his property
   (D) The teacher has a legal responsibility to refrain from furnishing alcohol to a minor who is not his or her child

89. Teaming an experienced educator with a new teacher so that the new teacher has a resource for adjusting into the profession is an example of

   (A) vertical teaming.
   (B) horizontal teaming.
   (C) mentoring.
   (D) team teaching.

90. A fourth-grade school teacher starts a class wiki. She has students keep notes throughout the week on things they want to share with their parents about what is happening in class. During free-time sessions, students can work on the class wiki, and she sets aside 30 minutes every Thursday afternoon for students to finalize their contributions for the week. On Friday morning, she has printed copies available for students to take home if their parents are unable to access the wiki electronically. This initiative primarily addresses which of the following educator responsibilities?

   (A) Using technology to promote student learning
   (B) Using technology to interact effectively with families
   (C) Using technology to promote students' abilities to work cooperatively
   (D) Using technology to integrate productive play time into the students' school day

PRACTICE TEST 2
ANSWER KEY

1. (B)	24. (A)	47. (B)	69. (C)
2. (A)	25. (A)	48. (C)	70. (D)
3. (D)	26. (C)	49. (B)	71. (D)
4. (C)	27. (A)	50. (B)	72. (A)
5. (A)	28. (C)	51. (B)	73. (C)
6. (B)	29. (B)	52. (B)	74. (B)
7. (A)	30. (A)	53. (A)	75. (C)
8. (C)	31. (A)	54. (C)	76. (C)
9. (B)	32. (B)	55. (A)	77. (B)
10. (C)	33. (A)	56. (D)	78. (C)
11. (D)	34. (C)	57. (B)	79. (D)
12. (A)	35. (C)	58. (C)	80. (A)
13. (B)	36. (D)	59. (C)	81. (C)
14. (C)	37. (B)	60. (A)	82. (B)
15. (B)	38. (C)	61. (C)	83. (A)
16. (D)	39. (A)	62. (C)	84. (D)
17. (D)	40. (C)	63. (B)	85. (B)
18. (C)	41. (A)	64. (C)	86. (C)
19. (A)	42. (C)	65. (C)	87. (A)
20. (C)	43. (C)	66. (A)	88. (D)
21. (B)	44. (B)	67. (C)	89. (C)
22. (A)	45. (D)	68. (C)	90. (B)
23. (A)	46. (D)		

1. **(B)** The correct response is (B). By dressing up as historical characters, the teacher is showing enthusiasm for the subject. (A) is incorrect because the teacher's actions do not indicate that multiple perspectives are involved or not addressed by other materials. (C) and (D) are likely to occur as a result of the teacher's action, but the underlying motivation for dressing up as historical characters is best expressed by response (B).
    Competency 005

2. **(A)** The correct response is (A). Integrating lyrics from songs with which the students are familiar is a prior knowledge activity designed to make learning relevant and meaningful. (B) does not explain how the lyrics represent an instructional strategy. (C) is not the primary focus of the activity. (D) misrepresents the instructional intent in this activity.
    Competency 008

3. **(D)** The correct response is (D). Having businesspeople identify real-world applications of course content is a good example of integrating outside resources to enhance student learning. (A) is not the instructional intent of the field trip. (B) is incorrect because the field trips are not intended as criticism of textbook materials but as a means to enhance students' learning. (C) incorrectly presents the field trips as field research.
    Competency 003

4. **(C)** The correct response is (C). Having students write math problems based on what they learned during their field trip illustrates assessment that reflects real-world applications. (A) and (B) are not reflected by the problem-creation scenario. (D) is incorrect because the teacher has planned the activity beforehand.
    Competency 010

5. **(A)** The correct response is (A). Small-group activities that are effectively structured are considered an excellent strategy for helping all students develop social skills needed for academic success. (B) would unfairly punish the unresponsive students and would not solve the problem of increasing their participation. (C) is not likely to happen; the students need direct support from the instructor. (D) is likely to make the students uncomfortable and create a classroom environment that ignores these students' developmental needs.
    Competency 001

6. **(B)** The correct response is (B). Working across disciplines at the same instructional level to achieve jointly valued teaching goals illustrates horizontal teaming. (A) is incorrect because the scenario does not suggest that the teachers are teaching jointly in their classrooms. (C) is not the primary focus of this activity; the project seems focused on enriching the children's appreciation of the topic. (D) misrepresents the instructional intent in this activity although it could seem that the teachers involved are effective leaders.
    Competency 012

7. **(A)** The correct response is (A). The Individualized Education Program is mandated by IDEA, and it stipulates the establishment of measurable goals for each child and provisions for helping disabled children make educational progress. (B), (C), and (D) are incorrect explanations of IEP.
    Competency 013

8. **(C)** The correct response is (C). Questions that call for analysis, synthesis, evaluation, consideration, speculation, and other higher-order thinking skills require generous wait time so that students can think about their

responses. (A) demonstrates an inefficient approach to using questions to promote student learning; instead of moving on to the next question, the teacher should rephrase the original question. (B) is incorrect because the list of questions represents discussion points that the teacher wants to explore more deeply so all the questions need to be addressed during discussion. (D) misrepresents the instructional intent in this activity; the teacher created the questions for whole-class discussion.

Competency 007

9.   **(B)**   The correct response is (B). Results of mandated exams should be used to identify students' strengths and weaknesses in the standards addressed by the exams. Instruction can be adjusted to ensure that strengths and weaknesses are appropriately addressed as part of exam readiness. (A) and (D) do not effectively address the teachers' goals; making sure that students know the answers to sample test questions is not an instructional improvement activity. (C) should have been done at the beginning of the year when teachers were creating the curriculum.

Competency 003

10.   **(C)**   The correct response is (C). In this scenario, the teacher already has created rules and solicits student input to collaboratively change some of the rules. (A) is not reflected in the scenario; in contract approaches, students sign a statement indicating that they understand the rules and consequences. (B) is not reflected in the scenario; in low-control scenarios, students are given a great deal of autonomy for the behavioral decisions they make in the classroom. (D) is not reflected in the scenario; in high-control situations, the teacher actively reinforces appropriate behavior and penalizes undesired behaviors.

Competency 006

11.   **(D)**   The correct response is (D). Research shows that initiating and maintaining positive communication with parents leads to higher levels of student achievement and promotes students' positive feelings about school and education. (A) casts communication with parents as a preemptive effort to avoid potential conflict. (B) casts parents in the role of class procedures police. (C) suggests communication with parents is motivated by an expectation that, on their own, students will not fulfill basic class responsibilities; while parents can be valuable partners, the concerns listed in this item should be the students' responsibility.

Competency 011

12.   **(A)**   The correct response is (A). If the teacher has used appropriate wait time and students still do not respond, a good, initial strategy is to rephrase the question and give students another opportunity to respond. (B) is incorrect because putting students on the spot when no one seems able to respond to a question turns class discussions into a high-risk endeavor for students. (C) is probably what most teachers do, but if there is no response, a good first step is to rephrase the question rather than repeat it. (D) suggests that the unanswered question was not important to begin with; if the teacher is using whole-class questioning to help students explore content, then the question should not be ignored.

Competency 007

13.   **(B)**   The correct response is (B). Making this initiative work calls for vertical teaming, with teachers from different levels working to achieve a common goal. (A) is not the instructional intent of the field trip activity. (C) is not supported by the scenario since the field trip is clearly intended to introduce students to the middle-school environment. (D) is not supported by the scenario.

Competency 012

14.   **(C)**   The correct response is (C). Sequencing assignments breaks up the assignments into smaller components, a strategy that allows all learners to work at their best individual pace. This response most effectively allows

for recognition of learner diversity. (A) pulls other students away from their own work. (B) is not in the spirit of IEP. (D) isolates the special education students and very likely makes it impossible for the teacher to attend equitably to all learners' needs.
Competency 002

15. **(B)** The correct response is (B). The timer, the cardboard number, and the large clock are age-appropriate strategies for teaching students time management. (A) is an outcome of the activity but not the prime intention. (C) is not supported by the scenario. (D) is not age-appropriate; learners this age are beginning to discover their work paces and any suggestion that they should work faster is likely to cause anxiety.
Competency 004

16. **(D)** The correct response is (D). Play is an important component of students' learning experiences and should be used to support instruction. (A) partially represents the teacher's intention, but providing a video games center suggests that the teacher values play as an important learning tool. (B) is incorrect because the students are likely to need the teacher's assistance during the video game sessions; thus, the teacher cannot count on this time for noninstructional duties. (C) is not supported by the scenario.
Competency 004

17. **(D)** The correct response is (D). Under *Family Education Rights and Privacy Act* (FERPA), parents are entitled to see their own children's academic records but not those of other students. (A) ignores the parents' concern. (B) and (C) are violations of FERPA.
Competency 013

18. **(C)** The correct response is (C). The teacher is modeling a prereading skill that will enable students to be efficient, focused readers. (A) and (B) do not apply in this scenario. (D) is incorrect because the activity is not a prior-knowledge activity.
Competency 004

19. **(A)** The correct response is (A). The question invites students to consider several sides of an issue and make a value judgment. (B), (C), and (D) are not the cognitive strategies targeted by the teacher's question.
Competency 007

20. **(C)** The correct response is (C). The collaborative activity allows learners to support each other's learning in an equitable way. (A) does not apply in the scenario. (B) incorrectly represents the activity. (D) is not suggested by the scenario.
Competency 001

21. **(B)** The correct response is (B). This activity is a good example of authentic assessment that can be integrated smoothly into a learning activity. The activity allows the teacher to determine the students' general understanding of, and engagement with, the story. (A) is incorrect because the activity is not set up as summative assessment. (C) does not apply because there is no indication the teacher will provide feedback. (D) is not supported by the scenario.
Competency 010

22. **(A)** The correct response is (A). The phonics programs offer a good technological application to support the instructor's goals for this age level. (B) and (C) are incorrect because the computer work is an instructional activity. (D) is likely to be a result of the activity but not the focus as presented in the stem.
Competency 009

23. **(A)** The correct response is (A). This is an appropriate adjustment for this ELL level. (B) and (C) do not provide appropriate scaffolding to help the students become independent learners. (D) does not support the learners' needs.
    Competency 004

24. **(A)** The correct response is (A). This activity provides an indication of the students' understanding of key terms and their basic ability to apply them. (B) is an inquiry activity. (C) is a higher-level thinking and creating activity. (D) is an assessment activity based on basic understanding.
    Competency 003

25. **(A)** The correct response is (A). This activity allows the ELL students to see how other students contribute to class discussions and to practice with support from their classmates. (B) does not give students the practice they need to develop confidence as participants. (C) is a high-stress activity for ELL students and does not address the immediate problem presented in the scenario. (D) also does not address the problem.
    Competency 002

26. **(C)** The correct response is (C). The groups are formed by allowing students to select their topic preferences. (A), (B), and (D) do not correctly identify the grouping strategy.
    Competency 006

27. **(A)** The correct response is (A). This activity will promote students' own construction of knowledge and make the learning experience meaningful. (B) is an aspect of the teacher's goal, but the focus of the scenario is having students teach the new information to the class. (C) is incorrect because the scenario does not indicate that the teacher is directly responding to a perceived student need. (D) is incorrect because the assignment is not set up to convey designated information delivered by the teacher.
    Competency 004

28. **(C)** The correct response is (C). This activity allows students to use technology to collaborate and synthesize information within a wide-ranging community of learners. (A) does not acknowledge the impact of technology. (B) misrepresents the intent of the assignment. (D) addresses only part of the impact of the learning activity.
    Competency 009

29. **(B)** The correct response is (B). This option actively involves the family in the child's educational experience. (A) creates an inequitable situation since the children cannot control whether their parents show up. (C) does not address the students' concerns. (D) might get some parents to attend but the approach seems coercive.
    Competency 011

30. **(A)** The correct response is (A). Several items are simple recall items, but others ask students to evaluate and analyze information about the countries. (B), (C), and (D) do not correctly assess the type of knowledge covered by the items.
    Competency 009

31. **(A)** The correct response is (A). Having the student assume the role of teacher in this activity promotes a high level of learner engagement. (B) is not considered a means of genuinely enhancing student engagement. (C) does not apply because, according to the scenario, inviting the parents was the students' suggestion *after* they were already into the project. (D) addresses the teacher's responsibility to assess her own instructional methods.
    Competency 008

32. **(B)** The correct response is (B). Having students pick a topic they are interested in will involve them meaningfully in the project. (A) is incorrect because research papers are not personal experience papers. (C) and (D) are not relevant to the scenario.
     Competency 008

33. **(A)** The correct response is (A). This option is developmentally appropriate; it provides hands-on learning. (B) does not effectively address the learners' needs. (C) provides a low level of learner engagement. (D) does not effectively address the learners' developmental needs.
     Competency 001

34. **(C)** The correct response is (C). Having the students look around their homes for objects in the shapes of their figures creates a real-world application of the lesson. In (A), the lesson integrates a fun component, but it is an academic lesson, not play. (B) is incorrect because the scenario focuses on actions by the students, not the teacher's presentation. (D) misrepresents the intent of the assignment although some of the children will very likely ask their parents and siblings for help.
     Competency 010

35. **(C)** The correct response is (C). The assignment calls for using knowledge to carry out a learning task. (A), (B), and (D) do not correctly describe the learning task.
     Competency 003

36. **(D)** The correct response is (D). The think-pair-share will actively involve students in the shorter lesson segments and is very likely to promote comprehension. (A) does not address the engagement problem identified in the scenario. (B) is incorrect because the scenario does not suggest that the students are not listening. (C) would work if the teacher knew for certain that the students are capable of understanding the material on their own. The scenario suggests that the problem is lack of basic comprehension.
     Competency 007

37. **(B)** The correct response is (B). The placement of the desk and the teacher's active lecturing style facilitates learning by varying the typical expectation that the teacher will be at the front of the room. By moving about the room, the teacher enters the students' space and becomes more accessible to the learners. (A) and (C) will likely result when the teacher moves about the room but do not represent the primary intent of the teacher's action. (D) does not correctly represent the scenario.
     Competency 005

38. **(C)** The correct response is (C). Texas educators are required to contact the hotline in cases of suspected abuse. The TEA website includes a letter from the Commissioner of Education on the seriousness of this issue. (A), (B), and (D) are incorrect responses to reporting suspected child abuse.
     Competency 013

39. **(A)** The correct response is (A). This option best incorporates all of the teacher's objectives. (B) is a research task that does not address the teacher's learning objectives. (C) and (D) only partially address the teacher's objectives.
     Competency 009

40. **(C)** The correct response is (C). The activity incorporates ELPS expectations for narrating, describing, and explaining. (A) and (B) are not addressed by ELPS and also incorrectly represent the scenario. (D) is not the intent of the activity.
     Competency 002

41.   **(A)**   The correct response is (A). Sitting next to the student at his or her eye level will create a nurturing, productive learning environment. This teacher behavior also shows understanding of the child's developmental needs at this age. (B) misrepresents the teacher's intent. (C) is possibly integrated into the teacher's behavior but the scenario does not suggest that the students are uncomfortable about working at the teacher's desk at the front. (D) also misrepresents the teacher's intent.
Competency 005

42.   **(C)**   The correct response is (C). A wiki provides opportunities for students to generate, change, and collaborate in creating an electronic document. (A) and (B) allow contributions but no modifications. Additionally, these are not considered documents. (D) does not fit the definition; a web page is controlled by the creator.
Competency 009

43.   **(C)**   The correct response is (C). The variety of tasks and interest areas reflects the teacher's understanding that the children are discovering skills they can excel at and activities they enjoy. (A), (B), and (D) do not apply to this age group.
Competency 001

44.   **(B)**   The correct response is (B). The teacher has created an opportunity for students to choose to improve their grades. The teacher offers external motivation with the possibility of a higher grade, and the assumption is that a one-on-one student conference will motivate the students to try for the higher score. (A) explains the teacher's contribution during the conference but does not address the whole scenario. (C) and (D) misrepresent the scenario.
Competency 008

45.   **(D)**   The correct response is (D). Providing materials in highly illustrated books at various reading levels is a good strategy for promoting ELLs' content-area knowledge. (A) is likely to make the ELLs feel comfortable but will not promote their content-area knowledge since they are at beginning and intermediate levels. (B) is pedagogically unsound. (C) does not promote the ELLs acquisition of content-area knowledge; additionally, assigning more homework seems punitive.
Competency 002

46.   **(D)**   The correct response is (D). The scenario points to a problem in instructional planning that is addressed by sequencing and structuring lessons with attention to time available. (A) does not address the time-management problem. (B) still does not allow time for students to reflect on the lesson and ask questions as part of the lesson. (C) shows a misunderstanding of how slide presentations impact instructional delivery.
Competency 003

47.   **(B)**   The correct response is (B). This option allows the teacher to show the students how to perform the desired behavior in the actual context. Additionally, stopping a few minutes before lunch calms the students' anxieties about getting to lunch in a hurry. (A) is incorrect because students at this age need more than just a verbal explanation of behavioral rules. (C) takes a negative reinforcement approach that does not reward students for observing the desired behavior. (D) might be a good follow-up after the students perform the desired behavior as described in (B).
Competency 006

48.   **(C)**   The correct response is (C). Getting teaching advice from a trusted, experienced colleague via observation is considered an excellent strategy for new teachers to develop professionally. (A) lacks the interactive possibilities of the observation. (B) is very limited in possibilities for improvement; the teacher needs feedback from other teachers. (D) misrepresents technology as an automatic improvement in instructional delivery.
Competency 012

49.   **(B)**   The correct response is (B). The cut-and-paste function allows student writers to effectively revise throughout the writing process. (A) is a problematic application because relying on these functions keeps student writers from critically editing their work. Additionally, structures such as misused words and homonyms are not tagged. (C) represents very limited application of word-processing software. (D) is relevant to formatting rather than to the writing process.
  Competency 009

50.   **(B)**   The correct response is (B). Semantic maps are considered excellent scaffolding for helping ELLs acquire content-area vocabulary. (A) does not provide linguistic support for the ELLs. (C) might occasionally be a helpful strategy but it does not actively promote the ELLs' acquisition of content-area vocabulary. (D) is a good prereading strategy but does not address the focus of the scenario.
  Competency 004

51.   **(B)**   The correct response is (B). The types of centers created by this teacher suggest an attempt to address different ways of learning. (A) accurately addresses a reality of classroom experience but it does not represent the teacher's intent in setting up centers that recognize diverse ways of learning. (C) incorrectly targets the autonomy aspect; in selecting center activities, the learners have autonomy in the center selection but what they learn is fluid and cannot be determined beforehand. (D) is not suggested by the scenario.
  Competency 004

52.   **(B)**   The correct response is (B). The scenario suggests that the teacher is actively trying to promote students' appreciation of diversity and to equitably represent men's and women's contributions. (A) is likely to result when a variety of scientists are represented, but it is not the focus of the scenario. (C) suggests that there are deficiencies in textbook materials. (D) is not supported by the scenario. It is likely that the information about the scientists will target lower-level cognitive skills.
  Competency 002

53.   **(A)**   The correct response is (A). The teacher is facilitating students' progress through the center activities by actively engaging students in comments about their work. (B) suggests a nonparticipatory, directorial function. (C) and (D) do not reflect the teacher's activities as described in the scenario.
  Competency 008

54.   **(C)**   The correct response is (C). Hands-on activities promote learners' ability to shape their understanding through active, immediate application of new knowledge. (A) addresses part of the learning benefit of hands-on activities, but we cannot legitimately claim that such activities increase intelligence. (B) also stretches the benefits of hands-on activities to include social growth, but such activities might as likely be acquired completely independently. (D) does not reasonably apply to hands-on activities.
  Competency 001

55.   **(A)**   The correct response is (A). A good guiding principle for conducting parent conferences is to stay positive; this response also addresses the reality of providing family support as the ELL child adjusts to an L2 learning environment. (B) suggests that parent conferences have a superficial quality and that they are triggered by problems. (C) presents a deficit view of the child's home language experience. (D) is incorrect because technical terms are likely to intimidate parents rather than promote the allegedly positive response suggested by this choice.
  Competency 011

56.   **(D)**   The correct response is (D). This is the typical description of a rubric. (A) and (B) are tools that enable students to independently check their work against expectations. (C) is an approach to scoring, not an assessment tool.
  Competency 010

57.　**(B)**　The correct response is (B). No Child Left Behind (NCLB) is the driving force behind ESL programs in elementary and secondary schools. (A), (C), and (D) are not supported by NCLB. These features of special language programs are managed by states and local districts.
　　Competency 013

58.　**(C)**　The correct response is (C). Although the student may not be forthcoming about what is bothering her, the teacher should make an attempt to reach out to the student before trying other options. (A) may make the situation worse, especially if the student's behavior is triggered by problems at home. (B) should not be the first thing the teacher does; without information about the cause of the student's behavior, this is a preemptive, possibly invasive option. (D) also is unwarranted; if the student is not fulfilling basic expectations, extra work will not address the problem.
　　Competency 005

59.　**(C)**　The correct response is (C). Identifying learning objectives should always be the first step in planning instruction. (A), (B), and (D) are logical steps *after* objectives are identified.
　　Competency 004

60.　**(A)**　The correct response is (A). The teacher's unit sounds challenging, but if students do not feel that success is possible, they will not feel motivated to try. Knowing that success is possible creates a positive learning environment. (B) is not supported by the scenario. (C) is only partially relevant; the scenario suggests that cooperative learning is a delivery method that the teacher has not yet integrated. (D) is a possibility, but the students may in fact be able to adeptly handle this pressure and the demands of day-to-day schoolwork.
　　Competency 001

61.　**(C)**　The correct response is (C). The teacher knows that the students' ability to concentrate on the unit may be impacted by their upcoming college entrance exams. (A) describes the impact of the teacher's approach not environmental factors. (B) is incorrect because external factors are likely to interfere with students' attention to school work. (D) misrepresents cooperative learning.
　　Competency 005

62.　**(C)**　The correct response is (C). Gifted students may be able to see angles of the unit that they want to explore on their own. (A) does not address the exceptionality of gifted students. (B) does not create a learning challenge for gifted students; instead, it casts them in the role of tutors for low-achieving students. (D) creates a unit that does not create equitable opportunities for all learners.
　　Competency 002

63.　**(B)**　The correct response is (B). Cooperative learning does not eliminate the teacher from the learning process, but it does provide opportunities for increased learner responsibility for constructing knowledge. (A) partially explains a benefit of cooperative learning—socialization—but the suggestion that the teacher is intrusive makes this response incorrect. (C) does not fully explain cooperative learning because the teacher's role varies in cooperative learning. (D) misrepresents the intent of cooperative learning by suggesting that it makes students responsible for instructional planning.
　　Competency 007

64.　**(C)**　The correct response is (C). Portfolio assessment allows students to select and refine the work that they submit for evaluation. Portfolio assessment generally requires certain types of submissions, but there is a great deal of student choice in making and refining the submissions. (A) incorrectly suggests that a portfolio is cumulative

rather than selective. (B) is incorrect because portfolios, like any other assessment, include deadlines for submission. (D) does not accurately reflect the most salient features of portfolio assessment.
Competency 010

65. **(C)** The correct response is (C). Although classroom rules govern behaviors and expectations in specific classrooms, all rules must reflect campus and district policies. (A) is an important guideline, but in this scenario, the teacher first needs to pay attention to district and campus policies. (B) contradicts most guidelines about setting classroom rules and procedures. (D) does not have to be included in the rules but should be explained to students.
Competency 006

66. **(A)** The correct response is (A). Having a hand in creating classroom rules makes students feel like valuable participants in the community and in maintaining order in that community. (B) contradicts the impact of having students contribute to creating rules. (C) is irrelevant to rule creation. (D) presents contradictory perspectives on how students respond to rules: if students have the ability to do the right thing, there should be no need for rules.
Competency 006

67. **(C)** The correct response is (C). This response presents two pillars of cooperative learning: collaboration and individual responsibility. (A) incorrectly presents criticism as a pivotal component of group work. (B) suggests that group members always need to be vigilant about a group member taking over. (D) suggests that group efforts are ultimately competitive rather than collaborative.
Competency 006

68. **(C)** The correct response is (C). This response shows the new teacher interacting with an experienced colleague, a choice considered an important part of enhancing professional knowledge and skills. In (A), without someone to talk about these parts of the campus, the new teacher may not learn anything from a tour. (B) casts the teacher as dependent rather than self-motivated. (D) has a place in the teacher's preparation, but (C) is the most pragmatic, most potentially beneficial professional development choice in the context of the scenario.
Competency 012

69. **(C)** The correct response is (C). Clustering students according to ability is not a common approach to cooperative learning. (A), (B), and (D) describe important features of cooperative learning activities that contribute to enhancing students' engagement in learning.
Competency 008

70. **(D)** The correct response is (D). Inviting colleagues to share their expertise with your class is an important component of professional development. (A) and (C) do not value the guest speakers' expertise and ability to help students achieve their learning goals. (B) may be a side effect of the guest speaker strategy, but simply introducing students to other teachers and resources is not the primary objective in this initiative.
Competency 012

71. **(D)** The correct response is (D). Although the teacher does not know the source of the conflict among the students, he should take time to illustrate desired community-building behaviors. (A) would exacerbate the stress among the students involved. (B) is incorrect because the teacher has to act immediately to reduce or eliminate the conflict. (C) is incorrect because until the conflict is resolved the students will be unable to work together.
Competency 005

72. **(A)** The correct response is (A). Adjusting assignments to reflect the ELLs' abilities is a first step in moving them toward higher levels of proficiency. (B) looks at ELLs as deficient, incompetent students. (C) does not promote

self-sufficiency. (D) is not viable under Texas procedures for channeling students into special language programs.
   Competency 002

73.   **(C)**   The correct response is (C). A spreadsheet is the best choice for the assignment requirements described in the scenario. (A), (B), and (D) do not enable students to perform the calculations mentioned in the scenario.
   Competency 009

74.   **(B)**   The correct response is (B). This option provides the best approach for helping students become savvy researchers in the context of Internet information. (A) accurately identifies a major problem in search-engine-based research but it does not provide guidelines for determining which hits are reliable. (C) is incorrect. Students need to be taught that websites are updated only if the creator keeps it updated. (D) is an interesting exercise, but it does not teach students how to evaluate the validity of web-based sources.
   Competency 009

75.   **(C)**   The correct response is (C). Providing the objectives and procedures should be standard, but the teacher also provides a model (paradigm) to shape students' conceptualization of the final product. (A) and (D) incorrectly suggest that results of science experiments can be manipulated so that the experiment can be successfully completed. (B) is also incorrect because work pace is a separate issue from procedures and models.
   Competency 008

76.   **(C)**   The correct response is (C). Observation-based assessment enables the evaluator to see the student's performance in a variety of contexts. (A) and (B) offer "snapshot," or summative, assessments. (D) offers a variety of student artifacts but it lacks in-progress, contextualization of observation.
   Competency 010

77.   **(B)**   The correct response is (B). Multiple-choice exams offer the most pragmatic means of objectively connecting test items to specific learning objectives. (A), (C), and (D) are subjective assessments.
   Competency 010

78.   **(C)**   The correct response is (C). This assignment shows logical sequencing that reflects best practices in teaching process-based activities. (A) and (B) present reductive explanations of the teacher's instructional activities. (D) is not supported by the scenario.
   Competency 003

79.   **(D)**   The correct response is (D). Although this is a writing assignment, the teacher is also promoting students' abilities to explore their behavioral assets. (A) is incorrect because the activity calls for students to think about their personal qualities rather than consider background knowledge of a new content-area topic (which is the general description of prior knowledge). (B) and (C) misrepresent the parameters of the scenario.
   Competency 001

80.   **(A)**   The correct response is (A). Inviting college professors to lecture on content-area information expands the teacher's presentation and provides fuller coverage of the instructional objectives. (B), (C), and (D) are not supported by the scenario. There is no direct indication that the teacher is preparing students for college or that she is looking for real-world applications of science content.
   Competency 003

81.   **(C)**   The correct response is (C). The scenario describes a developmentally appropriate research assignment. A session at the library for Internet research supports the teacher's objectives. (A) is not supported by the scenario. (B) seems partially relevant since the teacher is taking students to the library and the computer lab, but the scenario

does not indicate that the librarian or computer lab director are actively involved in the project. (D) is not supported by the scenario.
Competency 004

82. **(B)**   The correct response is (B). Providing examples of the expected product is an excellent strategy for promoting student success. (A) and (C) will result when a teacher does the same assignment as the students, but it is not the focus of the scenario. (D) takes a negative approach to the activity. Providing a model is intended to help students feel more comfortable about what is expected.
Competency 007

83. **(A)**   The correct response is (A). By scaffolding class discussion on terms such as *collaboration* and *innovation* in the context of the film clip, the teacher is promoting students' ability to think deeply about these concepts. (B) and (C) are results of the activity but not the focus. (D) is not supported by the scenario.
Competency 007

84. **(D)**   The correct response is (D). At this age, students need parental support to stay on-task with home-based academic activities. Asking parents to initial the students' reading log gives the learner autonomy in completing the assignment but still relies on the parent for supervisory support. (A), (B), and (C), do not actively promote the teacher's objective.
Competency 003

85. **(B)**   The correct response is (B). The timer seems an optimal solution to the parent's objection: the child can monitor her own at-home reading time and the parent can still authenticate that the reading occurred. (A) does not support the teacher's instructional objective. (C) is inappropriate since the parent is already indicating that she does not have time to simply monitor the child's reading. (D) does not address the problem: the child's willingness or unwillingness to read at home is not the problem. The problem is the parent's participation.
Competency 011

86. **(C)**   The correct response is (C). Inviting librarians to share library resources with the students forges a good relationship between the teacher and community resource representatives. (A) is a good intention but informing students about library resources does not facilitate their access. (B) and (D) are not supported by the scenario.
Competency 013

87. **(A)**   The correct response is (A). Wait time means giving students an appropriate time period to craft a response to a question; wait time should be mediated by the cognitive level of the discussion question. (B), (C), and (D) are incorrect representations of wait time.
Competency 008

88. **(D)**   The correct response is (D). The Code of Ethics and Standard Practices for Texas Educators stipulates that teachers cannot furnish alcohol to minors unless they are the parents of the minors involved. (A), (B), and (C) are incorrect interpretations of the Code of Ethics.
Competency 013

89. **(C)**   The correct response is (C). A mentor teacher provides professional insights, shares experiences, and generally eases a new teacher's entry into the profession. (A), (B), and (D) are collaborative teaching experiences that allow teachers to work together to achieve instructional goals and experiment with teaching innovations.
Competency 013

90. **(B)** The correct response is (B). While a wiki is a technological application, the teacher needs to accommodate families who do not have access to technology. (A) is not supported by the scenario. The wiki described here suggests that the teacher's intent is communicative rather than academic. (C) is a side effect but not the focus of the wiki activity. (D) misrepresents the scenario.
       Competency 011

ANSWERS SORTED BY DOMAIN AND COMPETENCY

Domain	Competency	Question	Answer	Did You Answer Correctly?
I	001	5	A	
I	001	20	C	
I	001	33	A	
I	001	43	C	
I	001	54	C	
I	001	60	A	
I	001	79	D	
I	002	14	C	
I	002	25	A	
I	002	40	C	
I	002	45	D	
I	002	52	B	
I	002	62	C	
I	002	72	A	
I	003	3	D	
I	003	9	B	
I	003	24	A	
I	003	35	C	
I	003	46	D	
I	003	78	C	
I	003	80	A	
I	003	84	D	
I	004	15	B	
I	004	16	D	
I	004	18	C	
I	004	23	A	
I	004	27	A	
I	004	50	B	
I	004	51	B	
I	004	59	C	
I	004	81	C	
II	005	1	B	

Domain	Competency	Question	Answer	Did You Answer Correctly?
II	005	37	B	
II	005	41	A	
II	005	58	C	
II	005	61	C	
II	005	71	D	
II	006	10	C	
II	006	26	C	
II	006	47	B	
II	006	65	C	
II	006	66	A	
II	006	67	C	
III	007	8	C	
III	007	12	A	
III	007	19	A	
III	007	36	D	
III	007	63	B	
III	007	82	B	
III	007	83	A	
III	008	2	A	
III	008	31	A	
III	008	32	B	
III	008	44	B	
III	008	53	A	
III	008	69	C	
III	008	75	C	
III	008	87	A	
III	009	22	A	
III	009	28	C	
III	009	30	A	
III	009	39	A	
III	009	42	C	
III	009	49	B	

(continued)

237

Domain	Competency	Question	Answer	Did You Answer Correctly?
III	009	73	C	
III	009	74	B	
III	010	4	C	
III	010	21	B	
III	010	34	C	
III	010	56	D	
III	010	64	C	
III	010	76	C	
III	010	77	B	
IV	011	11	D	
IV	011	29	B	
IV	011	55	A	
IV	011	85	B	
IV	011	90	B	
IV	012	6	B	
IV	012	13	B	
IV	012	48	C	
IV	012	68	C	
IV	012	70	D	
IV	013	7	A	
IV	013	17	D	
IV	013	38	C	
IV	013	57	B	
IV	013	86	C	
IV	013	88	D	
IV	013	89	C	

ANSWERS SHEET FOR PRACTICE TEST 1

1. (A) (B) (C) (D)
2. (A) (B) (C) (D)
3. (A) (B) (C) (D)
4. (A) (B) (C) (D)
5. (A) (B) (C) (D)
6. (A) (B) (C) (D)
7. (A) (B) (C) (D)
8. (A) (B) (C) (D)
9. (A) (B) (C) (D)
10. (A) (B) (C) (D)
11. (A) (B) (C) (D)
12. (A) (B) (C) (D)
13. (A) (B) (C) (D)
14. (A) (B) (C) (D)
15. (A) (B) (C) (D)
16. (A) (B) (C) (D)
17. (A) (B) (C) (D)
18. (A) (B) (C) (D)
19. (A) (B) (C) (D)
20. (A) (B) (C) (D)
21. (A) (B) (C) (D)
22. (A) (B) (C) (D)
23. (A) (B) (C) (D)

24. (A) (B) (C) (D)
25. (A) (B) (C) (D)
26. (A) (B) (C) (D)
27. (A) (B) (C) (D)
28. (A) (B) (C) (D)
29. (A) (B) (C) (D)
30. (A) (B) (C) (D)
31. (A) (B) (C) (D)
32. (A) (B) (C) (D)
33. (A) (B) (C) (D)
34. (A) (B) (C) (D)
35. (A) (B) (C) (D)
36. (A) (B) (C) (D)
37. (A) (B) (C) (D)
38. (A) (B) (C) (D)
39. (A) (B) (C) (D)
40. (A) (B) (C) (D)
41. (A) (B) (C) (D)
42. (A) (B) (C) (D)
43. (A) (B) (C) (D)
44. (A) (B) (C) (D)
45. (A) (B) (C) (D)
46. (A) (B) (C) (D)

47. (A) (B) (C) (D)
48. (A) (B) (C) (D)
49. (A) (B) (C) (D)
50. (A) (B) (C) (D)
51. (A) (B) (C) (D)
52. (A) (B) (C) (D)
53. (A) (B) (C) (D)
54. (A) (B) (C) (D)
55. (A) (B) (C) (D)
56. (A) (B) (C) (D)
57. (A) (B) (C) (D)
58. (A) (B) (C) (D)
59. (A) (B) (C) (D)
60. (A) (B) (C) (D)
61. (A) (B) (C) (D)
62. (A) (B) (C) (D)
63. (A) (B) (C) (D)
64. (A) (B) (C) (D)
65. (A) (B) (C) (D)
66. (A) (B) (C) (D)
67. (A) (B) (C) (D)
68. (A) (B) (C) (D)

69. (A) (B) (C) (D)
70. (A) (B) (C) (D)
71. (A) (B) (C) (D)
72. (A) (B) (C) (D)
73. (A) (B) (C) (D)
74. (A) (B) (C) (D)
75. (A) (B) (C) (D)
76. (A) (B) (C) (D)
77. (A) (B) (C) (D)
78. (A) (B) (C) (D)
79. (A) (B) (C) (D)
80. (A) (B) (C) (D)
81. (A) (B) (C) (D)
82. (A) (B) (C) (D)
83. (A) (B) (C) (D)
84. (A) (B) (C) (D)
85. (A) (B) (C) (D)
86. (A) (B) (C) (D)
87. (A) (B) (C) (D)
88. (A) (B) (C) (D)
89. (A) (B) (C) (D)
90. (A) (B) (C) (D)

ANSWERS SHEET FOR PRACTICE TEST 2

1. Ⓐ Ⓑ Ⓒ Ⓓ
2. Ⓐ Ⓑ Ⓒ Ⓓ
3. Ⓐ Ⓑ Ⓒ Ⓓ
4. Ⓐ Ⓑ Ⓒ Ⓓ
5. Ⓐ Ⓑ Ⓒ Ⓓ
6. Ⓐ Ⓑ Ⓒ Ⓓ
7. Ⓐ Ⓑ Ⓒ Ⓓ
8. Ⓐ Ⓑ Ⓒ Ⓓ
9. Ⓐ Ⓑ Ⓒ Ⓓ
10. Ⓐ Ⓑ Ⓒ Ⓓ
11. Ⓐ Ⓑ Ⓒ Ⓓ
12. Ⓐ Ⓑ Ⓒ Ⓓ
13. Ⓐ Ⓑ Ⓒ Ⓓ
14. Ⓐ Ⓑ Ⓒ Ⓓ
15. Ⓐ Ⓑ Ⓒ Ⓓ
16. Ⓐ Ⓑ Ⓒ Ⓓ
17. Ⓐ Ⓑ Ⓒ Ⓓ
18. Ⓐ Ⓑ Ⓒ Ⓓ
19. Ⓐ Ⓑ Ⓒ Ⓓ
20. Ⓐ Ⓑ Ⓒ Ⓓ
21. Ⓐ Ⓑ Ⓒ Ⓓ
22. Ⓐ Ⓑ Ⓒ Ⓓ
23. Ⓐ Ⓑ Ⓒ Ⓓ

24. Ⓐ Ⓑ Ⓒ Ⓓ
25. Ⓐ Ⓑ Ⓒ Ⓓ
26. Ⓐ Ⓑ Ⓒ Ⓓ
27. Ⓐ Ⓑ Ⓒ Ⓓ
28. Ⓐ Ⓑ Ⓒ Ⓓ
29. Ⓐ Ⓑ Ⓒ Ⓓ
30. Ⓐ Ⓑ Ⓒ Ⓓ
31. Ⓐ Ⓑ Ⓒ Ⓓ
32. Ⓐ Ⓑ Ⓒ Ⓓ
33. Ⓐ Ⓑ Ⓒ Ⓓ
34. Ⓐ Ⓑ Ⓒ Ⓓ
35. Ⓐ Ⓑ Ⓒ Ⓓ
36. Ⓐ Ⓑ Ⓒ Ⓓ
37. Ⓐ Ⓑ Ⓒ Ⓓ
38. Ⓐ Ⓑ Ⓒ Ⓓ
39. Ⓐ Ⓑ Ⓒ Ⓓ
40. Ⓐ Ⓑ Ⓒ Ⓓ
41. Ⓐ Ⓑ Ⓒ Ⓓ
42. Ⓐ Ⓑ Ⓒ Ⓓ
43. Ⓐ Ⓑ Ⓒ Ⓓ
44. Ⓐ Ⓑ Ⓒ Ⓓ
45. Ⓐ Ⓑ Ⓒ Ⓓ
46. Ⓐ Ⓑ Ⓒ Ⓓ

47. Ⓐ Ⓑ Ⓒ Ⓓ
48. Ⓐ Ⓑ Ⓒ Ⓓ
49. Ⓐ Ⓑ Ⓒ Ⓓ
50. Ⓐ Ⓑ Ⓒ Ⓓ
51. Ⓐ Ⓑ Ⓒ Ⓓ
52. Ⓐ Ⓑ Ⓒ Ⓓ
53. Ⓐ Ⓑ Ⓒ Ⓓ
54. Ⓐ Ⓑ Ⓒ Ⓓ
55. Ⓐ Ⓑ Ⓒ Ⓓ
56. Ⓐ Ⓑ Ⓒ Ⓓ
57. Ⓐ Ⓑ Ⓒ Ⓓ
58. Ⓐ Ⓑ Ⓒ Ⓓ
59. Ⓐ Ⓑ Ⓒ Ⓓ
60. Ⓐ Ⓑ Ⓒ Ⓓ
61. Ⓐ Ⓑ Ⓒ Ⓓ
62. Ⓐ Ⓑ Ⓒ Ⓓ
63. Ⓐ Ⓑ Ⓒ Ⓓ
64. Ⓐ Ⓑ Ⓒ Ⓓ
65. Ⓐ Ⓑ Ⓒ Ⓓ
66. Ⓐ Ⓑ Ⓒ Ⓓ
67. Ⓐ Ⓑ Ⓒ Ⓓ
68. Ⓐ Ⓑ Ⓒ Ⓓ

69. Ⓐ Ⓑ Ⓒ Ⓓ
70. Ⓐ Ⓑ Ⓒ Ⓓ
71. Ⓐ Ⓑ Ⓒ Ⓓ
72. Ⓐ Ⓑ Ⓒ Ⓓ
73. Ⓐ Ⓑ Ⓒ Ⓓ
74. Ⓐ Ⓑ Ⓒ Ⓓ
75. Ⓐ Ⓑ Ⓒ Ⓓ
76. Ⓐ Ⓑ Ⓒ Ⓓ
77. Ⓐ Ⓑ Ⓒ Ⓓ
78. Ⓐ Ⓑ Ⓒ Ⓓ
79. Ⓐ Ⓑ Ⓒ Ⓓ
80. Ⓐ Ⓑ Ⓒ Ⓓ
81. Ⓐ Ⓑ Ⓒ Ⓓ
82. Ⓐ Ⓑ Ⓒ Ⓓ
83. Ⓐ Ⓑ Ⓒ Ⓓ
84. Ⓐ Ⓑ Ⓒ Ⓓ
85. Ⓐ Ⓑ Ⓒ Ⓓ
86. Ⓐ Ⓑ Ⓒ Ⓓ
87. Ⓐ Ⓑ Ⓒ Ⓓ
88. Ⓐ Ⓑ Ⓒ Ⓓ
89. Ⓐ Ⓑ Ⓒ Ⓓ
90. Ⓐ Ⓑ Ⓒ Ⓓ

References

Ambrose, S.A. et al. *How Learning Works: Seven Research-Based Principles for Smart Teaching*. San Francisco, CA: Jossey-Bass, 2010.

Anderson, L. W. and D.R. Krathwohl, Eds. *A Taxonomy for Learning, Teaching, and Assessing: A Revision of Bloom's Taxonomy of Educational Objectives*. New York, NY: Longman, 2000.

Brewer, J. A. *Introduction to Early Childhood Education: Preschool Through Primary Grades*, 6th Ed. Boston, MA: Pearson/Allyn & Bacon, 2007.

Burden, P. *Classroom Management: Creating a Successful K–12 Learning Community*. Hoboken, NJ: John Wiley & Sons, Inc., 2006.

Burden, P. and D. M. Byrd. *Methods for Effective Teaching: Meeting the Needs of All Students*, 6th Ed. Boston, MA: Pearson, 2013.

DeVito, D., Shamberg, M., and Sher, S. *Freedom Writers*. USA: Paramount Pictures, 2007.

Education Service Center Region 13. Professional Development Appraisal System Workshops and Additional Workshops, 2013. *www4.esc13.net/pdas/workshops/additional-workshops*

Eggen, P. and D. Kauchak. *Strategies and Models for Teachers: Teaching Content and Thinking Skills*. Boston, MA: Pearson, 2012.

Erikson, E. *Identity Youth and Crisis*. New York, NY: Norton, 1968.

Evans, E. C. "History in the Secondary School: The Use of the Blackboard in the Teaching of History." *The Social Studies* 2(5), 1910. Reprinted in *The Social Studies*, May/June 2009, 100–101.

Fein, G. G. and N. W. Wiltz. "Play as Children See It." In D. P. Fromberg and D. Bergen. Eds. *Play from Birth to Twelve and Beyond: Contexts, Perspectives, and Meanings*: 37–49. New York, NY: Garland Publishing, Inc., 1998.

Freeman, Y. S. and D. E. Freeman. *ESL/EFL Teaching: Principles for Success*. Portsmouth, NH: Heinemann, 1998.

Freire, P. *Pedagogy of the Oppressed*. New York, NY: Continuum Publishing Company, 1970.

Gale, X.L. *Teachers, Discourses, and Authority in Postmodern Composition Classroom*. Albany, NY: State University of New York, 1996.

Haines, R. *The Ron Clark Story*. Alberta Film Development Program of the Alberta Foundation for the Arts. USA: TNT, 2006.

Hiller, A. *Teachers*. USA: United Artists, 1984.

Jacobsen, D. A., P. Eggen, and D. Kauchak. *Methods for Teaching: Promoting Student Learning in K–12 Classrooms*, 7th Ed. Upper Saddle River, NJ: Pearson, 2006.

Johnson, S. *Where Good Ideas Come From: The Natural History of Innovation*. New York, NY: Riverhead Books, 2010.

Kauchak, D. and P. Eggen. *Learning and Teaching: Research-Based Methods*, 6th Ed. Boston: MA: Pearson, 2012.

Manning, M. L. "Play Development from Ages Eight to Twelve." In D.P. Fromberg and D. Bergen. Eds. *Play from Birth to Twelve and Beyond: Contexts, Perspectives, and Meanings:* 154–161. New York, NY: Garland Publishing, Inc., 1998.

National Dissemination Center for Children with Disabilities (NICHCY), Disability and Education Laws, 2012. *nichcy.org/laws*

National Science Teachers Association, Browse Journal Articles: *Science and Teaching, 2013. www.nsta.org*

Patrikakou, E. N. *The Power of Parent Involvement: Evidence, Ideas, and Tools for Student Success.* Lincoln, IL: Center for Innovation and Improvement, 2008. *www.centerii.org/techassist/solutionfinding/resources/PowerParInvolve.pdf*

Peregoy, S. F. and O.F. Boyle. *Reading, Writing, and Learning in ESL: A Resource Book for Teaching K–12 English Learners,* 5th Ed. Boston, MA: Pearson, 2008.

Piaget, J. and B. Inhelder. *The Psychology of the Child.* H. Weaver, Trans. New York, NY: Basic Books, Inc., 1969.

Pressley, M. and C.B. McCormick. *Child and Adolescent Development for Educators.* New York: NY: The Guildford Press, 2007.

Ramos, F. "Keeping Class in Order." *Language Magazine 12*(5), 2013, 28–30.

Reis, N. M., R. Quintanar, and L. Cabral. "Teaching English Language Learners—Best Practices for Schools and Teachers." *NABE News* 30(3), 2008, 19–22.

Russo, A. *Teachers.* USA: United Artists, 1984.

Santrock, J. W. *Child Development,* 12th Ed. New York, NY: McGraw Hill, 2009.

Simpson, D. *Dangerous Minds.* USA: Hollywood Pictures, 1995.

Suskie, L. *Assessing Student Learning.* San Francisco, CA: Jossey-Bass, 2009.

Texas Constitution and Statutes, Texas Education Code. *§§21.351*–21.356, 2011. *www.statutes.legis.state.tx.us/index.aspx*

Texas Constitution and Statutes, Texas Education Code. Chapter 37. Discipline; Law and Order, 2011. *www.statutes.legis.state.tx.us/index.aspx*

Texas Constitution and Statutes, Texas Education Code, 2013. *www.statutes.legis.state.tx.us/?link=ED*

Texas Education Agency (TEA), English Language Proficiency Standards, 2007. *ritter.tea.state.tx.us/rules/tac/chapter074/ch074a.html#74.4*

Texas Education Agency (TEA), Texas Essential Knowledge and Skills. English Language Proficiency Standards, 2013. *www.tea.state.tx.us*

Texas Education Agency (TEA), Texas Essential Knowledge and Skills for Technology Applications, 2013. *ritter.tea.state.tx.us/rules/tac/chapter126/index.html*

Texas Education Agency (TEA), Limited English Proficiency Initiatives, 2013. *www.tea.state.tx.us*

Texas Education Agency (TEA), No Child Left Behind/Elementary and Secondary Education Act, 2013. *www.tea.state.tx.us/index4.aspx?id=4261&menu_id=2147483742*

Texas Education Agency (TEA), *Professional Development and Appraisal System Teacher Manual.* Austin, TX: Region XIII Education Service Center. Certification Programs, 2005.

Texas Education Agency (TEA), *Educator Guide to TELPAS, 2011*.
www.tea.state.tx.us/student.assessment/ell/telpas

Texas Education Agency (TEA), Texas Essential Knowledge and Skills for Social Studies. Subchapter B Middle School, 2011.
ritter.tea.state.tx.us/rules/tac/chapter113/ch113b.html

Texas Education Agency (TEA), *A Guide to the Admission, Review, and Dismissal Process,* Special Education in Texas A–Z Index, 2012.
www.tea.state.tx.us/index2.aspx?id=2147491399

Texas Education Agency (TEA), STAAR Resources, 2013.
www.tea.state.tx.us/student.assessment/staar

Texas Education Agency (TEA), Chapter 37–Safe Schools, 2013.
www.tea.state.tx.us/index2.aspx?id=262&menu_id=2147483656

Texas Education Agency (TEA), Child Abuse and Neglect Reporting and Requirements, 2013.
www.tea.state.tx.us/index4.aspx?id=25769803997

Texas Education Agency (TEA), Technology Application Standards for All Beginning Teachers. Approved Educator Standards, 2013. *http://www.tea.state.tx.us*

Texas Education Agency (TEA), Texas Education Service Centers, 2013.
www.tea.state.tx.us

Texas Education Agency (TEA), Texas Essential Knowledge and Skills. Chapter 126. Technology Applications, 2013. *www.tea.state.tx.us*

Texas Secretary of State. Texas Administrative Code. Title 19. Education. Part 7. State Board for Educator Certification. Chapter 247. Educators Code of Ethics, 2013.

U.S. Copyright Office, *Reproduction of Copyrighted Works by Educators and Librarians*. Washington, DC: Library of Congress, 2009.

U.S. Department of Education. *Digest of Education Statistics*. Table 92. Staff Employed in Public Elementary and Secondary School Systems By Type of Assignment, Selected Years 1947–1950 through Fall 2012. National Center for Education Statistics, Washington DC. 2013.
nces.ed.gov/programs/digest/d12/tables/dt12_092.asp

U.S. Department of Education. *Digest of Education Statistics*. Table 95. Staff, Teachers, and Teachers as a Percentage of Staff in Public Elementary and Secondary School Systems, by State or Jurisdiction: Selected Years, Fall 2000 through Fall 2010, Washington DC, 2013.
nces.ed.gov/programs/digest/d12/tables/dt12_095.asp

U.S. Department of Education. *Family Educational Rights and Privacy Act*, 2013.
www.ed.gov/policy/gen/guid/fpco/ferpa/index.html

U.S. Department of Education, Building the Legacy: IDEA 2004, 2013. http://idea.ed.gov

Wesch, M. A., "Vision of Students Today." Video produced by Kansas State University students, 2007. Retrieved from *youtube.com*.

Index

NOTES

NOTES

NOTES

NOTES

NOTES